D0121413

RESEARCHING ORGANIZATIONS

RESEARCHING ORGANIZATIONS

The Practice of Organizational Fieldwork

by MATTHEW JONES

Los Angeles | London | New Delhi
Singapore | Washington DC

Los Angeles | London | New Delhi
Singapore | Washington DC

SAGE Publications Ltd
1 Oliver's Yard
55 City Road
London EC1Y 1SP

SAGE Publications Inc.
2455 Teller Road
Thousand Oaks, California 91320

SAGE Publications India Pvt Ltd
B 1/I 1 Mohan Cooperative Industrial Area
Mathura Road
New Delhi 110 044

SAGE Publications Asia-Pacific Pte Ltd
3 Church Street
#10-04 Samsung Hub
Singapore 049483

Editor: Katie Metzler
Assistant editor: Lily Mehrbod
Production editor: Thea Watson
Copyeditor: Rose James
Proofreader: Elaine Leck
Marketing manager: Ben Griffin-Sherwood
Cover design: Francis Kenney
Typeset by: C&M Digitals (P) Ltd, Chennai, India
Printed in Great Britain by Henry Ling Limited at
The Dorset Press, Dorchester, DT1 1HD

MIX
Paper from
responsible sources
FSC
www.fsc.org FSC™ C013985

Library of Congress Control Number: 2013946899

British Library Cataloguing in Publication data

A catalogue record for this book is available from
the British Library

ISBN 978-1-4462-5721-0
ISBN 978-1-4462-5722-7 (pbk)

Contents

List of Figures and Tables

Preface

The original idea for this book emerged from my experiences in teaching research methods to graduate students, many of whom had just completed an undergraduate degree without having spent much time working in organizations, but who aspired to pursue research in organizational settings to Ph.D. level, and potentially to an academic career. Most of the available research methods textbooks, however, while sometimes very good on techniques of data-gathering (especially via experiments, surveys or occasionally interviews), data analysis (especially of the quantitative variety) and in a few cases on the philosophy, and occasionally ethics, of research, were notably silent on what is actually involved in doing fieldwork in organizations.

Like an instruction manual for a device that omits crucial steps in the process, therefore, or a children's craft programme that moves from the disassembled components to 'here's one that I made beforehand' with only the barest hint of what goes on in between, most methods textbooks tend to focus on abstract description of general principles and final products rather than how research happens in practice. They may therefore be useful, as Bell and Newby (1977: 9) suggest, in providing '*some* standard, *some* set of procedures, *some* method by which research practice could be evaluated', but they are of limited help in actually doing research, as opposed, say, to planning it or judging its conformance to accepted norms. Despite the observation of Bell and Newby in 1977 that 'it is common knowledge that there is considerable divergence between how sociological research has actually been done and what is found in the textbooks', moreover, little would appear to have changed in the intervening years. Thus Walford (2001: 2) comments:

> Many social science and educational research methods textbooks still abstract the researcher from the process of research in the same way as have natural science textbooks. The social dimension of research is largely omitted and the process is presented as an analytic practice where any novice researcher can follow set recipes and obtain predetermined results.

As a supervisor of M.Phil and Ph.D. students conducting largely qualitative studies in a range of organizational settings, moreover, most of whom were more than competent in learning techniques as required, it was precisely this practical aspect of research that many seemed to find the hardest to get to grips with. The description given by Gans (1968: 312) of the anxieties of fieldwork, would seem to resonate with their experience (as well as my own at times):

> the constant worry about the flow of research activities: Is one doing the right thing at the right time, attending the right meeting, or talking to the right people? ... [the feeling that] one must be in many places at the same time. This being impossible, one must make the right choice of what to study every day, and even so there is always the danger of having missed something and of never being able to retrieve an event that has already become history.

Finding no guidance from textbooks on these issues, however, the students would talk of 'wandering in the dark', 'making it up as I go along' and 'learning the hard way'.

Although to some extent the students' difficulties could be ascribed to the 'craft' character of fieldwork (Punch, 1986), and qualitative research in particular, that means that it can only really be learned through doing it, there was also a sense that it should be possible to provide some information on what organizational fieldwork involves, which might offer guidance and reassurance to those undertaking research in organizations for the first time.

Aware of various 'confessional' methodological appendices in organizational ethnographies such as those of Atkinson (1997), Kunda (1992) and Luke (2003), I therefore started to look for additional fieldwork accounts, as well as any literature that might draw some common threads between these contributions, or offer suggestions on how fieldwork might best be approached. My first discovery was the edited collection *Doing Research in Organizations* (Bryman, 1988), but I found that this was long out of print. Further investigation revealed some sociological literature, albeit much of it dated, such as Wax (1971), Johnson (1975) and the edited collections of Hammond (1964), Bell and Newby (1977) and a range of articles in specialist research methods journals, such as *Journal of Contemporary Ethnography* and *Qualitative Research in Organizations and Management*. While this suggested that the topic was not as wholly neglected as it had seemed at first, the literature appeared to be quite fragmented and had, for whatever reason, rather fallen out of favour in recent years. A synthesis and updating of this literature seemed, therefore, like it might be a worthwhile contribution.

In terms of updating, there are certainly some aspects of the earlier literature, such as the gendered language, that would seem likely to disconcert the contemporary reader, but there are also a lot of specific observations on the issues faced in conducting research in organizations that are still very much applicable today. In drawing quite extensively on this literature, some of which dates back to the 1950s, therefore, the aim has been explicitly to counter the general neophilia and parochialism of much research, especially in management, which, with a few exceptions, regards anything published more than five years ago or outside a coterie of discipline-specific journals as not worthy of any attention. If matters of contemporary concern were well addressed fifty years ago, or may be of relevance to one discipline despite being published in a journal from another field, we may do better to acknowledge this, rather than reinvent the wheel.

At the same time, it is evident that attitudes to the research process are now considerably more formalized than they were when some of this literature was written. A particularly striking example of this is to be found in the account given by Sir Edward Evan Evans-Pritchard of the guidance on conducting field-work that he received from various distinguished anthropologists at the start of his career (Evans-Pritchard and Gillies, 1976: 240).

> When I was a serious young student in London I thought I would try to get a few tips from experienced fieldworkers before setting out for Central Africa. I first sought advice from Westermarck. All I got from him was 'don't converse with an informant for more than twenty minutes because if you aren't bored by that time he will be.' Very good advice, even if somewhat inadequate. I sought instruction from Haddon, a man foremost in field-research. He told me that it was really all quite simple; one should always behave as a gentleman. Also very good advice. My teacher, Seligman, told me to take ten grains of quinine every night and to keep off women.

If it is to be hoped that the novice researcher might receive somewhat more substantive and more helpful advice today, it is still surprising how casual the approach to research is, even in literature of the 1970s and 1980s. The researchers' sense of superiority and entitlement in relations with their research 'subjects' can also be grating. It is difficult to imagine, for example, that Dalton's trading of advice to a secretary on how she might attract the romantic interest of a senior company specialist in exchange for access to confidential income data (Dalton, 1959) would be viewed with such equanimity today, or that contemporary students would profess admiration for miners' 'spontaneity' as Gouldner (1955) reports.

What also comes across strongly in this literature, and served to reinforce the belief in the merits of paying greater attention to the practice of fieldwork, though, is the sense that, as Gans (1968: 309) puts it, fieldwork generally, and participant observation in particular, 'provides great satisfactions: discovering new facts, coming up with new ideas, watching people act ... being in the middle of things, meeting new kinds of people'. Gouldner (1955: 250) similarly describes fieldwork as 'simply having a wonderful time' – a view I found echoed in my own experience and also that of many students for whom, notwithstanding the difficulties they sometimes went through, it was often the highpoint of their studies.

It should be acknowledged, however, that the experience of fieldwork is not necessarily so positive for all researchers. Thus Shaffir and Stebbins (1991: 1) write, of anthropological fieldwork, that it 'must certainly rank with the more disagreeable activities that humanity has fashioned for itself. It is usually inconvenient, to say the least, sometimes physically uncomfortable, frequently embarrassing, and, to a degree, always tense.' Nevertheless, Shaffir and Stebbins (1991: 7) argue,

> field research is accompanied by a set of experiences that are, for the most part, unavailable through other forms of social scientific research. These experiences are bound together with satisfactions, embarrassments, challenges, pains, triumphs, ambiguities, and agonies, all of which blend into what has been described as the field research adventure. (Glazer, 1972)

The hope of this book is that it may be of some assistance to those setting out on this adventure.

References

Atkinson, P. (1997) *The Clinical Experience: The Construction and Reconstruction of Medical Reality*. Aldershot: Ashgate.

Bell, C. and Newby, H. (1977) 'Introduction: The rise of methodological pluralism', in C. Bell and H. Newby (eds), *Doing Sociological Research*. London: Allen and Unwin, pp. 9–29.

Bryman, A. (1988) *Doing Research in Organizations*. London: Routledge.

Dalton, M. (1959) *Men who Manage: Fusions of Feeling and Theory in Administration*. New York: Wiley.

Evans-Pritchard, E.E. and Gillies, E. (1976) *Witchcraft, Oracles and Magic Among the Azande*, abridged edn. Oxford: Oxford University Press.

Gans, H.J. (1968) 'The participant observer as a human being: observations on the personal aspects of fieldwork', in H.S. Becker, B. Geer, D. Riesman and R.S. Weiss (eds), *Institutions and the Person*. Chicago, IL: Aldine Publishing Company, pp. 300–17.

Glazer, M. (1972) *The Research Adventure: Promise and Problems of Field Work*. New York: Random House.

Gouldner, A.W. (1955) *Patterns of Industrial Bureaucracy*. London: Routledge and Kegan Paul.

Hammond, P.E. (1964) *Sociologists at Work*. New York: Basic Books.

Johnson, J.M. (1975) *Doing Field Research*. New York: Free Press.

Kunda, G. (1992) *Engineering Culture: Control and Commitment in a High-tech Corporation*. Philadelphia, PA: Temple University Press.

Luke, H. (2003) *Medical Education and Sociology of Medical Habitus: 'It's Not About the Stethoscope!'* London: Kluwer Academic.

Punch, M. (1986) *The Politics and Ethics of Fieldwork*. London: SAGE.

Shaffir, W.B. and Stebbins, R.A. (1991) *Experiencing Fieldwork: An Inside View of Qualitative Research*. Newbury Park, CA: SAGE.

Walford, G. (2001) *Doing Qualitative Educational Research: A Personal Guide to the Research Process*. London: Continuum International Publishing Group.

Wax, R.H. (1971) *Doing Fieldwork: Warnings and Advice*. London: University of Chicago Press.

1

Introduction

Chapter objectives

- to identify the scope of topics covered in the book
- to explain the book's focus on the practice of organizational fieldwork
- to introduce the 'getting in, getting on, getting out and getting back' framework around which the main chapters are structured
- to present an overview of the book

For researchers in a wide range of disciplines, not just those in organization studies, the primary site for their research, that is, the place where they collect their data, is an organization of some sort or another. By an organization we mean a relatively enduring group of people with some degree of coordination around a common principle or objective that has a more or less identifiable boundary. As this definition suggests, many different types of social group may be considered as an organization – a small charity set up to raise funds for a local hospice, a transnational corporation, a network of consultants who offer their services under a common name, or a high-security prison. Just from these examples we can also see that organizations may vary widely in terms of aspects such as their size, motivation, location and degree of formalization. Whatever these differences, the potential significance of which will be considered in the next chapter, the common features of organizations (coordination, collective orientation and boundaries) tend to make them distinctive research sites, compared to studying other social groups such as families, street-corner gangs or residents of a neighbourhood. This book is about the practical issues that may arise when carrying out research fieldwork[1] in organizational settings and what can be done to try to address them.

---

[1] *The Oxford Dictionary of Sociology* (Scott and Marshall, 2009) defines fieldwork as 'Data collection for any study that involves talking to people or asking them questions about their activities and views, sometimes including attempts at systematic observation of their behaviour. Fieldwork ranges from large-scale survey interviewing by hundreds of professional interviewers, to the lone researcher recording information collected through participant observation in a small-scale case-study. The term is sometimes extended to any research activity that takes one out of the office and into the "field" that is the subject of study.' For the purposes of this book the extended definition will be employed, with the 'field' that is the subject of study being an organization or organizations.

In focusing on practical issues, the intention is not to suggest that researchers do not need to know about philosophical, theoretical or more traditional 'methodological' issues, such as survey or experimental design or statistical analysis. There is already such a wealth of literature available on these topics, however, that it would seem more useful to focus on supplementing, rather than attempting to replicate it. References will therefore be provided, as appropriate, to relevant literature on the philosophy and methods of research in organizations, so that the focus can be maintained on the practical issues of undertaking research in organizational settings. A sound understanding of the philosophical assumptions of the study and a well-thought out design, for example, may be essential prerequisites of effective research, but it is also important to be able to put these into practice.

Most of the philosophical, theoretical and methodological issues faced by organizational researchers, moreover, can also be argued to be common to social research in general and therefore addressed by general social research methods texts, whereas practical issues often arise from what will be suggested are the distinctive characteristics of organizations. Thus, while there may have been a 'strong tradition of collections of "inside" views of the process of social research' (Bryman, 1988: 1), some of which include chapters on research on organizational settings, there would not seem to be a comparable literature focusing specifically on organizational research. Nor would the tradition that Bryman refers to seem to have been particularly active since the publication of *Doing Research in Organizations*, with the main contributions being domain-specific works, such as Walford (1991) and Delamont (2002) in education, Gellner and Hirsch (2001) in social anthropology, Randall et al. (2007) in computer-supported cooperative work and Halliday and Schmidt (2009) in law.

Researchers undertaking fieldwork in organizations therefore largely have to rely either on trial and error, improvising solutions to issues as they encounter them; searching for guidance on specific issues in specialist journals; relying on such discussion of issues as may be divulged in papers and monographs (often in confessional appendices rather than in the main body of the text); or seeking the personal advice of more experienced colleagues. While none of these approaches is necessarily inappropriate, locating suitable guidance or developing relevant experience can be costly and there is a risk that lack of broader awareness of issues and ad hoc solutions may inadvertently cause irreparable harm to the research, for example when a mishandled approach to an organization for access results in exclusion from a key research site. This is not to claim that this book offers infallible guidance or that factors beyond the researcher's control may not prevent the successful implementation of even the best-laid plans, but that providing a systematic discussion of potential issues across the whole research process may help to avoid, or at least anticipate, some of the more common problems that can derail research.

A useful way of thinking about this aspect of research in organizations is provided by a widely cited chapter in Bryman (1988) by David Buchanan, David Boddy and James McCalman, which is entitled 'Getting in, getting on, getting out and getting back'. This framing provides the main structure of this book. Discussion of 'getting in' explores the issues of access to organizations, 'getting on' addresses issues that may be encountered in sustaining access, 'getting out' examines when and how to end fieldwork and potential considerations when reporting on such work and 'getting back' looks at possible reasons why a researcher may wish to revisit a research site and how this may be facilitated.

The primary focus of discussion of the research process is practical. This is partly because there are relatively few principles on which it may be considered to be based (and probably even fewer that all researchers would agree on). What is often presented as the guiding consideration in undertaking fieldwork is therefore 'what works' (Buchanan et al. (1988) refer to this as an 'opportunistic approach'). Even if there are principles, however, another reason for a pragmatic approach to researching organizations is that there is so much variability between sites that generalized prescriptions are rarely possible. Organizational research can thus be considered as much of a craft as a science, relying on experience, sensitivity to context and the individual researcher's social skills, even if guided by more systematic principles.

Some, perhaps much, of the guidance offered in this book may therefore appear to be obvious to researchers with substantial experience of working in organizations. If this is the case, all well and good, and sections can be skipped (although it may be advisable to check whether your experience is supported by other researchers' reports). It cannot be assumed, however, that all organizational researchers will necessarily have such experience or will have reflected on it in ways that enable them to identify solutions to the issues discussed. The book also does not claim to offer a magic formula that will ensure that any organizational research project will proceed without a hitch. Rather, by alerting researchers to potential issues and discussing possible solutions, in many cases by reference to published examples of how they have been overcome, the aim is to provide some reassurance that the quagmire of fieldwork, as it can sometimes appear, can be safely traversed and that there is a body of experience available that can avoid each researcher having to 'reinvent the wheel'.

In emphasising the practical, craft-based nature of the research process and the issues involved in getting in, on and out of organizations, this book might be viewed as being applicable only to 'intensive' observational research carried out over a long period of time. While many of the issues discussed in the book are perhaps brought most strongly to the fore in what is sometimes referred to as organizational ethnography, however, a lot of them also apply, albeit maybe to a different degree or in a different way, to more 'distant' forms of organizational

Table 1.1 Key issues in the practice of organizational fieldwork

	Getting in	Getting on	Getting out	Getting back
Field experiments	• Identifying sites • Negotiating organizational participation	• *Gaining subjects' trust* • *Organizational politics* • Ethics	• Ethics of reporting	• Response to findings • Research fatigue
Surveys	• Identifying respondents • Engaging individual participation	• *Gaining respondents trust* • *Organizational politics* • *Ethics*	• Ethics of reporting	• Response to findings • Research fatigue
Analysis of internal documentation	• Identifying sources • Negotiating access	• Gaining organization's trust • Organizational politics • Ethics	• Ethics of reporting	• Response to findings • Research fatigue
Interview-based case studies	• Identifying interviewees • Engaging individual participation	• *Gaining interviewees' trust* • Organizational politics • Emotions • Ethics	• Ethics of reporting	• Response to findings • Research fatigue
Ethnomethodological work study	• Identifying sites • Negotiating organizational participation	• Fitting in • Gaining organization members' trust • Building rapport • Recording data • Observer effects • Organizational politics • Ethics	• Personal relationships • Planning disengagement • Ethics of reporting	• Response to findings • Research fatigue
Organizational ethnography	• Identifying sites • Negotiating access	• Fitting in • Gaining organization members' trust • Building rapport • Finding a role • Recording data • Observer effects • *Observation bias* • Organizational politics • Emotions • Ethics	• Personal relationships • Planning disengagement • Fulfilling the bargain • Ethics of reporting	• Response to findings • Research fatigue

research. This is the case not just with interview-based studies (some of which may even call themselves ethnographic), but also with surveys and, indeed, with research based on published data.

Problems of access, for example, apply to a researcher undertaking a survey perhaps just as much as a researcher wishing to undertake interviews, although they may be less visible to the former and may be framed as an issue of response rates. Nevertheless both researchers face the challenge, as organizational outsiders, of making contact with relevant respondents/interviewees and of persuading them to engage with the study. Similarly, the issues faced in 'getting on' in an organization, such as incentives for participation and organizational politics, apply just as much to survey respondents as they do to interviewees, even if they are not visible to the researcher sending the survey. Nor, despite their apparent objectivity, are these issues necessarily avoided by research relying on secondary data or published statistics, the possible influences on the original collection of which are rarely considered at the point of use. Highlighting these issues may therefore encourage greater awareness of these influences and their possible implications for research findings.

Table 1.1. presents an overview of some of the key issues in the practice of organizational fieldwork (which are discussed in subsequent chapters) that may arise in different forms of organizational research across the four phases of the Buchanan et al. framework. This is not intended as a comprehensive listing of all possible forms of research or issues that a particular form of research may encounter, but as an illustration of the potential relevance of the topics covered in the book across a range of different forms of organizational research. Italics are used to indicate issues that may not always be immediately evident when carrying out particular forms of research, but which may nevertheless be a potential influence on how the research proceeds.

Overview of the book

Broadly speaking, the structure of this book follows that of the process of organizational research, as described by Buchanan et al. (1988). Before we can begin to think even about 'getting in' to an organization, however, it would seem important to establish an understanding on a number of points that inform the approach to organizational fieldwork that is adopted in the subsequent chapters.

The first of these is to consider what it is about organizations that makes organizational research a potentially distinctive domain of study. Chapter 2 therefore sets out some of the characteristics that could be considered to differentiate organizations from other forms of social research site and explores their implications for the conduct of research. One of these implications can be seen to be the existence of a range of forms of organizational research, from 'scientific inquiry' to consultancy, each with their different outlook and expectations. Organizations vary too, in terms such as their size, industry, history and location and this may affect how they can be researched. Consequently, it is argued that there is no 'one right way' to study organizations, and that the responses to the issues raised in the book are likely to depend on the interaction between the researchers' approach and the type of organization.

Chapter 3 discusses the research process as it is represented in many research methods textbooks, in order to locate the particular focus of this book and to relate this to the more general methodology literature. The key features of each stage of the process and the methods employed in these stages are identified and their strengths and weaknesses in particular types of study discussed. It will be argued that while such texts may sometimes acknowledge that there can be practical difficulties in conducting empirical research, their primary focus tends to be on the principles of research design, data-gathering and analysis. A more detailed breakdown of the research process will then be presented to highlight the stages that will be the main focus of the book.

Organizational researchers face increasing public expectations that their work will be demonstrably ethical and this is particularly the case in any discussion of fieldwork, where a researcher's practice may be most visible to members of the public. Chapter 4 sets out the nature, scope and principles of social research ethics and identifies four stances on ethics that may be found in organizational research. The chapter also considers the (contested) process of ethical regulation of organizational research in terms of ethical codes, ethical guidance and review and research governance. Discussion of the ethics of organizational fieldwork is not confined to Chapter 4, however. Rather the particular ethical issues that may be encountered at each stage of the research process are considered in the subsequent chapters.

With these understandings established, Chapters 5 to 8 discuss the process of organizational research, following the 'getting in, getting on, getting out and getting back' framework. Thus, working on the assumption that a suitable research topic and research question have been defined, the first stage of fieldwork will involve finding a suitable organization, or organizations, in which to study the chosen topic. Chapter 5 establishes the starting point for the framework. Various ways of identifying potential research sites and establishing contacts are described and their advantages and disadvantages considered, illustrated by examples from the literature.

Assuming that successful contact has been made with a relevant organization, the focus then turns to potential barriers to access and how to overcome them, including such issues as degrees of access; different roles in the access process, such as gatekeepers and sponsors; and the organizational politics of access. Gaining access is presented as a matter of negotiating, formally or informally, the terms of a 'bargain' with the organization. A number of potential terms of this bargain, such as the price of entry, any financial arrangements and possible returns to the organization, will be considered, with particular discussion of confidentiality agreements. Successful negotiation of access, it is argued, is likely to depend on the researcher's interpersonal skills and their ability to persuade gatekeepers that the rewards of allowing access exceed the costs.

After what can be the difficult process of gaining access to an organization, there can be a tendency to assume that the researcher's troubles are over. As Chapter 6 discusses, however, many issues may be encountered even after formal access has been granted. For example, individual and organizational incentives for members of an organization to participate in research and possible reasons for non-participation are explored. Research also often has a political dimension and researchers need to be aware that they may face hostility and encounter manipulation and deceit. The pressures this can create for researchers are discussed and possible measures to address these are presented.

Chapter 7 considers the circumstances of the researcher's withdrawal from the research site. Some potential causes of early termination of fieldwork are discussed and ways to avoid this suggested. When and how to withdraw in a more managed way are then discussed and the need to fulfil the 'bargain' made when negotiating access and the potential consequences of 'cut and run' research are emphasized. Reasons for maintaining access and how this may be achieved are also considered.

As most researchers studying organizations are likely to be interested in publishing their findings, the question of what, how and where work is published, or even proposed to be published, can be a source of considerable tension. Issues surrounding the reporting of organizational research are therefore highlighted, distinguishing between reporting to research participants and reporting to a wider audience, whether in an academic journal or the mass media. Various options for reporting organizational research to participants are considered in terms of what is reported. For example this might be research components, such as transcripts of interviews or summaries of analyses, or research outputs, such as reports or recommendations. Next, those to whom these reports may be made – the organization's management, the research sponsor, research 'subjects' – are identified and potential issues with reporting to each discussed.

Arguments for a right to publish are then presented and some examples of organizations seeking to prevent or restrict publication are described. These are countered with arguments for seeking approval and different approaches to getting approval are discussed. Some problems of reporting organizational research to particular audiences, for example in relation to anonymity and confidentiality and the accuracy of accounts, are highlighted and the ethics of reporting are explored.

Even when fieldwork is considered to have been completed, a researcher may still wish to gain access to the same organization again at a later date. In Chapter 8, possible reasons for such a return to the field are discussed, some barriers to achieving this are outlined and suggestions are made on how these might be overcome.

Research on and in organizations is constantly evolving as organizations themselves change, and discussion in the literature can take some time to catch up with these developments. Chapter 9 seeks to address some of these emerging topics in researching organizations. One of the most prominent of these relates to the various forms of Internet research. Such research raises issues from the use of email and video-conferencing for interviews, or studies of virtual organizations that conduct all, or much, of their business via the Internet, to researching organizations that predominantly exist online. There is some overlap between Internet research and the issues faced in international research, where the increasingly global distribution of research sites, even within a single organization, may preclude face-to-face interaction in some, or even most, locations. International research also faces cultural and linguistic challenges, which, while not new in the context of international business research, are increasingly made more complex by the distribution of staff over multiple locations even within a single function. Finally the chapter discusses research in non-conventional organizations, reflecting the growing attention to the third sector, but also research in difficult-to-access settings, such as the military, in which many of the issues discussed in the book may be particularly marked.

One of the assumptions of this book, discussed in Chapter 2, is that organizations constitute a distinctive domain of research. This claim is revisited in Chapter 10 in the context of an overview of the book's argument. While it is acknowledged that organizational research poses few, if any, unique challenges, it is argued that researching organizations faces a number of issues to a greater degree than other forms of social research. Similarly, while acknowledging that many of the issues are not necessarily new, it will be argued that they have tended to be neglected in much contemporary discussion of research methods and deserve greater attention. Finally it is suggested that the expanding role of organizations in contemporary society, the changing nature of the employment relationship and the growth in the global workforce mean that organizations are becoming increasingly important as research sites and that the issues raised in this book are therefore likely to be of continuing significance for researchers across a range of disciplines, not just management.

━━━━━━━━━━━━━━━ **EXERCISE** ━━━━━━━━━━━━━━━

1 Fieldwork in organizations

- for each of the types of study listed at (a) to (e) consider whether they may face difficulties in:
  - o identifying suitable organizations to study
  - o getting agreement from suitable organizations to participate in the research
  - o locating and contacting potential participants in those organizations
  - o gaining entry to an organization's site
  - o persuading organization members to participate
  - o knowing whether data collected accurately reflect the situation in the organization
  - o maintaining engagement with the organization over many months
  - o reporting on 'sensitive' findings
  - o gaining re-entry to an organization

  (a) An industry-wide survey of the adoption of particular human resource practices
  (b) An evaluation of the implementation of a new production technology
  (c) An experiment to investigate the effect of workload on creativity in advertising agencies
  (d) A study of the negotiation of a new international agreement on green-house gas emissions
  (e) A study of how companies respond to new health and safety legislation.

Further reading

In addition to the works cited in the references for this chapter, a further selection of classic articles on fieldwork in the social sciences are included in this four-volume edited collection:

Pole, C. (2005) *Fieldwork*. London: SAGE.

References

Bryman, A. (1988) 'Introduction: "inside" accounts and social research in organizations', in A. Bryman (ed.), *Doing Research in Organizations*. London: Routledge, pp. 1–20.

Buchanan, D., Boddy, D. and McCalman, J. (1988) 'Getting in, getting on, getting out and getting back', in A. Bryman (ed.), *Doing Research in Organizations*. London: Routledge, pp. 53–67.

Delamont, S. (2002) *Fieldwork in Educational Settings: Methods, Pitfalls and Perspectives*, 2nd edn. London: Routledge.

Gellner, D. and Hirsch, E. (2001) *Inside Organizations: Anthropologists at Work*. Oxford: Berg.

Halliday, S. and Schmidt, P.D. (2009) *Conducting Law and Society Research: Reflections on Methods and Practices*. Cambridge: Cambridge University Press.

Randall, D., Harper, R. and Rouncefield, M. (2007) *Fieldwork for Design: Theory and Practice*. London: Springer.

Scott, J. and Marshall, G. (2009) *A Dictionary of Sociology*, 3rd revised edn. Oxford: Oxford University Press.

Walford, G. (1991) *Doing Educational Research*. London: Psychology Press.

2

Research and Organizations

Chapter objectives

- to identify the distinctive characteristics of organizations as sites of social research
- to identify some key forms of organizational research
- to identify some key dimensions of variation between types of organization

Calling a book *Researching Organizations* might seem to suggest, at the very least, that organizations constitute a distinct context for research – a book called *Researching Nothing in Particular* might be expected to have rather less appeal. The title could also be seen to suggest, however, that organizations are relatively homogenous as a research context and that organizational researchers face a common set of issues. In this chapter various characteristics of organizations, forms of organizational research and dimensions on which organizations may vary are discussed to explore the extent to which either of these assumptions is valid.

Just what is it that makes organizations so different as sites for research?

Most organizational behaviour textbooks, generally written for students taking business and management courses, are surprisingly short on definitions of what an organization is, perhaps because the answer is seen as so self-evident as to require no discussion (although their assumptions are often revealed in their focus on 'firms', 'companies' and occasionally public sector bodies). Where they do discuss the nature of organizations (e.g. Mullins, 2010) it seems to be much easier to identify examples of organizations than to suggest how they differ from other forms of social group. Such texts may also seek to identify 'common factors in organizations', e.g. people, objectives, structure and management (Mullins, 2010: 78–9), although, again, these may be seen as reflecting the interests of their audience rather than providing a comprehensive definition.

In Chapter 1, therefore, organizations were defined as a relatively enduring group of people with some degree of coordination around a common principle that has a more or less identifiable boundary. This was intended to avoid the rather functionalist assumptions of the organizational behaviour textbooks, while providing some basis for differentiating organizations from other types of social group. Transient groupings, such as commuters passing through a railway station, are therefore not an organization, nor are a group of teenagers who hang around a village bus stop, even though they may do this regularly for quite a period of time. The same commuters or teenagers could become an organization, however, if circumstances led them to coordinate in, say, agitating for better facilities at the station or leisure activities in the village. Coordination around principles also allows churches or clubs and societies to be considered as organizations, where the more common language of objectives may be seen as inappropriate. In many larger organizations this coordination is likely to be formalized in hierarchical power relationships, but this would not seem a necessary feature of organizations per se (and such relationships may also be found in other forms of social group).

While the boundaries of an organization may not always be clear-cut, it would seem an important characteristic of an organization that it should be possible to identify the people who form part of this group (if not all to the same degree). The boundaries of organizations need not be physical, although in some cases (think of a high-security prison), this may be a key characteristic. Boundaries may also be legal, for example in the form of a contract of employment, or simply by personal subscription or mutual identification.

Although it may be helpful to adopt a broad definition of organizations for the purposes of distinguishing organizations from other forms of social group, the sorts of business and public sector organizations that are the focus of organizational behaviour textbooks are probably the most common sites for research in organizations. Such organizations tend to be relatively formal in their structuring, to have clear physical boundaries, to have more explicit objectives and to be seen as persisting over a reasonable span of time. The larger and better-established of these organizations also tend to be economically powerful and may have their own capability for, and interest in, research.

Although individually these characteristics are not exclusive to organizations (a family, village or street-corner gang may be relatively persistent and well-bounded, for example) it is their combination that distinguishes organizations from other types of social group. These characteristics may also affect how research may be undertaken in organizations.

Table 2.1 The distinctive character of organizations

Characteristics of organizations that make them distinctive as research sites:

- coordination
- common principle
- boundary
- relative persistence.

In business and public sector organizations these characteristics may be more formalized and they may also exhibit:

- economic power
- capability for, and interest in, research.

The coordination exhibited by organizations, for example, is often viewed in terms of structure and management. In larger organizations this may be highly formalized and even expressed in an official organigram, defining the organizational hierarchy and the places of particular individuals within it. As will be discussed in later chapters this structure may be important in research, for example in determining the scope of access that an individual may be able to grant or how an association with particular individuals may be viewed by others in the organization. It is not that there is no equivalent structure in other social groups, but that the bureaucratic character of many organizations means that these effects pertain to the structural positions of the individuals as much as to the individuals themselves. A Head Teacher acquires a certain status by virtue of their role that does not depend on their personal qualities as an individual. Management also implies some formal power relationship of particular individuals over others (even if this may not always be informally observed). Sensitivity to both the formal and informal structure may therefore be important in the conduct of organizational research.

The common principle(s) of an organization may be symbolically important as values with which researchers may need to present their work as aligned, or at the very least not in conflict. Gaining access to a commercial organization, for example, may require a case to be made that the costs of participation in the research will be minimal and that it may indeed have economic benefits, while a healthcare organization may be more persuaded by arguments that research will improve patient care. That there are common principles that an organization is said to subscribe to, need not imply that all individuals in the organization do so with the same enthusiasm, or even that some organization members do not reject them. Organizations are not necessarily unitary and sensitivity to conflict and factions within an organization may be essential to effective research practice.

The boundaries of formal organizations are often clearly demarcated and access inside them tightly controlled. There may be literal gatekeepers (such as receptionists or security personnel) whose role it is to police these boundaries. It is therefore often difficult to undertake research in organizations without formal permission because their practices are often not visible in the public realm.

While organizational boundaries may be a barrier, the persistence of organizations may facilitate research. Most organizations are likely to remain in existence for the duration of a research study. This is not to say that this apparent stability may not mask considerable internal change (departments may be restructured, individuals join and leave the organization, or change jobs), but the formal entity endures.

The economic power of organizations, especially large commercial ones, enables them to exert a degree of potential control over research that can weaken the researchers' position. It means, for example, that they can afford to resort to the law to protect their interests against research findings that they are unhappy with, or can enforce non-disclosure agreements. Such power need not be solely restrictive on research, however. For example it may be used to help the researcher with the expenses of their study (although this may be considered to compromise their independence) or mean that the organization has access to data that it may be beyond the resources of a researcher to gather.

Many large organizations also have their own research capacity. Sometimes this is directed solely at scientific development of their products, but in others it may also be directed at organizational improvement. This capacity can help researchers by making organizations informed consumers of research who appreciate its importance and understand what is involved. Their internal research activities may be seen as a benchmark, however, against which external research may be measured (and found wanting, for example where qualitative social research is proposed to an organization with a strong culture of scientific research, such as in medical settings). Organizations may also show an active interest in research they consider relevant to their situation. Researchers may therefore encounter what Giddens (1993) terms the 'double hermeneutic', whereby organizational members frame their understanding of their own activities in terms of concepts that are the product of prior research.

We will return to consider whether the effects of these characteristics are actually sufficient to designate organizations as a distinct domain of social research in Chapter 10, but we will now turn our attention to whether, as a consequence of these characteristics, research on organizations may involve distinctive forms of research.

Forms of organizational research

An examination of the literature reporting research in organizations reveals a wide diversity of different forms of practice being included within this designation and also a diversity of terminology to describe these. Thus, as Buchanan and Bryman (2009: xxviii) note, 'many commentators use the terms methodology, design, strategy and methods synonymously, inclusively ... and often without precise definition'. For their part, Buchanan and Bryman (2009: xxvii) make the case for restricting the term method to 'a tool or technique or approach for collecting data', but this would only apply to a subset of the forms of practice undertaken by organizational researchers and be inconsistent, as they acknowledge, with much writing on research methods. Rather than enter these debates, therefore, this book will refer to 'forms of organizational research' to describe the types of research practice that may be employed in researching organizations. This will be taken to be more than just the 'framework for the collection and analysis of data' that Bryman and Bell refer to as 'research design', and includes the philosophical assumptions influencing these practices.

Many of these forms of research that are used to study organizations have been adopted, and often adapted, from practices in other disciplines and are not therefore specific to the study of organizations. These include studies emulating the practices of the natural sciences, such as experiments and population analyses, studies drawing on the ethnographic tradition from anthropology and sociologically informed ethnomethodological and symbolic-interactionist studies. There are also a number of forms of research practice, however, that may be argued to be more distinctive to research in organizations, such as action research and consultancy, that capitalize on the particular characteristics of organizations such as their economic power and research capacity, or that specifically question those characteristics, such as critical research.

Given the concern of this book with the practice of organizational fieldwork, discussion will be focused on those forms of research that involve the researcher getting 'out of the office and into the "field"', as Scott and Marshall (2009: 256) put it. A number of significant forms of organizational research practice in which the researcher does not have direct contact with any organization, will therefore only receive passing mention. These include: studies reviewing or undertaking meta-analyses of existing studies or re-analysing their data (Hakim, 2000); studies making use of secondary data provided by third parties such as national statistical bureaux and commercial database companies; and studies analysing documentation relating to organizations that is available in the public domain, such as company reports; laboratory experiments with student subjects (Colquitt, 2008); and simulations (Harrison et al., 2007).

It should be noted, however, that despite not involving any fieldwork, analysis of published statistics, such as those produced by national statistical bureaux or by commercial data services, do not entirely avoid the issues discussed in this book. Rather the significance, or otherwise, of these issues is likely to be inaccessible to the researcher who needs to take it on faith that they were appropriately addressed in the original data-gathering exercise. Even where data are apparently objective outputs from highly regulated and even automated reporting systems, such as stock price indices or company accounts, it cannot be assumed that they are necessarily a valid and reliable measure of the phenomenon of interest, as financial scandals and changing reporting standards may reveal.

Excluding organizational research that does not involve fieldwork does not significantly reduce the variety of forms of research to be considered though, as variants of most of the non-fieldwork forms of research may be carried out in field settings or drawing on primary data. There is a significant tradition of field experiments in organizational research, for example, such as the classic Hawthorne experiments (Roethlisberger and Dickson, 1939), and of the use of surveys in place of, or as a supplement to, secondary data. It would therefore seem necessary to consider other ways of categorizing organizational research to distinguish different approaches.

One common categorization is between quantitative and qualitative strategies/designs/methods (see, for example, Bryman and Bell, 2011; Cooper and Schindler, 2011; or Easterby-Smith et al. 2008). This would seem misleading, however, as it implies that the type of data used in a study is the key determinant of the research approach and that using numbers is fundamentally different from, and perhaps even incompatible with, research using 'people's own written or spoken words and observable behaviour' (Taylor and Bogdan, 1998: 7). This is not to deny that research using numbers often tends to adopt a rather different approach and to make different assumptions about the nature of reality (ontology) and our knowledge of it (epistemology), than that found in many, but certainly not all, studies that employ qualitative data, but to argue that the association is not a necessary one and that data type is not therefore a robust basis on which to categorize research. Rather, it would seem more helpful to categorize research in terms of the epistemological assumptions on which it is based (Johnson and Duberley, 2000).

At the risk of over-simplification, two main epistemological positions may be identified. On the one hand, there is what is often termed positivism (Bryman and Bell, 2011; Easterby-Smith et al., 2008; Gill and Johnson, 2010). This proposes that the methods of organizational research should be modelled on those of the natural sciences (methodological monism), following a hypothetico-deductive approach (using theory to develop hypotheses that are tested against specifically gathered data) and seeking to establish law-like generalizations about organizational phenomena. On the other, following the hermeneutic and phenomenological traditions in the humanities and social sciences, there is what is often termed interpretivism, which argues that the methods of the natural sciences are inappropriate for the understanding of social (and organizational) phenomena and that alternative, inductive research methods (developing understanding from data gathered without necessarily having a predefined theory) are required that seek to engage with the way that social actors inter-pret their world.[1]

Thus, while positivist organizational researchers tend to gather quantitative data (because these are amenable to statistical analysis which can enable their hypotheses to be definitively tested) their assumptions do not preclude the gathering of qualitative data. Indeed there is a significant tradition in positivist research in organizations, such as the case methods of Eisenhardt (1989) or Yin (2003) or the descriptive inference of King et al. (1994), that relies predomi-nantly on qualitative data. Nor, conversely, does the rejection of the methods of the natural sciences as a model for social research mean that interpretive researchers cannot use quantitative data, even if they might tend to argue that such data tend to obscure the interpretations involved in their gathering and analysis and that qualitative data provide more insight on the interpretations of social actors that they seek to understand.

Another dimension of differentiation of research in organizations was pro-posed by Burrell and Morgan (1979), who categorized social theories along two dimensions: subjectivism/objectivism and the sociology of regulation/sociology of radical change. The resulting 2×2 matrix identified four 'paradigms' that they called interpretivist, functionalist, radical humanist and radical structuralist. Although controversial in its attempt to fit all social theory into its categories and in its argument that the paradigms are incommensurable (i.e. no synthesis between them is possible), their regulation/radical change dimension enables the differentiation of critical organizational research (subjectivist/radical

Table 2.2 Forms of relationship between researchers and organizations

Relationship	Guiding principles
Research in organizations	Researcher independence Research aims to meet the researcher's objectives
Research with organizations	Partnership between researcher and organization members Research aims to meet mutually beneficial objectives
Research for organizations	Research instigated by the organization Research aims to meet the organization's objectives

---

[1]Just to complicate matters, some interpretive researchers propose that even if the natu-ral science methods are not applicable to social research, the principles that the natural sciences are seen to aspire to, such as objectivity, rigour, and reliability, should neverthe-less guide social research (in order that it can be more scientific). It may therefore be helpful to distinguish between such a 'weak' interpretivist position, e.g. Lofland (1995), Flick (2009), and that of other, 'strong' interpretivists, e.g. Law (2004), who would reject both the methods and the principles of the natural sciences (because they would argue that the two are inseparable).

change), from traditional interpretivism (subjectivist/regulation – according to Burrell and Morgan [1979]).

A third way in which organizational research may be categorized concerns the relationship between the researcher and the organization, that is, whether the research is conducted in, with or for an organization as shown in Table 2.2. The latter two forms of research may, broadly speaking, be considered to correspond to action research and consultancy.

These three dimensions (epistemology, regulation/radical change and relationship between researcher and organization) are orthogonal to one another so there is no necessary relationship between particular forms of research and any one position on any dimension, although certain forms may tend to adopt a particular epistemological position and some combinations (critical consultancy?) may be highly unlikely. Table 2.3 maps the association between a number of forms of organizational research and these dimensions. The forms of research listed are not intended to be comprehensive, but cover most of the 'key methods' (Gill and Johnson, 2010) or 'types of study' (Hakim, 2000) that may involve the carrying out of fieldwork. Rather than attempt to review the technicalities of carrying out these approaches in practice, the discussion below will focus on their implications for organizational fieldwork. References to sources that are able to offer the depth of specialist guidance that is needed to undertake these forms of research, however, are given in the further reading list at the end of this chapter.

Experimental research

Experimental research involving direct interaction with organizations may be of three types: true, field and natural experiments. All are based on a positivist epistemology that draws on the natural sciences. In *true experiments* the researcher is able to: control which of the (randomly selected) subjects receives the treatment or not; identify and measure the effects of the treatment; and control any other possible influences on the effects being measured. Achieving such conditions will require the establishment of a 'laboratory' in which all relevant variables can be controlled and measured. While this will typically be located away from the the organization being studied, usually in a university or research institute, in principle it could be located 'on site' in the organization.

The strength of a true experiment will be in the replicability of findings and in their internal validity (as the researcher is able to control all potentially confounding factors). Where it is not possible to set up fully controlled conditions in an organization it may nevertheless be possible to conduct *quasi-experiments* that follow the principles of experimental design, but in which the assignment of subjects to the treatment and comparison groups is not random, for example by taking a series of measurements of a single group before and after the

Table 2.3 Association between forms of organizational research and dimensions of differentiation

	Positivist	Interpretivist	Regulation	Radical change	In organization	With organization	For organization
Experiments	4		4		2	1	1
Surveys	3	1	4		2	1	1
Ethnographic		4	3	1	2	1	1
Ethnomethodological		4	4		2	1	1
Case study	2	2	2	2	3	1	
Critical research		4		4	3	1	
Action research	2	2	2	2	1	3	
Consultancy	2	2	4				4

Key: 1 = possible association, 2 = probable association, 3 = highly likely association, 4 = (almost) certain association.

administration of a treatment. This has the advantage of being less disruptive to the organization. Such intervention may take place in the workplace setting without establishing control of the conditions (*field experiments*), or the researcher may seek to find *natural experiments* in which different groups, not necessarily within the same organization, happen to experience some treatment (or not) and their respective outcomes are compared. While sacrificing internal validity (the researcher has no control over the conditions), the external validity of such studies is improved (as the effects occur in a 'natural' setting or are naturally occurring).

As the talk of variables and measurement implies, experimental studies tend to favour quantitative data, and their pursuit of control implies an a priori theory about the phenomenon of interest that the experiment seeks to test. It is possible, however, for experimental researchers to collect qualitative observational data and verbal reports, although such data are likely to be highly structured and may be converted to numerical indices for ease of data analysis.

Setting up a laboratory to undertake experimental studies 'in the field' would seem impossible without the active support of the host and the resources involved would seem likely to be beyond the reach of all but the largest of organizations. Even the conduct of field experiments or the collection of data on natural experiments, however, may be expected to require extensive cooperation. Researchers seeking to pursue field-based experimental studies would therefore seem likely to be working with or for the organization they are studying, either in a collaborative action research mode or as consultancy, and will need to be able to demonstrate clear benefits of the study that significantly outweigh the potentially high costs. Recruiting potential partner organizations and maintaining good relationships with them over the duration of the study is thus likely to be no less important for such research than for extensive observational fieldwork, although the researcher may seek to adopt a more distant role, especially with experimental subjects, so as not to compromise their objectivity.

Survey research

Survey studies involve researchers eliciting information from a relatively large number of individuals, either in a personal capacity or as representatives of an organization or a subgroup within an organization, through the administration of a structured questionnaire. Analytic (or explanatory) surveys that seek to test a theory will require careful design of questions to ensure that relevant variables are appropriately measured and the selection of a suitable sample to enable inferences to be drawn about the population being investigated. Descriptive (or exploratory) surveys are more concerned with characterizing a particular phenomenon (perhaps as a prelude to developing theory for subsequent testing), and may include more open questions seeking qualitative responses, but still need to pay attention to sampling to enable generalization of their findings. Analytical surveys are likely to be associated with a positivist epistemology, but a descriptive survey could be conducted as part of an interpretivist study.

Surveys may be administered face-to-face, by post, telephone, email or, increasingly, online. In all cases the researcher will need to gain access (directly or indirectly) to potential respondents, but only face-to-face and telephone surveys involve some direct interaction between the researcher and respondents. While the researcher may need the cooperation of the organization to be able to contact respondents and to get into the organizational setting to conduct a face-to-face survey, the amount of interaction between the researcher and respondent will generally be limited to completion of the questionnaire. Indeed the researcher may seek to restrict and standardize their interaction so as not to bias the responses.

Ethnographic research[2]

A very different approach is adopted by ethnographic researchers, reflecting their interpretive epistemology. They typically assume that understanding of organizational phenomena requires close engagement with the research site, usually over an extended period of perhaps one year or more, involving the gathering[3] of data through unobtrusive observation and informal conversation. While it is acknowledged that individuals in the research setting may change their behaviour as a result of being studied, it is believed that they will find it difficult to sustain this for very long and that any effect is likely to diminish over time as they get used to the presence of the researcher. Because ethnographic data rely on what the researcher sees and hears and how they interpret and record it, they are considered to be inevitably subjective, however hard the researcher may try to be objective. As Clifford Geertz puts it, 'what we call our data are really our own constructions of other people's constructions of what they and their compatriots are up to' (Geertz, 1973: 9).

While claiming to eschew generalization in favour of 'thick description' of the detail of specific settings, ethnographic researchers often make statements

---

[2]Watson (2011: 205) argues that it is helpful to view ethnography not as a research method, but as the output from a particular type of research practice (involving 'close observation of and involvement with people in a particular setting'). Ethnographic research would therefore include studies that exhibit such characteristics, whether or not they identify themselves as ethnographies.

[3]Some researchers would question whether data are 'out there' to be gathered or are created in the process of research.

from their findings that go beyond the immediate setting (Hammersley, 2008; Payne and Williams, 2005; Williams, 2000).

Ethnomethodological research

In contrast to ethnographers' efforts to describe the richness and complexity of a setting as a whole, ethnomethodologists typically focus on how it is that people 'get on in the world' in everyday life, seeking to surface the taken-for-granted assumptions that produce and sustain a shared sense of social order. One way in which they may do this is through the detailed study of organizational practices. Rather than attempting to produce a description that can express the totality of a year's observation, therefore, ethnomethodologists might seek to analyse every nuance of two minutes of video of everyday practice in an organizational setting to explore how work is accomplished. In their insistence on the essentially situated character of all organizational practice, ethnomethodologists generally reject generalization of their findings (at least in the form conventionally understood in social research, as Sharrock and Randall [2004] discuss).

Case study research

A common form of organizational research is that of the case study of one or a small number of organizations. In such research, topics are defined broadly, not narrowly, contextual conditions are considered, not just the phenomenon of study, and multiple sources of evidence, both quantitative and qualitative, are used (Yin, 2003). Multiple case studies generally follow a replication, rather than sampling, logic with cases being selected on grounds of criticality, topicality or feasibility and access. Although Yin (1993) proposes that case studies may be descriptive, exploratory or explanatory, he is clear that case studies that emulate the scientific method are to be preferred. This positivist view of case studies has been taken up by other authors such as Eisenhardt (Eisenhardt, 1989; Eisenhardt and Graebner, 2007), as has been noted, who propose them as a valuable tool in the exploration of new topic areas that can lead to the development of a novel, testable and empirically valid theory.

Interpretive organizational researchers also use case studies, however, placing more emphasis on the rich theoretical insights that may be obtained from the in-depth study of particular settings (Dyer and Wilkins, 1991). Such research often bears some similarity to more traditional ethnographic research, indeed such studies may describe themselves in such terms, although it often involves fieldwork of a shorter duration and the use of interviews, rather than observation, as the primary data-gathering method.

Critical research

The structured character of organizations, with their positional power relationships and alignment to particular principles, provides the impetus for another form of research in organizations that seeks to provide resources that can enable these relationships and principles to be challenged. Such research is distinguished more by its emancipatory objectives than by methodology, but generally adopts an interpretivist epistemology (Alvesson and Deetz, 2000). Critical organizational researchers therefore do not have a distinctive methodological approach, but employ other methods such as surveys or case studies as appropriate. In its questioning of existing organizational practice, however, critical research may have an effect on how fieldwork is conducted (Alvesson and Deetz, 2000), for example by eschewing cooperation with senior figures in the organizational hierarchy. If, as was suggested, it would seem unlikely that critical research would be adopted as a form of consultancy, critical researchers could potentially engage in action research, perhaps with groups in a subordinate position in the organization.

Action research

Most organizational research, however, does not necessarily contest the motivating principles of the organizations it studies, and indeed in action research intervention by the researcher may be directed towards improving their achievement. Compared to the objectivity and detachment sought in scientific research, or ethnographers' attempts to avoid their presence altering the behaviour of organizational participants, action researchers deliberately initiate change in the organization. Their research therefore depends on the organization's agreement to the intervention and the collaboration of members of the organization in carrying out the study. The cooperative character of such research is particularly emphasized in some approaches to action research, such as participative inquiry (Reason and Bradbury-Huang, 2007).

Consultancy

There is some debate in the literature as to whether consultancy can be considered a valid form of research. Proponents, e.g. Klein (1976), Gummesson (2000), argue that consultancy offers a way to study aspects of an organization, such as strategic decision-making, that may be inaccessible to other forms of research. They also question whether there is any substantive difference between consultancy and action research, except that, capitalizing on the economic power of organizations, the consultant gets paid for their efforts and may have considerably greater resources at their disposal to carry out the research. Indeed it is argued that the payment can be seen as evidence of the importance and relevance of the research to the organization.

Others, however, question whether payment inevitably compromises the researcher's independence and point to the fact that the research problem and goals are generally set by the organization (although they may be open to subsequent negotiation), and that both the researcher and the organization may be committed to the successful outcome of any intervention, making any objective assessment difficult. Concerns are also raised about the ownership of results and the publication of findings being restricted by commercial confidentiality. Whether or not these concerns are seen to disqualify consultancy as a form of research, it is the case that some work reported as research in the organizational literature is the product of consultancy assignments (even if this is not always acknowledged).

This variety of forms of practice would seem enough to make it hard to generalize about research in organizations as a whole, but the situation is made considerably more complex by the enormous diversity in types of organization. While it is not possible to consider all possible ways in which organizations may vary from each other and how this may affect research, some discussion of a number of the possible dimensions of variation would seem necessary in order to appreciate the sorts of contexts in which organizational research is carried out.

Types of organization

Conventional typologies of organizations generally categorize them in terms of characteristics such as industry or size. While there is no universally agreed taxonomy of industries, most countries adopt a standardized classification of economic activity in their national statistics that can be used to define the industry in which a particular organization operates. These classifications can be highly specific, for example category C of the European Union Statistical Classification of Economic Activities in the European Community (NACE)[4] is designated as 'Manufacturing', within which category C.10 is 'Manufacturing of food products', C.10.7 is 'Manufacturing of bakery and farinaceous products' and C.10.7.1 is 'Manufacture of bread; manufacture of fresh pastry goods and cakes'.

Size may have a major influence on organizational structuring, with larger organizations tending to be more formalized and with more layers of hierarchy. A distinction is often made between small- and medium-sized enterprises (SMEs) and large organizations, but there is no internationally agreed definition of the cut-off point between the two. While this is usually measured in terms

---

[4]http://ec.europa.eu/eurostat/ramon/nomenclatures/index.cfm?TargetUrl = LST_NOM_ DTLandStrNom = NACE_REV2andStrLanguageCode = ENandIntPcKey = andStrLayoutC ode = HIERARCHIC

of the number of employees, with organizations having less than somewhere between 100 and 250 employees being classed as SMEs, it is sometimes also measured in terms of financial turnover.

Other ways in which organizations may differ from each other include their location (single or multi-site) and whether multiple sites are distributed within a small geographical area, across a country, or internationally. Within this last group a distinction is also usually made between multinational organizations, with a head office in one country and more or less autonomous foreign subsidiaries and transnationals that seek to operate at a global level.

Where an organization has multiple sites or operating units it may be possible to distinguish between different ways in which these component elements are organized. Decision-making in decentralized organizations is likely to be distributed to the component sites or units. In divisionalized organizations components are grouped, perhaps around product or geographical markets, while in centralized organizations all components are subordinated to a single authority.

Another important distinction between organizations may be in their ownership. This may be split into private and public sector, but other categories include family firms and third-sector organizations such as voluntary and community organizations, charities, social enterprises, cooperatives and mutuals. This last category may sometimes be referred to as non-profit or not for profit organizations, although this designation, which brings tax advantages in many jurisdictions, may not be restricted to small voluntary or community organizations, but may include large foundations and regular business organizations that choose to operate on a non-profit basis.

Finally, organizations may be classified in terms of their age, with a distinction between start-ups and established organizations. While this may have some connection with size, not all established organizations are large and spin-offs and spin-outs may be large in size from an early stage. Table 2.4 summarizes these dimensions of variation among organizations.

Table 2.4 Dimensions of variation between types of organization

Dimension	Categories
Industry	Standard industrial classification codes
Size	SMEs/large
Location	Localized/national/multinational/transnational
Structure	Decentralized/divisional/centralized
Sector	Public/private/family/not for profit/third sector
Age	Start-up/established

While the dimensions listed in Table 2.4 are not necessarily the only ways in which to categorize organizational types, they may be significant when conducting research in organizations. Industry, for example, is likely to influence the type of personnel found and the range of practices carried out – a coal mine, a pharmaceutical company and a bank, say, will have a very different mix of manual and non-manual labour with different skills carrying out different tasks. It is also often a criterion used in selecting research sites, e.g. a study of innovation practices in the automotive industry. Industries vary too in terms of their stability, with some, such as the IT sector, characterized by high rates of turnover of organizations, while others, such as basic goods manufacturing, show lower levels of change. This will affect the ease with which it is possible to identify suitable organizations in which to undertake research, as the potential population of target organizations may be continually changing, and the likelihood of target organizations' survival over the course of a longitudinal study. Industry conditions may be another influence on the opportunities for research, with organizations generally being more receptive when their industry is experiencing rapid growth (as resources are less constrained, so the potential costs of participation are less of a concern, and the likelihood of findings being considered as evidence of success are greater) and more defensive and reluctant to allow access during an industry downturn. Defensiveness may not just be a product of economic conditions, though, and industries are likely to vary in terms of the confidentiality of their practices. A proposal to undertake a study in the retail sector may encounter fewer difficulties and restrictions than one studying a research laboratory where commercial secrecy may be a concern.

The formalization that is often associated with increasing size (and perhaps also, to some extent, longer history) may be significant in the ease with which access may be gained to an organization. Access to smaller (and younger) organizations may be possible on the informal permission of perhaps a single individual, especially if they are a key actor in the organization such as the founder, whereas in larger (and more established) organizations there may be formal procedures in place requiring the involvement of several different departments (maybe not just those likely to be involved in the research, but also human resource and legal departments) before approval can be granted. Practically speaking, too, larger organizations are more likely to have clearly defined boundaries and to have staff specifically employed to police them.

The stronger structuring of large organizations may also restrict the scope of research even after access has been achieved, as organizational subunits (divisions, departments, sites) may set internal boundaries on research that may be absent in more informal, fluid and unitary SMEs, where staff are more likely to know each other and to accept a researcher on a colleague's recommendation. Further constraints on research may arise from the economic power of (generally larger) organizations, for example through the enforcement of non-disclosure agreements or contesting of what are perceived to be unfavourable findings.

The location of an organization may limit research access, as visiting more than a few sites of a large organization may be beyond the means of many researchers. If the research design requires study of more than the sites that are immediately accessible then other forms of contact with the organization, such as phone or email interviews, may be necessary to gather data, but may create problems of comparability with the findings from sites in which face-to-face interaction is possible. A further complication may be created in transnational companies where the phenomena of interest may be distributed across many locations, with perhaps even the staff involved having little or no face-to-face interaction, but carrying out their work through information and communication technology networks. If research sites or participants are located in different countries then there may be additional issues of cultural and linguistic differences.

The sector within which an organization operates need not necessarily influence its receptiveness to research; a private sector organization, for example, may be as welcoming or discouraging of a potential piece of research as one in the public or third sectors. Where it may have more influence, however, is on the principles around which an organization is coordinated, which may be important in shaping how it may be most effectively approached.

The most significant effect of organizational age on research in organizations is in organizations' persistence over time. Data on the survival rate of start-ups vary widely between countries, industry sectors and periods of time, but findings that about 20 per cent of start-ups fail within the first year and 50 per cent within five years are widely reported (Cook et al., 2012). From a research perspective this means that longitudinal studies face a high mortality rate and studies of individual start-ups have a high risk of premature termination. It is not that more established organizations are necessarily more stable, but that change is accommodated internally and the survival of the whole organization is not at stake. Nevertheless this changeability may create difficulties for research in established organizations where changes in personnel (sometimes through deliberate policies of job rotation) and internal reorganization may make it hard to maintain continuity. As a result research agreements may be subject to periodic renegotiation over the course of a longitudinal study.

▓▓▓▓▓▓▓▓▓▓▓▓▓▓▓ EXERCISES ▓▓▓▓▓▓▓

1 Which of the characteristics of organizations are exhibited by the following types of social group?

	Common Coordination principle	Boundary	Relative persistence	Economic power	Research capability
The audience at a concert					
Guests at a wedding					
A fire crew					
Contributors to Wikipedia					
Contractors on a building site					
Members of a surgical team					
A government inquiry					

2 Identify the relationship between these combinations of categories/forms of research as

(a) fundamentally incompatible
(b) compatible, but infrequently found in practice
(c) compatible and typically found in practice
(d) necessarily related

Combination	a	b	c	d
Positivism + qualitative data				
Quantitative data + ethnography				
Experiments + positivism				
Surveys + critical research				
Case studies + qualitative data				
Action research + ethnomethodology				
Consultancy + ethnography				

In each case, explain the reasons for the relationship identified? Where the relationship is identified as (a) or (b), what categories/forms of research might be more typically associated with the first named category/form? Why?

Further reading

Characteristics of organizations

For examples of other characterizations of organizations see:

Knights, D. and Willmott, H. (2012) *Introducing Organizational Behaviour and Management*, 2nd revised edn. Andover: Cengage Learning EMEA.

Forms of organizational research

There is a substantial literature on most of the forms of research referred to in this chapter. The following are among the more thorough and accessible discussions of particular forms.

Experiments

Although it is focused on research on 'sensitive topics', this article provides some useful guidance on the conduct of field experiments:

King, E.B., Hebl, M.R., Morgan, W.B. and Ahmad, A.S. (2012) 'Field experiments on sensitive organizational topics', *Organizational Research Methods*, 00(0): 1–21.

Similar advice for quasi-experiments is provided by:

Grant, A.M. and Wall, T.D. (2009) 'The neglected science and art of quasi-experimentation why-to, when-to, and how-to advice for organizational researchers', *Organizational Research Methods*, 12 (4): 653–86.

Surveys

Although it is now quite dated, a comprehensive discussion of most aspects of the design and conduct of surveys in social research is provided by:

Moser, S.C. and Kalton, G. (1985) *Survey Methods in Social Investigation*, 2nd edn. Aldershot: Dartmouth Publishing Co. Ltd.

For a more accessible overview, see:

Fowler, F.J. (2009) *Survey Research Methods*. London: SAGE.

For more information on online surveys see:

Dillman, D.A., Smyth, J.D. and Christian, L.M. (2009) *Internet, Mail, and Mixed-mode Surveys: The Tailored Design Method*, 3rd edn. Chichester: Wiley.
Sue, V.M. and Ritter, L.A. (2012) *Conducting On Line Surveys*. London: SAGE.

Ethnographic

Hammersley, M. and Atkinson, P. (2007) *Ethnography: Principles in Practice*, 3rd edn. London: Routledge.
Provides a general overview of the practice of ethnographic research.

Ybema, S., Yanow, D., Wels, H. and Kamsteeg, F. (2009) *Organizational Ethnography: Studying the Complexity of Everyday Life*. London: SAGE.
Includes chapters discussing a range of issues in the conduct of specifically organizational ethnography as well as an annotated bibliography of both classic and more contemporary organizational ethnographies.

Ethnomethodological

Rouncefield, M. and Tolmie, P. (2011) *Ethnomethodology at Work*. Farnham: Ashgate.
Includes a range of papers discussing the practice of workplace ethnomethodological research.

Randall, D., Rouncefield, M. and Harper, R. (2007) *Fieldwork for Design: Theory and Practice*. London: Springer.
Although focused on computer-supported cooperative work, this provides useful insight on the practice of ethnomethodological fieldwork.

Case study

Thomas, G. (2011) *How to Do Your Case Study: A Guide for Students and Researchers*. London: SAGE.
Provides a general introduction to the conduct of case study research.

Simons, H. (2009) *Case Study Research in Practice*. London: SAGE.
More geared to the practical issues of conducting case studies.

Critical research

Alvesson, M. and Deetz, S. (2000) *Doing Critical Management Research*. London: SAGE.
Quite theoretical, but also addresses some of the practical issues.

Action research

There is a wide variety of literature on action research, especially as it is applied in educational studies.

McNiff, J. and Whitehead, J. (2011) *All You Need to Know About Action Research*. London: SAGE.
Offers a general introduction to the topic (and the same authors have written a number of other introductory texts).

James, E.A., Slater, T. and Bucknam, A. (2012) *Action Research for Business, Nonprofit, and Public Administration: A Tool for Complex Times*. London: SAGE.
Adopts a slightly more organizational focus.

Consultancy

Gummesson, E. (2000) *Qualitative Methods in Management Research*. London: SAGE.
Makes the argument for consultancy as a form of organizational research.

Crowther, D. and Lancaster, G. (2008) *Research Methods: A Concise Introduction to Research in Management and Business Consultancy*. Oxford: Elsevier Butterworth-Heinemann.
Although primarily oriented towards student projects, addresses the overlap between management research and consultancy.

References

Alvesson, M. and Deetz, S. (2000) *Doing Critical Management Research*. London: SAGE.
Bryman, A. and Bell, E. (2011) *Business Research Methods*, 3rd edn. Oxford: Oxford University Press.
Buchanan, D.A. and Bryman, A. (2009) *The SAGE Handbook of Organizational Research Methods*. London: SAGE.
Burrell, G. and Morgan, G. (1979) *Sociological Paradigms and Organizational Analysis: Elements of the Sociology of Corporate Life*. London: Heinemann Educational.
Colquitt, J.A. (2008) 'Publishing laboratory research in AMJ: a question of when, not if', *Academy of Management Journal*, 51 (4): 616–20.
Cook, R., Campbell, D. and Kelly, C. (2012) 'Survival rates of new firms: an exploratory study', *Small Business Institute Journal*, 8 (2): 35–42.
Cooper, D.R. and Schindler, P.S. (2011) *Business Research Methods*, 11th edn. Singapore: McGraw-Hill.
Dyer, W.G. and Wilkins, A.L. (1991) 'Better stories, not better constructs, to generate better theory: a rejoinder to Eisenhardt', *Academy of Management Review*, 16 (3): 613–19.
Easterby-Smith, M., Thorpe, R. and Jackson, P.R. (2008) *Management Research*, 3rd edn. London: SAGE.
Eisenhardt, K.M. (1989) 'Building theories from case study research', *Academy of Management Review*, 14 (4): 532–50.
Eisenhardt, K.M. and Graebner, M.E. (2007) 'Theory building from cases: opportunities and challenges', *Academy of Management Journal*, 50 (1): 25–32.
Flick, U. (2009) *An Introduction to Qualitative Research*, 4th edn. London: SAGE.

Geertz, C. (1973) *The Interpretation of Cultures*. New York: Basic Books.

Gill, J. and Johnson, P. (2010) *Research Methods for Managers*, 4th edn. London: SAGE.

Giddens, A. (1993) *New Rules of Sociological Method*, 2nd edn. Cambridge: Polity Press.

Gummesson, E. (2000) *Qualitative Methods in Management Research*. London: SAGE.

Hakim, C. (2000) *Research Design: Successful Designs for Social and Economic Research*, 2nd edn. London: Routledge.

Hammersley, M. (2008) *Questioning Qualitative Inquiry: Critical Essays*. London: SAGE.

Harrison, J.R., Carroll, G.R. and Carley, K.M. (2007) 'Simulation modelling in organizational and management research', *Academy of Management Review*, 32 (4): 1229–45.

Johnson, P. and Duberley, J. (2000) *Understanding Management Research: An Introduction to Epistemology*. London: SAGE.

King, G., Keohane, R.O. and Verba, S. (1994) *Designing Social Inquiry: Scientific Inference in Qualitative Research*. Princeton, NJ: Princeton University Press.

Klein, L. (1976) *A Social Scientist in Industry*. Epping: Gower Press.

Law, J. (2004) *After Method: Mess in Social Science Research*. London: Routledge.

Lofland, J. (1995) 'Analytic ethnography: features, failings, and futures', *Journal of Contemporary Ethnography*, 24 (1): 30–67.

Mullins, L.J. (2010) *Management and Organizational Behaviour*, 9th edn. London: Financial Times/Prentice Hall.

Payne, G. and Williams, M. (2005) 'Generalization in qualitative research', *Sociology*, 39 (2): 295–314.

Reason, P. and Bradbury-Huang, H.B.-H. (2007) *The SAGE Handbook of Action Research: Participative Inquiry and Practice*, 2nd edn. London: SAGE.

Roethlisberger, F.J. and Dickson, W.J. (1939) *Management and the Worker: An Account of a Research Program Conducted by the Western Electric Company, Hawthorne Works, Chicago*. Cambridge, MA: Harvard University Press.

Scott, J. and Marshall, G. (2009) *A Dictionary of Sociology*, 3rd revised edn. Oxford: Oxford University Press.

Sharrock, W. and Randall, D. (2004) 'Ethnography, ethnomethodology and the problem of generalisation in design', *European Journal of Information Systems*, 13 (3): 186–94.

Taylor, S.J. and Bogdan, R. (1998) *Introduction to Qualitative Research Methods: A Guidebook and Resource*, 3rd edn. Chichester: Wiley.

Watson, T.J. (2011) 'Ethnography, reality, and truth: the vital need for studies of "how things work" in organizations and management', *Journal of Management Studies*, 48 (1): 202–17.

Williams, M. (2000) 'Interpretivism and generalisation', *Sociology*, 34 (2): 209–24.

Yin, R.K. (1993) *Applications of Case Study Research*. London: SAGE.

Yin, R.K. (2003) *Case Study Research: Design and Methods*, 3rd edn. London: SAGE.

3

The Research Process

Chapter objectives
• to identify the main stages of the research process
○ to identify issues at each stage that may influence the practice of fieldwork in organizations
○ to review the advantages and disadvantages of different data-gathering methods in organizational research
○ to highlight activities in the research process that may be important in the practice of fieldwork in organizations

Many research methods textbooks sometimes explicitly but more often implicitly by their chapter headings (e.g. Cooper and Schindler, 2011: 11; Gill and Johnson, 2010: 9; Robson, 2011: xxi), present the process of research in organizations as following the sorts of stages depicted in Table 3.1.

Although, as discussed in Chapter 1, this book will not attempt to present a comprehensive account of this whole process, it would nevertheless seem desirable to consider some of the key features of each stage to set the context for the subsequent discussion of the practicalities of organizational fieldwork. This also provides an opportunity to signpost literature that does offer such an account and that therefore complements the coverage in this volume.

Table 3.1 Stages of the research process

Stage	
0	Identify broad area of interest
1	Define the research topic
1a	Define the research question(s)
1b	Choose the research design
2	Gather data
3	Analyse data
4	Present findings

Stage 0 Identify a broad area of interest

Research typically starts from a general area of interest, some aspect of organizations that piques the researcher's curiosity. There is no principle, however, that can tell us what this may be. What particular area interests any individual researcher tends to be highly personal. For some people human resource management, public policy-making or military strategy, say, are endlessly fascinating, while others may be unable even to understand what anybody could possibly see in them. Although it may be possible to identify a variety of influences that may shape a researcher's interests, such as personal experience, academic training or opportunity (although these may themselves be products of an interest rather than sources of it), therefore, it makes little sense to try to prescribe the area of an individual's research. Rather it may be better to treat this as a given (hence its designation as stage 0) and to focus on the implications of this interest.

Areas of interest are often broadly defined in terms of a particular subfield within an academic discipline, such as penal theory in criminology, international relations in politics, or finance within management or by a domain of study such as healthcare, sustainable development or primary education. The two ways of defining an area are not necessarily mutually exclusive; a subfield may be associated with a particular domain, but studies starting from a subfield would seem likely to be more focused on their contribution to academic debates, for example the development or testing of theory, while domain-oriented studies may be more concerned with practical relevance.

For any particular academic subfield, moreover, there is often a dominant methodology, so it can appear that the choice of area of interest predetermines whether or not the researcher is likely to engage in fieldwork in organizations. In management, for example, studies in finance are predominantly quantitative, relying on data from public databases of company and stock market performance, and fieldwork in organizations is relatively rare. For many finance scholars, therefore, issues such as those discussed in this book may be excluded from consideration. This is not to say, however, that there is no place for fieldwork in studies of finance, as work in behavioural finance (e.g. Forbes, 2009) and the sociology of markets (e.g. Knorr-Cetina and Preda, 2006; MacKenzie, 2006) illustrates. Thus, while an area of interest may historically have been associated with particular methodologies this can be considered a matter of custom and practice rather than a necessary characteristic, and alternative approaches need not be ruled out.

Defining an area of interest at the level of an academic subfield, moreover, still leaves a huge scope for different interests within that field. Indeed the challenge for a researcher is more often that of choosing between perhaps many different areas of interest. How to narrow down to a specific topic will be addressed in the next section, but for the present the concern is how choosing an area of interest may already have implications for the conduct of fieldwork. This may operate in both directions. On the one hand, choice of an area of interest may be shaped by awareness of opportunities for fieldwork. For example the researcher may be keen to study an organization that is seen as particularly innovative in its field and may define their area of interest in a way that makes this organization a prime site in which to pursue their work. On the other hand, an area of interest may be chosen because of particular theoretical considerations and fieldwork opportunities pursued in the light of these.

Stage 1 Define the research topic

Getting from a broad area of interest to a specific research topic can be challenging and much time can be wasted in pursuing ideas that do not lead to viable topics. One way to try to avoid this is to look for 'ready-made' topics that have already been identified by others. It is a common trope of research papers and dissertations, for example, to include in their conclusions recommendations for 'further research'. Whether these are a viable source of topics for a particular researcher, however, will depend on the recommendations' alignment with the researcher's interests and the quality of the previous research. It is also the case that such lists of further research are sometimes a description of the research that the authors have been conducting during the time it takes to get their earlier work published and are simply priming the audience for their next papers. Even if the topic has not been subsequently studied, the fieldwork implications of such further research may not have been considered by the authors. Rather it may be a wish list of studies that the authors have been unable to pursue themselves and the feasibility of which they have not assessed.

In practice, feasibility is often a major consideration in the choice of research topic, even when researchers may present their work as driven by theoretical concerns or real-world significance. Feasibility may be viewed in terms of a number of aspects such as the possibility of access, likelihood of achieving outcomes, required resources, personal interest and competence (and in the case of students, the support of their supervisor). Such considerations may lead to a narrowing of the scope of the research topic in terms of the time frame, range of phenomena or variables addressed, or the number of cases to be considered. For example a study may focus on the adoption of environmental reporting systems by firms in a particular industry, in a particular country, over a particular period, perhaps relating only to particular measures rather than attempting to study environmental reporting in general. These aspects of feasibility will be considered in more detail in later chapters, but for the present it is sufficient to observe the extent to which issues relating to fieldwork may influence the path of research even in its very initial stages.

Other considerations that may influence the choice of a topic may relate to the significance of the expected contribution (a topic should be non-trivial, but realistic in its ambitions), ethical concerns (which will be discussed further in Chapter 4) and the amount of previous research on the topic. In terms of the last of these, it may be best to avoid topics with both a lot of previous research and little previous research. In the first case it can be difficult to find a distinctive contribution and there may be a risk in a popular area of other studies covering similar ground that may pre-empt the planned research. Little prior research, on the other hand, could indicate an overlooked area that may be a fertile niche for a researcher who identifies it, but it may also be a warning that the topic poses unanticipated difficulties that have deterred other researchers. Moreover, a lack of other studies in an area may limit the potential audience for the research. Table 3.2 summarizes the characteristics of a good topic. Similar considerations are discussed in Gill and Johnson (2010).

Stage 1a Define the research questions

Choosing a research topic is rarely sufficient to guide the actual conduct of research, both because there may be many ways to investigate a particular topic and because the description of a topic is often still too broad to define a specific plan of investigation. It is therefore often recommended that the first step in researching a topic should be to specify it more precisely in the form of one or more research questions. The emphasis placed on this and the form and detail with which research questions need to be specified are likely to reflect the researchers' epistemological assumptions. Studies adopting a positivist epistemology, for example, would normally expect the researcher to formulate precise research questions that are capable of being expressed as falsifiable hypotheses before undertaking any research activities. Only when it is clear what is being studied and how data will answer the questions should further planning of the research take place.

Social constructivist, or more broadly interpretivist, researchers, in contrast, may consider it acceptable for the research question to be refined in the course

Table 3.2 Characteristics of a good research topic

Feasible in terms of:
    Access
    Resources
    Researcher's competence
    Researcher's personal interest
Plausible contribution
Ethical
Moderate level of prior research

---

of the research as it becomes evident how social actors understand their situation. Indeed, in some interpretive approaches, such as narrative methods (Boje, 2001; Czarniawska, 2004), the very idea of a priori formulation of research questions may be considered as constraining the researcher's interpretations. Nevertheless, even in many interpretive studies it is considered good practice to present research questions (whether or not these were defined before the research was conducted) as a way of concisely framing the research topic, setting boundaries on what is done and demonstrating the success of the research in answering them.

Getting from a broad topic of interest to specific questions can be challenging because it is difficult to know where to start. Marx (1997) suggests a number of sources of potential questions:

- intellectual puzzles and contradictions
- the literature
- replication (applying an existing approach in a new context)
- structures and functions (how do these relate)
- opposition (challenging an existing approach)
- a social problem or an unrealized value
- gaps between official versions of reality and the facts on the ground
- the counter-intuitive
- empirical examples that trigger amazement
- new methods and theories
- new social and technical developments and social trends
- personal experience
- sponsors and teachers

Even having identified a suitable question, however, it may require several iterations to get it right.

Robson (2011) offers some useful advice on the characteristics of good research questions. They should, he argues: be clear and unambiguous; indicate the type of research being undertaken (exploratory, explanatory, descriptive, emancipatory); answerable; and non-trivial. Where there is more than one research question, there should be a clear logic linking them. Robson also warns against allowing research questions to be determined by methodological preferences (looking for questions that suit the characteristics of methods that the researcher is familiar with), that cannot be answered with available methods or that have already been answered (unless there are strong grounds for suggesting that the existing answers may be wrong).

Stage 1b Choose the research design

Research design is the main topic of many research methods textbooks. In some (e.g. Hakim, 2000) it is presented almost as a catalogue of ready-made options, available 'off-the shelf' and ready to be put into practice with little or no further modification. Other texts, however, view research design as an activity, rather than a packaged solution, emphasising the assembly of a coherent set of 'design processes of research' (Cresswell, 2009), comprising questions, theoretical lens, data collection, data analysis, writing up and validation, that are consistent in terms of the types of evidence and level of analysis that they address and the philosophical assumptions on which they are based.

Quite apart from differences over whether research design should be considered as a noun or a verb, an entity or a process, as was noted in discussing forms of research in Chapter 2, discussion of the topic is also bedevilled by a profusion of inconsistent terminology that places the emphasis variously on the character of the research process, types of data and philosophical assumptions. Robson (2011), for example, distinguishes between fixed, flexible and multi-strategy designs. In the first of these, which Robson also refers to as a quantitative strategy (reflecting its almost exclusive reliance on quantitative data), methodological choices are tightly specified before data are collected. 'Flexible' designs, in contrast, may evolve during data collection and are seen as typically involving qualitative data and hence are labelled as a qualitative strategy. Multi-strategy designs combine elements of the other two in sequence (typically, Robson suggests, flexible first and then fixed). Bryman and Bell (2011), on the other hand, place the emphasis on types of data, distinguishing between quantitative, qualitative and mixed-methods strategies and matching these against different designs, or 'frameworks for the collection and analysis of data' (experimental, cross-sectional, longitudinal, case study and comparative). Cresswell (2009) adopts a similar categorization of research designs in terms of quantitative 'methods' (comprising experiments and surveys), qualitative 'procedures' (ethnography, case studies, phenomenological research and narrative research) and mixed method 'procedures' (sequential, concurrent and transformative). Easterby-Smith et al. (2012), in contrast, plot a number of 'typical research designs', including action research, grounded theory and participant observation, on a 2×2 matrix with axes of positivist/social constructionist (epistemology) and detached/involved (role of the researcher).

The confusion created by this inconsistency within the literature can be a problem for researchers, especially where, it was argued in Chapter 2, what are secondary characteristics, such as data types or researcher roles, are elevated to a primary consideration. This is not to say that certain designs do not predominantly use particular types of data; experimentalists, for example, tend to use numbers as this allows them to make precise and robust statistical claims about the relationships they are studying, but that this association is not a necessary one. Similarly the involvement or detachment of a researcher is to some extent a matter of the researcher's self-perception, as it can be argued that all research involves some degree of intervention, whether or not the researcher pays attention to it.

The same problems also contribute to the long-standing debates about combining designs in so-called mixed methods studies. In focusing on the type of data it uses as the defining characteristic of a piece of research, for example, studies that use both are presented as transcending a significant philosophical or ideological divide. What this obscures, however, is that any incommensurability, if it exists, is in the researcher's assumptions in gathering (or perhaps as some would have it constructing) and analysing the data, rather than in the data themselves. A number, or a statement in an interview, collected by a researcher who believes that they are accessing some relatively enduring indication of a phenomenon that exists independently of their investigation and that this can be used to establish causal statements about phenomena that are to some degree generalizable and enduring, would seem to have a very different status for that researcher from that same number or statement 'collected' by a researcher who takes the view that data are 'really our own constructions of other people's constructions of what they and their compatriots are up to' (Geertz, 1993: 9).

Thus, that a researcher records both that 22 pupils out of a class of 30 expressed positive views about the efficacy of a new pedagogic technique and the words the pupils used in expressing these views does not necessarily involve any inconsistency. For the same researcher, however, to believe both – that the pupils' views can be construed as an objective measure of the technique's efficacy the validity of which is enhanced the greater the proportion of the pupils expressing views that are deemed positive; and that the views expressed by the pupils were specific, situated responses to the researcher's particular form of questioning in the particular context of that class at that particular time, the translation of which into an assessment of the technique's efficacy depends less on the number of pupils making particular types of comment than on the researcher's interpretations of these comments – would seem to require that they can understand the same phenomenon in quite different ways at the same time. While such mental dexterity may not be impossible, a variety of psychological theories, such as cognitive dissonance, suggest that it is unlikely.

This is not to say that people are always wholly consistent in their beliefs, or that researchers pursuing mixed-methods research are being disingenuous in asserting that they are not concerned about philosophical consistency (Bryman, 2006). Rather the point is that these assertions do not show that philosophical consistency is unnecessary. Just as it may be possible to produce grammatically meaningful sentences without awareness of the rules of grammar, this does not mean that such rules do not exist (even if they may be subject to change over time). Indeed, research as an activity that seeks to make logically defensible statements about the world would seem to need to be particularly careful about those rules. A British tourist in Rome, for example, may be able to find their way to the Trevi Fountain with a few mispronounced words of Italian, some slowly enunciated English and a few gestures, but they would not be considered by most observers to be communicating in Italian. So, it may be possible to conduct a research project by freely combining components from different approaches, but this does not mean that the findings will make sense in terms of any of the approaches being drawn on. Nor, as Bryman (2006: 118) states, can 'the adequacy of particular methods for answering research questions' be the crucial arbiter of which methodology to adopt, since researchers from different philosophical positions may not share the same notions of what makes a method adequate or agree on what sort of questions research can or should address.

To suggest that a research design involves philosophical assumptions that influence what is, or is not, considered valid research and that any design should seek to ensure that a common understanding informs the choice of the various components of the design, is also not to insist that some sort of philosophical driving licence is required before researchers should be allowed to conduct research in organizations. It may be that, as Robson (2011) suggests, the researchers who deny the relevance of philosophical considerations in research design are actually conducting philosophically consistent research without being aware of it, but this may be because their philosophical assumptions are so deeply ingrained in their training that they cannot conceive of research in ways that are not consistent with their assumptions, rather than because they are able to transcend any inconsistencies. The point is therefore not to require some sort of badge of adherence to a universal, or even community, standard of philosophical righteousness, but to suggest that a research design will benefit from reflection on the assumptions on which it is based and that these assumptions should be applied consistently to all components of the design.

Even such a modest proposal may be something of a counsel of perfection, however, in relation to research design in practice, much of which adopts the off-the-shelf approach referred to earlier, in which the emphasis is on following prescribed procedures rather than reflecting on their underlying assumptions. This is particularly prevalent in fixed-design, positivist research, generally using quantitative data, where the suitability of assumptions is rarely considered, let alone called into question. There is accepted to be a 'one right way' to conduct research, with the randomized controlled trial being the 'gold standard' and all other designs being measured against their conformance to it. This is not to say that issues of, for example, access to organizations or maintaining research relationships in longitudinal studies do not arise in such research, but to the extent that they are recognized, it is assumed that they can be anticipated and pre-empted by suitable measures at the design stage, such as adjustment of sample sizes.

As was mentioned in Chapter 1, researchers pursuing flexible design approaches would seem likely to be those most exposed to the issues addressed in this book. That these approaches allow that a research design may be adjusted in the light of these issues also increases their salience. Given that the particular combination of 'design processes' (Cresswell, 2009) employed in a study depend on the judgement of the researcher, rather than being fixed in advance, however, it is not possible to make any general comments about the practicalities faced in pursuing such designs, rather these will have to be inferred from the discussion of the individual components in the different sections of this chapter.

Stage 2 Gather data

Buchanan and Bryman (2009: xxvii) propose that '[s]ocial science has only three methods [of data collection]: observation, asking questions and inspecting documents', although the conditions under which these methods are employed may vary significantly – from highly controlled in experimental settings to 'naturally occurring' in ethnographic studies.

Observation methods

Several different types of observation may be used to gather data in research on organizations. These may be categorized in terms of the degree of standardization of the observation and the role of the observer (passive or participant). Positivist researchers are likely to favour highly standardized forms of observation and passive observer roles, in order to maximize the reliability and perceived validity of the observations recorded. Such *structured*, or *systematic*, observation typically involves the collection of behavioural data through a predefined, standardized observation protocol. The behaviour observed may occur under experimental conditions or in the everyday organizational setting. In both situations the protocol is intended to ensure that any observer will make the same observations in a consistent way, hence controlling for the effects of observation on the organization members' behaviour.

Different strategies may be adopted to organize data collection. For example, observations may be made at specific time intervals, such as every 15 minutes, or using time sampling (in which some, perhaps random, sampling procedure is used to determine when observations are carried out) or may be triggered by particular events, or incidents. While it is possible for such observation to be used to gather qualitative, inferential data, for example descriptions or assessments of behaviours, more typically a coding scheme (usually predefined) will be used to categorize observed behaviours such that they can be represented quantitatively, for example in terms of the frequency or duration of their occurrence. The advantages and disadvantages of structured observation are shown in Table 3.3.

Table 3.3 Advantages and disadvantages of structured observation as a data-gathering method in organizational research

Advantages	Disadvantages
Provides the researcher with direct access to behaviour, rather than relying on organization members' reports	Tends to focus on overt behaviour without reference to context
Provides access to non-verbal behaviour	Rarely able to access intentions behind behaviour
Does not rely on organization members' interpretations of questions	Tends to encourage disaggregation of behaviours to observable units
Influence of researcher on organization members' behaviour is standardized	Impossible to detect whether observation influences behaviour of organization members

In structured observation studies the researcher is usually a complete observer, but this is just one of the types of observation role identified by Gold (1957). Other, typically interpretive, researchers, may play a more active role in the setting they are observing. Gold identifies three such roles in terms of the increasing level of researcher involvement: 'observer as participant', 'participant as observer' and 'complete participant'. Observation of the negotiation of an international treaty, for example, might be conducted by a researcher acting in a support role to one of the delegations (observer as participant), by a researcher who was an expert adviser directly influencing the course of the negotiations (participant as observer), or by one of the actual negotiators who was coincidentally researching the negotiation process (complete participant).

Becker and Geer (1957: 28) argued that participant observation provides 'us with a yardstick against which to measure the completeness of data gathered in other ways, a model which can serve to let us know what orders of information escape us when we use other methods'. In particular they suggest that it enables the researcher to learn the native language, to access matters that interviewees are unable or unwilling to talk about, and to understand things that people see through distorting lenses. While their claims were challenged by Trow (1957), who argues that observation may not necessarily be superior to interviews for all types of data in all settings, participant observation is sometimes seen as the preferred method for the gathering of qualitative data, especially for ethnographic studies.

Despite its attraction as a source of rich data on social phenomena, however, participant observation may also place particular demands on the researcher. Not the least of these is time. Anthropologists tend to regard any study that involves less than a year 'in the field' as unworthy of being called ethnography, but even the sorts of 'quick and dirty' ethnography employed in computer-supported cooperative work research (Hughes et al., 1994) may involve an elapsed time of several

Table 3.4 Advantages and disadvantages of participant observation as a
data-gathering method in organizational research

Advantages	Disadvantages
Rich data	Time required to gather data
Get 'behind the scenes'	Difficult to negotiate access
Understand local meanings	Dual role of the researcher
Personal experience of research context	Reporting the observer's role [Intervention]

weeks or months.[1] Seeking access to organizations (and sustaining it once granted)
for such periods of time can be difficult, as discussed in Chapter 5. For the
researcher, the conduct of fieldwork (Chapter 6), with its juggling of the two roles
of participant and observer in whatever proportion is adopted, and the reporting
of findings (Chapter 7) in which they may have played a significant role can be
hard to balance. While proponents of observational research (Becker and Geer,
1957; Taylor and Bogdan, 1998) may suggest that researchers can observe unobtrusively, without affecting the behaviour of organization members, it is unclear that
the researcher can necessarily tell what effect they are having or that they can do
much to control this. From the perspective of more 'distant' research methods,
moreover, the researcher's personal involvement in the setting, their intervention,
if only by their presence as an observer changing people's practices, and the reliance on the subjective records of the researcher as evidence of unique events for
which there may be no independent witness, are likely to be considered problematic. The advantages and disadvantages of participant observation as a data-gathering method are summarized in Table 3.4.

Asking questions

If the researcher does not consider that observation will be effective in gaining
insight on the phenomena they are studying, they may seek to elicit data

---

[1]Bate (1997: 1150) is particularly scathing in his assessment of the anthropological quality of much of what passes for organizational ethnography:

> there is actually less to 'organizational ethnography' than meets the eye. On closer
> examination 'thick description' invariably turns out to be 'quick description'
> (Wolcott, 1995, p. 90), yet another business case study or company history, a pale
> reflection of the 'experientially rich social science' envisaged by early writers like
> Agar (1980, p. 6). 'Prolonged contact with the field' means a series of flying visits
> rather than a long-term stay (jet-plane ethnography). Organization anthropologists
> rarely take a tooth-brush with them these days. A journey into the organizational
> bush is often little more than a safe and closely chaperoned form of anthropological
> tourism. 'Organizational' often turns out to be yet another marginal group: football
> hooligans, funeral directors [or] dance companies.

through asking questions. These questions may be posed in a variety of ways, including self-completion questionnaires and diaries, structured interviews, focus groups and semi- or unstructured interviews.

Silverman (2009), however, questions the validity of such methods, describing the data they produce as 'researcher-provoked', i.e. the act of asking questions necessarily pushes the interviewee to report something that it is unlikely that they would have expressed had the question not been asked. Furthermore, it cannot be assumed that the respondent's answer is necessarily something that they were already thinking, as it may only have been brought to mind in response to questioning. Despite the data arguably being created as a result of the researcher's intervention rather than pre-existing it, however, asking questions remains a highly prevalent data 'gathering' method in social research (although, as Lee [2004] notes, perhaps not quite as ubiquitous as the 90 per cent level that some of its proponents, e.g. Gubrium and Holstein [2002: 10], quote).

Self-completion questionnaires

Whether administered by post, email or online, the self-completion questionnaire is a relatively cheap and quick way to gather data from a large number of respondents. As the questions need to be planned in advance it tends to be used in fixed, positivist studies and, with no direct interaction between the researcher and respondents, the critical issues tend to be gaining access to suitable respondents, devising questions that are effective in eliciting the required data and ensuring adequate response rates.

Access to respondents will involve many of the same issues of identifying and gathering contact information as is the case for more extended fieldwork (see Chapter 5 for further details). The positivist assumptions, however, mean that particular attention needs to be paid to devising suitable, representative samples if findings are to be generalized to the population as a whole. This may not always be straightforward, however, as it may be impossible to identify the total population of potential respondents or to know how representative actual respondents are of this population. For example there may be no definitive listing of organizations of a particular type, or way of verifying that any available list of organizations is complete.

A key difference between self-completion questionnaires and other methods of asking questions, such as interviews, is the amount of an organization member's time that participation in a study can be expected to take up. Without any personal interaction between the researcher and respondents it is often difficult to engage the respondent's commitment to answering questions and particular efforts therefore need to be made to ensure that the questionnaire is quick and easy to answer. While respondents may be willing to spend more time answering a questionnaire on a subject that is of particular interest to them, it may not be possible to judge their level of enthusiasm in advance, so it may be better to err on the side of brevity. An analysis of the data from a sample of 10,000 surveys undertaken by the online survey site SurveyMonkey, for example, found that completion rates declined by up to 20 per cent if surveys took more than 7–8 minutes to complete, with tolerance for longer surveys being lower for customer surveys than for work or school-related surveys (SurveyMonkey, 2011).

Even if it is possible to design a questionnaire that achieves high completion rates, the researcher will have little, if any, insight on whether the respondents' answers reflect their actual views or behaviours, or even perhaps whether the respondent is who they claim they are. Quite apart from reporting biases in relation to sensitive topics, such as the incidence of malpractice, or answers being swayed by social desirability (giving answers that make the respondent look good) or acquiescence (agreeing with all statements regardless of the respondent's real opinions), answers may be influenced by the practicalities of the response situation, such as the time available to complete the questionnaire, the respondent's feelings at the time or their judgement about how the information may be used (Johnson, 1975).

Although it is possible to include check questions, for example asking the same question in different ways at different points in the questionnaire or including two questions that may be expected to be correlated in some way, that may offer some insight on the reliability of responses, these do not necessarily show whether the answers are truthful or have been given by the person who is considered to be the respondent. There may therefore be questions about the validity of findings from self-completion questionnaires.

Response rates appear to be a particular issue in organizational research. Baruch and Holtom (2008) report that an analysis of 17 refereed academic journals between 2000 and 2005 indicated an average response rate for studies collecting data from organizations of 35.7 per cent with a standard deviation of 18.8 (the average response rate for data collected from individuals was 52.7 per cent, standard deviation 20.4). It is difficult to find definitive statements on what constitutes an adequate response rate for self-completion questionnaires, but among the few authors willing to put a figure to it Mangione (1995) describes 60–70 per cent as acceptable, 50–60 per cent as barely acceptable and anything below 50 per cent as unacceptable, while Fowler (2009) quotes a US government requirement of 80 per cent. On this basis the response rates of a large proportion of the organizational studies analysed by Baruch and Holtom would seem to fall considerably below these levels.

Bryman and Bell (2011) argue that response rates are less important in studies that do not employ probability sampling, because the findings cannot be generalized to the unknown population in any case. They also cite influential studies in highly regarded journals, the findings of which have been based on

Table 3.5 Advantages and disadvantages of self-completion questionnaires as a data-gathering method in organizational research

Advantages	Disadvantages
Gain information about many sites	No access to respondents
Standardized intervention	Simple answers to simple questions
Relatively low cost and low demands on respondents	No opportunity for follow-up/ supplementary data collection
High response rates can enable claims about whole population	May be difficult to achieve required response rates

responses from less than a quarter of those surveyed. While it may be correct, however, that low response rates do not preclude the use of self-completion questionnaires in practice (as the findings of Baruch and Holtom [2008] indicate), they do undermine claims to be able to generalize from the findings. Efforts to achieve 'acceptable' response rates are therefore necessary if one of the key reasons for the use of self-completion questionnaires is not to be abandoned. A range of measures that can be taken to address this issue in the administration and design of self-completion questionnaires are proposed in the literature (see the further reading at the end of this chapter for details). Table 3.5 summarizes the advantages and disadvantages of questionnaires as a data-gathering method in organizational research.

Diary studies

Diary studies, in which an organization member is asked to record certain types of data (for example on their mood, activities, or performance or on the occurrence, duration or circumstances of certain types of events) over a period of time, may be seen as a specialized type of self-completion questionnaire. Diaries may be structured, where the researcher predefines the categories to be recorded, or free text, in which the respondents write their own entries, perhaps in response to particular prompt from the researcher. Compared to a self-completion questionnaire, diaries allow the tracking of phenomena over time and may be relatively unobtrusive, as they can be completed at a time of convenience for the respondent. As such they may be seen as an alternative to observation (Zimmerman and Wieder, 1976).

Perhaps even more than with self-completion questionnaires, however, as the demands placed on the respondent and the opportunities for misreporting are correspondingly greater, the validity of the findings from diary studies is very much dependent on the respondent's reliability. However reliable the respondent, moreover, the completion of the diary depends on the respondent's perceptions of what it is they are recording, without any independent verification. The

Table 3.6 Advantages and disadvantages of diary studies as a data-gathering method in organizational research

Advantages	Disadvantages
Low demands on researcher	High demands on respondents
Relatively unobtrusive	Respondent attrition/declining diligence over time
Can obtain data on change/process over time	No independent verification of reports
May allow access to data on sensitive topics	Reliant on respondent's interpretation of the task

data will therefore reflect what the respondent chooses to record about what they believe they have been asked to record, which may not correspond to the researcher's understanding of the phenomenon. The greater commitment expected of respondents can also mean that: entries are more reliant on memory recall, if respondents do not have time to complete them in the course of their normal activities; participants may withdraw from the study because they find the demands too onerous; or the diligence with which they complete the diary may decrease over time. Table 3.6 summarizes the advantages and disadvantages of diary methods for data-gathering in organizational research.

Interviews

While interviews are commonly associated with face-to-face interaction between the researcher and interviewee, they may also be conducted by telephone or online. Three types of interviews may be identified, depending on the extent to which the questions are specified in advance. In structured interviews, the researcher follows a script of predefined questions to which specific answers are sought. In semi-structured interviews the researcher has a checklist of topics to be covered (and perhaps some key questions to be asked), but there is no specific guidance on how, or in what order, they should be explored. Often this will be left to the judgement of the researcher depending on the interviewee's responses. The particular form of the interview may therefore vary considerably between different respondents, but the researcher will be able to pursue topics in more or less depth and introduce new topics as the knowledge and interest of the respondent allows. In unstructured interviews the researcher will offer minimal guidance to the respondent on the direction the interview should take, perhaps just an opening question about what is, or has been, of importance to them in relation to the research topic, but will seek to facilitate the interviewee's responses, through open questions (Why did you do this? How did this work out?) as their interests lead them. As Halliday and Schmidt (2009: 179) report, for example, in McCann's study of litigation in pay equity reform an opening question of 'How did you become involved in this?' would often elicit 45 minutes of uninterrupted talk, in the course of which half the questions that he wanted to ask would be addressed.

Structured interviews are likely to be part of fixed research designs and to be oriented to the gathering of quantitative data (or qualitative data that can be converted to numbers, for example through Likert scales that invite respondents to rate their agreement or disagreement to a set of statements on a scale from 1 to 5). Given the emphasis on the reliability of responses, structured interviews are likely to be formally arranged. Semi-structured and particularly unstructured interviews, on the other hand, tend to be associated with flexible designs and interpretive studies where the focus is on the respondents' meanings. Particularly in the case of unstructured interviews, they may be ad hoc interactions during the course of a more extended piece of fieldwork.

Differences in the type of interview employed in a study may also be associated with different views on the types of knowledge that interviews give rise to. Alvesson (2003) identifies four such views which he refers to as neo-positivism, romanticism, localism and reflexivism. Neo-positivist researchers, he argues, view interviews as a means of gathering facts about a reality that is 'out there' and therefore seek to adopt transparent, standardized procedures that will yield the objective, context-free truth about this reality. For romantics, in contrast, interviews are about gaining access to the interviewee's social reality. Through the development of rapport, trust and positive interpersonal relations it is proposed the researcher can gain deep understanding of the truth as the interviewee sees it. Localists, however, question the assumption of both neo-positivists and romantics that interviews are able to access a reality beyond the immediate setting, seeing them rather as a social accomplishment, a particular genre of conversation that produces context-specific accounts, the applicability of which to other settings cannot be assumed. Lastly, reflexivists, while acknowledging the localists' argument that interviews should be considered as a situated practice, seek to understand the influence of the interview process on the accounts produced. They therefore consider that interviews can provide insight on organizational worlds, even as they recognize their biases.

Despite their prevalence in research in organizations, therefore, interviews may be viewed as having a number of limitations as a source of data. It is not just that interview data are provoked by the researcher, it cannot be assumed that what is said is necessarily an accurate reflection of the interviewee's views. Even if they are not deliberately lying (which may not always be easy to detect), the interviewee's perceptions may be inaccurate (especially if recollecting past events), and/or they may not be able to articulate their views clearly or explain their behaviour (especially if it relies on tacit knowledge).

From a practical perspective, though, interviews can be relatively low-cost, in terms of time at least, for both the researcher and interviewee. While some interviews can last many hours (but normally only at the instigation of the interviewee, rather than the researcher), one hour (plus or minus 30 minutes) would be more typical. Shorter interviews tend to be associated with fixed, positivist research designs in which the researcher has a specific set of predefined questions or topics to ask about, whereas researchers adopting more flexible, interpretive designs may favour more open-ended interaction. Chapman (2001: 24), for example, contrasts his own reactions, as an anthropologist by training, to a first interview with a manager that lasted 'about four hours including talk, lunch and a walk round the factory', with those of his co-researcher whose previous studies had been based on questionnaires and structured interviews. His colleague, accustomed to spending perhaps 30 minutes in an organization to complete a questionnaire, commented that they had spent a particularly long time in the company, whereas he considered that they had done nothing more than 'poke their head round the door', contrasting the four hours with the 'year-long total immersion that would have satisfied purist anthropological criteria'.

Whether lasting 30 minutes or 4 hours, however, a potentially large number of interviews can be carried out as part of a single study, although this may be limited by the logistics of arranging the interviews and travelling to and from the research site, which can take many times the duration of the interview itself. Phone and online interviews avoid this travel time and do not require the researcher to gain access to the organization site, but may reduce the interviewee's engagement with the research (Miller, 1995). Hales and O'Connor (2008), for example, suggest that while face-to-face interviews with business organizations are commonly around 60–90 minutes, telephone interviews should be only a third of that length. Proponents of telephone interviews, however, suggest that they may be preferred by interviewees when discussing sensitive topics, can access hard-to-reach respondents and avoid potential threats to interviewer safety (Sturges and Hanrahan, 2004).

Face-to-face interviews require the researcher and interviewee to be co-located, but this does not have to be at the site of the organization being studied. For example, Thomas (1993) talks of interviewing CEOs in airport departure lounges and limousines as this was a rare opportunity when they were not in a meeting and had time to talk to the researcher. In general, though, interviews may encounter issues of access (Chapter 5), of sustaining interaction (either over a series of interviews, or sometimes during the course of a single one), of reporting (Chapter 7) and of re-entry (Chapter 8). Table 3.7 lists the advantages and disadvantages of interviews in gathering data.

Table 3.7 Advantages and disadvantages of interviews as a data-gathering method in organizational research

Advantages	Disadvantages
Larger samples	'Researcher-provoked' data
Relatively low cost	Constraints on detection of local meanings, misrepresentation
Easier access	Reconstruction of past events
	Episodic/snapshot

Focus groups

One way of reducing the time demands of interviews, at least for the researcher, is by interviewing more than one person at a time. Such group interviews may sometimes be classified as 'focus groups', but the latter is generally taken to refer to a more specific form of data-gathering involving discussion among a group of six to ten people for perhaps 90 minutes to 2 hours, of a specific topic, that is facilitated by the researcher or a specialist moderator. While focus group sessions are often audio, or even video recorded, it can be difficult for the facilitator to monitor all interactions while running the group, so a second researcher may be present as a passive observer. Groups may be selected on the basis of the similarity or diversity of, for example, their views or organizational status. The emphasis is on the interaction between group members and their collective views on the topic.

Proponents of focus groups (e.g. Stewart et al., 2006) draw attention to their efficiency as a data-gathering method (although some argue that this should not be the primary reason for their use). Group dynamics and the longer duration of a focus group are seen as providing the opportunity for more in-depth exploration of a topic and for the emergence of new ideas and the questioning of existing understandings in a way that is not possible with interviews where respondents may just offer formulaic answers. Focus groups also enable observation of interaction among organization members and of the process of mutual influence.

Focus groups are not without their limitations, however. In particular they are seen to be highly dependent on the skill of the moderator and the dynamics of the particular group, with a risk that they may be dominated by a few individuals and that the views of less vocal members will not receive enough consideration. This may be a particular issue with heterogeneous groups involving individuals of different organizational status, such as managers and their subordinates. Although there is a danger of groupthink (Janis, 1982), such that the group does not question the assumptions of its collective position, there is also a risk that conflict between individuals or subgroups may undermine the group's effectiveness. Table 3.8 lists the advantages and disadvantages of focus groups in gathering data.

Table 3.8 Advantages and disadvantages of focus groups as a data-gathering method in organizational research

Advantages	Disadvantages
Efficient use of researcher's time	Responses tend to be constrained to the (researcher-selected) focus
Group members provide validity check on views expressed	Skilled facilitation required
New ideas can emerge and existing ideas can be questioned and modified	Risk of groupthink or destructive conflict
Views of all participants can be solicited	Risk of domination by more vocal individuals

'Inspecting documents'

Although Buchanan and Bryman (2009) refer to documents, this category may be extended to images, audio and video. Documents too may refer not just to printed texts, such as reports, books, memos, newspapers and magazines, but also to notices, handwritten notes and letters and to virtual texts such as web-pages or the screens displayed by a computer program. These materials may be collected from publicly available sources without the researcher undertaking any fieldwork themselves, or may be gathered through direct interaction with an organization, either as the primary source of data or as supplementary evidence collected during the course of fieldwork. Such interaction may also provide opportunities for the recording, by photography (or by written notes if photography is not permitted or would be considered too intrusive) of other forms of materials, such as the decor, furnishings and layout of the work space, or the collection of organizational ephemera (e.g. Post-Its, personal notes, preliminary sketches and drafts) that may provide insight on organizational work processes. Gathering of these documents may be systematic, following a pre-planned sampling strategy, or opportunistic.

Once a suitable corpus of documents has been assembled, their analysis may be either predominantly quantitative, for example recording the frequency of particular words or phrases, or qualitative, for example seeking to draw inferences about the message the document is intended to convey. Such *content analysis* is often highly structured, systematically applying what should aim to be an exhaustive and mutually exclusive list of categories to every document in the corpus. Table 3.9 lists the advantages and disadvantages of content analysis in gathering data.

Stage 3 Analyse data

Having 'gathered' data through one or more of the above methods, the next stage of the research is generally seen to be data analysis. Where the data are quantitative

Table 3.9 Advantages and disadvantages of content analysis as a data-gathering method in organizational research

Advantages	Disadvantages
Low cost	Collected documents may not be typical
Large samples	Often no access to reasons for creation of documents
Can be unobtrusive	Selective survival of documentation of past events
Can be longitudinal	Difficult to identify causality
Can provide data on phenomena for which there is no other access	Inferences drawn from documents may reflect researcher's bias

and have been collected electronically for example, through an online questionnaire, it may be possible to move directly to this stage, which will typically involve some form of statistical analysis appropriate to the characteristics of the data. Not all data, particularly if they are qualitative, however, will necessarily be collected in a form immediately suitable for analysis. There may be handwritten fieldnotes, audio or video recordings, or paper questionnaire returns that need to be collated and transcribed into an analysable, usually digital, form (if only to establish a consistent and searchable data repository). This may be quite straightforward for questionnaire data using primarily closed questions, but may be highly demanding and time-consuming for audio transcription and even more so for video (especially as there are few agreed standards for video transcription). Eight hours to transcribe one hour of audio is quite typical, with additional time needed if the interviews were not in the language in which they will be analysed or reported and have to be translated. Given the concentration required for a non-specialist to undertake such work it is also something that can be difficult to sustain for long periods continuously, and the elapsed time to complete transcription may considerably exceed that actually spent doing the transcription.

When a study may involve many tens of hours of audio recording, therefore, it is not surprising that researchers look for ways to speed the process up. Three options are generally available to do this: digital voice-recognition software, commercial transcription services or some measure of selectivity in what is transcribed. Although voice-recognition software is improving all the time it works best when it is used by a single person, enabling it to be trained to the particular characteristics of their voice, when the vocabulary size is limited, and in conditions in which there is little background noise. Transcription of interviews, however, typically involves continuous, spontaneous speech, with perhaps many different speakers who are paying no particular attention to the clarity of what they say, using an unrestricted vocabulary in potentially noisy settings. Accuracy of transcription may therefore be low. One technique to overcome these problems is for the researcher to listen to the recording and repeat what is said in their own voice, enabling suitably 'trained' voice recognition software to transcribe more accurately, although at the cost of some loss of the time benefits of voice recognition. Even if accuracy is high, however, it may still be necessary to review transcriptions to check the accuracy and to correct errors, so overall time savings may be less than anticipated.

Commercial transcription services are likely to be of higher accuracy than software, so long as there is not too much esoteric vocabulary, or the transcribers are familiar with specialist terminology. Costs can vary greatly and, generally speaking, the greater the accuracy and speed the higher the charges. Again, it may be necessary to review transcriptions against the original audio.

Selective transcription may be considered appropriate where only part of an interview is viewed as relevant to a particular research question. It is generally desirable to transcribe more than just the exact words that are seen as relevant, to enable the context within which they were said to be understood. It is also good practice to record notes on the topics covered in untranscribed portions of an interview so that these can be found more easily at a later date if it is subsequently decided that they may be relevant.

Whether speech-recognition software, commercial transcription services or selective transcription is used, the researcher's understanding of interviews transcribed by these methods will almost inevitably be less than if they had transcribed them themselves. In part this will be because a written transcript will usually not provide information on tone of voice, emphasis and pauses (and audio recording will already have lost information on non-verbal communication), but also because possession of the transcript is not the same as understanding its contents. Just as photocopying an article (or downloading the pdf) is not the same as reading it and reading it is not the same as understanding it, the effort involved in transcribing an interview requires an engagement with what is said that, while it does not necessarily lead to better understanding, is a necessary step towards such understanding.

Once data are in digital format, analysis can proceed by many different routes, the choice between which is likely to depend on the research approach, the characteristics of the data and the inclinations of the researcher rather than anything to do with the conduct of fieldwork (except, perhaps, insofar as fieldwork considerations may affect the data that are available to analyse). Quantitative data can be subject to a variety of different forms of statistical analysis of varying complexity, although this may sometimes be guided more by the available software and a desire to appear sophisticated than by the characteristics of the data. There is no shortage of good textbooks providing guidance on the choice and application of these methods.

Qualitative data analysis is generally recognized to be less formalized than quantitative analysis, although there are many authors who nevertheless argue that it can, and should, be made more systematic (Robson, 2011). Typically, it is seen as an iterative, three-part process, that Dey (1993) refers to in terms of 'describing', 'classifying' and 'connecting' and Miles and Huberman (1994) in terms of 'data reduction', 'data display' and 'drawing conclusions'. There are several different ways of doing qualitative analysis, including grounded theory, discourse analysis and narrative research (Wertz et al., 2011).

In grounded theory in particular a key element of the analysis is coding, that is labelling particular segments of the data (phrases, statements, instances of behaviour) as examples of a particular type. There are many different ways to do this, as Saldaña (2009) describes. These codes are then connected together and perhaps combined into higher-order codes to build up the analytic narrative.

Specialized Computer-Assisted Qualitative Data Analysis Software (CAQDAS) packages, such as Nvivo, MAXQDA and Atlas Ti, can provide some support for the process (Humble, 2012). Their main contribution, however, is in storing and managing large amounts of data in a consistent format, allowing easy and consistent coding of material and analysis and display of these codes. While the increasing sophistication of these packages has seen the introduction of features such as autocoding (of specified terms and structured source materials) and 'theory-building' capabilities (that search for co-occurrences of categories, for example, or chronological sequences of specified codes) they do not fully automate the process. Deciding what a particular data unit is an example of is still up to the researcher, so analysis may not be significantly simplified (in the way that statistical software automates the analysis of quantitative data).

Although some authors argue that the use of computer-assisted data analysis has 'revolutionised the way in which qualitative researchers now approach qualitative data analysis' (Johnston, 2006: 381) such that it is 'no longer an option' in qualitative research (Richards, 2009: 3), it has not been without its critics (Séror, 2005). Concerns have been raised, for example, that it is: changing the character of qualitative data analysis (Gilbert, 2002); leading to a McDonaldization and standardization of qualitative research, as the programs support one particular type of analysis, coding, rather than others (Brinkman, 2012); encouraging the quantification of qualitative data and threatening the craft skills of qualitative research (James, 2012).

Stage 4 Present findings

Discussion of the reporting of research in methods textbooks is often perfunctory and largely focused on the expectations, in terms for example of writing style, format and level of detail, of writing for different audiences, such as academic journals, research sponsors or members of the organization studied (usually described as a management report). This discussion also tends to present the process of reporting as a relatively unproblematic and largely transparent process of setting out an account of why the study was carried out, what it involved, what was found and what implications can be drawn from the findings. The completion of such reporting is generally presented as the end point of the research process.

The research process revisited

While such accounts of the process of research in organizations may be helpful in providing the researcher with a structure that can give them a sense of the overall shape of a piece of research, a checklist of the components that they will need to assemble and an idea of where they are in the process at any stage, they can also be misleading in presenting research as much more tidy, linear and smooth than it often seems to be in practice. Although this picture of a rigorous, systematic and carefully controlled activity is consonant with the logic underlying fixed designs in which messiness, iteration and deviation are excluded by meticulous planning, even the best-planned research cannot always avoid difficulties that can complicate or even derail the process. For researchers employing more flexible designs, in which, for example data-gathering and analysis may proceed in parallel with the latter feeding back to the former during the course of the research, it would seem even less relevant.

Such accounts also skate over many of the activities that can end up absorbing a significant proportion of the researcher's time and attention, even if they appear, particularly from the perspective of fixed designs, as incidental to the 'real work' of research in organizations. An alternative view of the research process might therefore look more like Table 3.10.

Table 3.10 Activities in the organizational research process

	Activity
Decide the research approach	Identify broad area of interest
	Define the research topic
	Define the research question(s)
	Choose the research design
Plan the fieldwork	Identify organizations relevant to the topic
	Assess the feasibility of obtaining access to the data needed to address the research question(s) from the organization(s) identified
	Approach organizations to seek access
Gain access	Negotiate access
'Gather' data	Conduct fieldwork
Conclude fieldwork	Organize departure from the field
Analyse data	Transcribe and collate data
	Carry out preliminary analysis
	Carry out detailed analysis
Report findings	Report findings to organization members from whom data were collected
	Report findings (and/or recommendations) to organizational sponsors of the research
	Report findings to other audiences
[Follow up	Negotiate a return to the field]

Rather than stages, implying a linear sequential process, Table 3.10 refers to activities to indicate that in flexible designs there may be, sometimes repeated, iterations between activities. For example, the organizations and data that it proves feasible to gain access to may lead to refinement of the research question, or difficulties in obtaining particular types of data may lead to a consideration of whether other data may offer insight on the phenomenon of interest. Activities may also be carried out in parallel, rather than necessarily in series. Analysis may commence with preliminary data, for example, and interim reports may be written up before the fieldwork is completed. Nor does the process necessarily have a clear end. The data analysis may suggest additional data that would strengthen findings, or the findings may lead to ideas for further studies. As a result the relationship with an organization may continue over several cycles of research.

These activities will be discussed in further detail in Chapters 5 to 8, but before that there is a discussion of ethics in organizational research. This is necessary both because of the emerging importance of this topic in relation to organizational fieldwork, and also because of its significance throughout the research process.

EXERCISES

1   The research process

- Find three standard methods textbooks for your subject area:

    o look at how they describe the stages of the research process (if they do)
    o look at the relative number of pages devoted to each stage
    o look at the relative number of pages devoted to discussing methodological principles compared to discussion of how these principles operate in practice
    o from your own experience, or that of other researchers, compare the relative attention devoted to different activities in the textbooks to the amount of attention devoted to the activities during a particular research project.

2   Research design

- From your own experience, or that of other researchers, consider how well the design of a particular research project corresponded to the principles of the relevant research design.

    o If the design that was followed in practice deviated from the principles, why was this?
    o How was this deviation reported (if it was)?

3   What data-gathering method might you choose if your research objective was to:

    (a) measure the diffusion of a new technology in a particular sector?
    (b) investigate the factors considered by managers when deciding whether to adopt the new technology?

(c) investigate how the characteristics of the new technology that were emphasized in reports in the trade press changed over time?

(d) investigate the process of adoption of the new technology?

(e) assess the organizational changes associated with the adoption of the new technology?

(f) evaluate the success of the adoption of the new technology by different organizations?

(g) identify the characteristics of organizations that are associated with successful adoption?

Further reading

General methods textbooks relevant to organizational research

Bryman, A. and Bell, E. (2011) *Business Research Methods*. Oxford: Oxford University Press.

Robson, C. (2011) *Real World Research*, 3rd edn. Chichester: John Wiley and Sons.

Questionnaires

Peterson, R.A. (2000) *Constructing Effective Questionnaires*. London: SAGE.

There is also some good discussion of questionnaire design in the further reading on surveys listed in Chapter 2.

Observation

DeWalt, K.M. and DeWalt, B.R. (2010) *Participant Observation: A Guide for Fieldworkers*. Plymouth: Altamira Press.

Primarily addressing anthropological fieldwork, it nevertheless provides useful practical advice relevant to organizational research.

Spradley, J.P. (1980) *Participant Observation*. London: Holt, Rinehart and Winston.

Diary studies

Ohly, S., Sonnentag, S., Niessen, C. and Zapf, D. (2010) 'Diary studies in organizational research', *Journal of Personnel Psychology*, 9 (2): 79–93.

Interviews

Alvesson, M. (2011) *Interpreting Interviews*. London: SAGE.
Kvale, S. (2008) *Doing Interviews*. London: SAGE.

Focus groups

Barbour, R. (2008) *Doing Focus Groups*. London: SAGE.

Krueger, R.A. and Casey, M.A. (2009) *Focus Groups: A Practical Guide for Applied Research*. London: SAGE.

Content analysis

Krippendorff, K. (2013) *Content Analysis: An Introduction to Its Methodology*. London: SAGE.
Schreier, M. (2012) *Qualitative Content Analysis in Practice*. London: SAGE.

Qualitative data analysis

Bazeley, P. (2007) *Qualitative Data Analysis with Nvivo*, 2nd edn. London: SAGE.
Richards, L. (2009) *Handling Qualitative Data: A Practical Guide*, 2nd edn. London: SAGE.

Quantitative data analysis

Field, A. (2009) *Discovering Statistics Using SPSS*, 3rd edn. London: SAGE.
Tarling, R. (2009) *Statistical Modelling for Social Researchers: Principles and Practice*. London: Routledge.

References

Alvesson, M. (2003) 'Beyond neopositivists, romantics, and localists: a reflexive approach to interviews in organizational research', *Academy of Management Review*, 28(1): 13–33.
Baruch, Y. and Holtom, B.C. (2008) 'Survey response rate levels and trends in organizational research', *Human Relations*, 61 (8): 1139–60.
Bate, S.P. (1997) 'Whatever happened to organizational anthropology? A review of the field of organizational ethnography and anthropological studies', *Human Relations*, 50 (9): 1147–75.
Becker, H.S. and Geer, B. (1957) 'Participant observation and interviewing: a comparison', *Human Organization*, 16 (3): 28–32.
Boje, D.M. (2001) *Narrative Methods for Organizational and Communication Research*. London: SAGE.
Brinkmann, S. (2012) 'Qualitative research between craftsmanship and McDonaldization'. A keynote address from the Seventeenth Qualitative Health Research Conference, *Qualitative Studies*, 3 (1): 56–68.
Bryman, A. (2006) 'Paradigm peace and the implications for quality', *International Journal of Social Research Methodology*, 9 (2): 111–26.
Bryman, A. and Bell, E. (2011) *Business Research Methods*. Oxford: Oxford University Press.
Buchanan, D.A. and Bryman, A. (2009) 'Preface', in D.A. Buchanan and A. Bryman (eds), *The SAGE Handbook of Organizational Research Methods*. London: SAGE, pp. xxiv–xxxvi.

Chapman, M. (2001) 'Social anthropology and business studies: some considerations of method', in D.N. Gellner and E. Hirsch (eds), *Inside Organizations: Anthropologists at Work*. Oxford: Berg, pp. 19–34.

Cooper, D.R. and Schindler, P.S. (2011) *Business Research Methods*, 11th edn. Singapore: McGraw-Hill.

Creswell, J.W. (2009) *Research Design: Qualitative, Quantitative, and Mixed Methods Approaches*, 3rd edn. Los Angeles, CA: SAGE.

Czarniawska, B. (2004) *Narratives in Social Science Research*. London: SAGE.

Dey, I. (1993) *Qualitative Data Analysis: A User-friendly Guide for Social Scientists*, 1st edn. London: Routledge.

Easterby-Smith, M., Thorpe, R. and Jackson, P.R. (2012) *Management Research*, 4th edn. London: SAGE.

Forbes, W. (2009) *Behavioural Finance*. Chichester: Wiley.

Fowler, F.J. (2009) *Survey Research Methods*, 4th edn. London: SAGE.

Geertz, C. (1993) *The Interpretation of Cultures*. London: Fontana.

Gilbert, L.S. (2002) 'Going the distance:' "closeness" in qualitative data analysis software', *International Journal of Social Research Methodology*, 5 (3): 215–28.

Gill, J. and Johnson, P. (2010) *Research Methods for Managers*, 4th edn. London: SAGE.

Gold, R.L. (1957) 'Roles in sociological field observations', *Social Forces*, 36: 217–23.

Gubrium, J.F. and Holstein, J.A. (2002) 'From the individual to the interview society', in J.F. Gubrium and J.A. Holstein (eds), *Handbook of Interview Research: Context and Method*. London: SAGE, pp. 3–32.

Hakim, C. (2000) *Research Design: Successful Designs for Social and Economic Research*, 2nd edn. London: Routledge.

Hales, J. and O'Connor, W. (2008) *Methodological Review of Research with Large Businesses Paper 3: Data Collection*. London: Her Majesty's Revenue and Customs.

Halliday, S. and Schmidt, P.D. (2009) *Conducting Law and Society Research: Reflections on Methods and Practices*. Cambridge: Cambridge University Press.

Hughes, J., King, V., Rodden, T. and Andersen, H. (1994) 'Moving out from the control room: ethnography in system design', in *Proceedings of the 1994 ACM Conference on Computer Supported Cooperative Work*. New York: Association for Computing Machinery, pp. 429–39.

Humble, A.M. (2012) 'Qualitative data analysis software: a call for understanding, detail, intentionality, and thoughtfulness', *Journal of Family Theory and Review*, 4 (2): 122–37.

James, A. (2012) 'Seeking the analytic imagination: reflections on the process of interpreting qualitative data', *Qualitative Research*, 1–16.

Janis, I.L. (1982) *Groupthink: Psychological Studies of Policy Decisions and Fiascoes*, 2nd edn. Boston, MA: Houghton Mifflin.

Johnson, J.M. (1975) *Doing Field Research*. New York: Free Press.

Johnston, L. (2006) 'Software and method: reflections on teaching and using QSR NVivo in doctoral research', *International Journal of Social Research Methodology*, 9 (5): 379–91.

Knorr-Cetina, K. and Preda, A. (2005) *The Sociology of Financial Markets*. Oxford: Oxford University Press.

Lee, R.M. (2004) 'Recording technologies and the interview in sociology, 1920–2000', *Sociology*, 38 (5): 869–89.

MacKenzie, D.A. (2006) *An Engine, Not a Camera: How Financial Models Shape Markets*. Cambridge, MA: The MIT Press.

Mangione, T.W. (1995) *Mail Surveys: Improving the Quality*. Thousand Oaks, CA: SAGE.

Marx, G.T. (1997) 'Of methods and manners for aspiring sociologists: 37 moral imperatives', *The American Sociologist*, 28 (1): 102–25.

Miles, M.B. and Huberman, A.M. (1994) *Qualitative Data Analysis: An Expanded Sourcebook*, 2nd edn. London: SAGE.

Miller, C. (1995) 'In-depth interviewing by telephone: some practical considerations', *Evaluation and Research in Education*, 9 (1): 29–38.

Richards, L. (2009) *Handling Qualitative Data: A Practical Guide*, 2nd edn. London: SAGE.

Robson, C. (2011) *Real World Research*, 3rd edn. Chichester: John Wiley and Sons.

Saldaña, J. (2009) *The Coding Manual for Qualitative Researchers*. London: SAGE.

Séror, J. (2005) 'Computers and qualitative data analysis: paper, pens, and highlighters vs. screen, mouse, and keyboard', *TESOL Quarterly*, 39 (2): 321–28.

Silverman, D. (2009) *Doing Qualitative Research*, 3rd edn. London: SAGE.

Stewart, D.W., Shamdasani, P.N. and Rook, D.W. (2006) *Focus Groups: Theory and Practice*, 2nd edn. London: SAGE.

Sturges, J.E. and Hanrahan, K.J. (2004) 'Comparing telephone and face-to-face qualitative interviewing: a research note', *Qualitative Research*, 4 (1): 107–18.

Survey Monkey (2011) http://blog.surveymonkey.com/blog/2011/02/14/survey_completion_times/

Taylor, S.J. and Bogdan, R. (1998) *Introduction to Qualitative Research Methods: The Search for Meanings*, 3rd edn. Chichester: John Wiley and Sons.

Thomas, R.J. (1993) 'Interviewing important people in big companies', *Journal of Contemporary Ethnography*, 22 (1): 80–96.

Trow, M. (1957) 'Comment on "Participant observation and interviewing: a comparison"', *Human Organization*, 16 (3): 33–5.

Wertz, F.J., Charmaz, K., McMullen, L.M., Josselson, R., Anderson, R. and McSpadden, E. (2011) *Five Ways of Doing Qualitative Analysis: Phenomenological Psychology, Grounded Theory, Discourse Analysis, Narrative Research, and Intuitive Inquiry*. New York: Guilford Press.

Zimmerman, D. and Wieder, D.L. (1976) 'The diary', *Urban Life*, 5 (4): 479–97.

4

Ethics in Organizational Research

Chapter objectives

- to identify the nature, scope and principles of social research ethics

  o to identify alternative stances on research ethics

- to outline the process of ethical regulation in organizational research

  o ethical codes
  o ethical guidance and review
  o research governance

Discussion of ethics in social research in general and in organizational research in particular has been marked by ongoing debates about the nature, scope and principles of ethical concern, about alternative stances on ethics that could, or should, be adopted and on the procedures and principles by which the ethics of social research should be regulated. While it is not the aim of this chapter to provide a definitive account of these debates, a number of the key themes will be critically reviewed to orient subsequent discussion. A central argument will be that ethics is not something to be considered separately from research practice or as a procedural obstacle to be surmounted before research can commence and that can subsequently be forgotten about. Rather it will be proposed that attention to ethics should pervade the research process and be actively addressed in research practice. To emphasize this point the majority of the discussion of ethics in organizational research practice will be presented in Chapters 5 to 8 in the context of the 'getting in, getting on, getting out, getting back' framework, and the focus of this chapter will be on setting out the terms of the debates and making the argument for the position just described.

The nature, scope and principles of ethics in social research

As Hammersley and Traianou (2012: 16) discuss, ethics in relation to research may be understood as being concerned either with 'the study of what researchers ought and ought not to do and how this should be decided', or, alternatively, with the 'principles that embody or exemplify what is good or right'. While the two are related, in the sense that judgements of what researchers ought and and ought not to do will be based on some principles of what is good or right, the emphasis of the former is more descriptive and procedural and the latter more broad-ranging and normative.

While it might seem straightforward to agree on a set of principles of what is good and right for researchers to do, in practice this can prove more complex. One reason for this complexity derives from the long-standing debate between whether ethical practice should be judged in terms of whether actions conform to some generally recognized rules that individuals should be expected to obey (deontology), or whether actions should be judged by their outcomes (consequentalism). Neither of these approaches, moreover, leads to unambiguous principles, since there may be debate about what rules actions should be expected to conform to and about the scope of application of these rules (do they apply universally, or could there be local variation), or about whose outcomes should be considered and how outcomes for different groups or individuals should be weighed against each other. Furthermore, even if it were possible to achieve consensus on the principles that researchers should subscribe to this would not necessarily solve the problem because principles may conflict with one another. For example, if a study identified incidents of bullying in a workplace then the maintenance of confidentiality might conflict with the avoidance of harm. Nor is there necessarily an ethically correct answer to such a dilemma, since reporting of bullying might lead to reprisals against the victim, making their situation worse.

Stances on ethics

Given the complexity of the ethical issues that may be faced, a range of different positions have been proposed on the appropriate ethical stance to be adopted in the conduct of research in organizations. Bryman and Bell (2011) identify four such stances: universalism, situation ethics, ethical transgression is pervasive, and anything goes.

Ethical universalism proposes that ethical principles are absolute and should be observed in all circumstances. An ethical universalist, for example, would argue that there are never any circumstances under which covert research or disguised observation, in which the researcher does not inform those they are researching that they are being studied, should be permitted.

As some researchers such as Erikson (1967: 372), who generally adopt a universalist stance, acknowledge, in practice it may be difficult to hold to such a position in all situations. As Bronfenbrenner (1952: 453) writes, 'the only safe way to avoid violating principles of professional ethics is to refrain from doing social research altogether'.

Situationism, on the other hand, argues that ethics should be judged on a case-by-case basis. Although this could imply a situation in which each individual decides their own principles, perhaps on the basis of personal expedience, it is more commonly presented as a form of 'principled relativism' (Fletcher, 1997: 31), a consequentialist position in which the justification of actions is based on an appeal to commonly held higher principles.

Bryman and Bell illustrate the stance that ethical transgression is pervasive, by reference to the argument of Gans (1968: 314) that 'often the only way to get honest data is to be dishonest in getting it'. That is, in an experiment it is often necessary to omit some details from the explanation of the aims of the study in order that subjects do not modify their responses, for example to 'help' the researcher or to make themselves look good. There may be similar issues with questionnaires, interviews and observations, and with participant observation there is the additional effect of the asymmetry in the relationship between the observer and participants. Thus Gans (1968: 314) argues,

> even though [the researcher] seems to give of himself [sic] when he participates, he is not really doing so, and thus deceives the people he studies. He pretends to participate emotionally when he does not; he observes even when he does not appear to be doing so.

This stance is not so much an attempt to argue for particular ethical principles, therefore, but rather, its proponents would argue, a pragmatic recognition of the reality of research practice.

The last ethical stance identified by Bryman and Bell (2011: 124) is described as 'anything goes (more or less)'. As with the previous stance this draws its justification from research practice, but emphasizes the social context within which research takes place. It is generally associated with the 'conflict paradigm' of society and its associated investigative field research (Douglas, 1976: 55). This argues that social life is characterized by 'profound conflicts of interest, feelings, values and actions' and that tactics such as infiltration and setting people up are reasonable ways to get behind the misinformation, evasions, lies and fronts that 'lie in the way of getting at social reality' (Douglas, 1976: 57). While acknowledging that such research may be ethically contentious, Douglas (1976: xiv) argues that, compared to 'what really goes on in American society', and the practices of journalists and the police, such fieldwork tactics are 'genteel and certainly harmless'. While there may be few studies that would explicitly adopt such a stance, Bryman and Bell (2011) suggest that a similar consequentialist argument may be recognized in claims of writers such as Denzin (1968) that the advancement of science, or knowledge, is sufficient justification for any research practice, so long as there is no evident harm to participants.

Ethical regulation

That there may be no general consensus on either ethical principles or ethical practice in organizational research, however, does not mean that organizational researchers are free to decide their own ethical position. As Bell and Bryman (2007) discuss, self-regulation of the ethics of research in organizations is increasingly giving way to more formal mechanisms, typically involving a requirement that researchers should demonstrate that their work conforms to a relevant code of ethics before commencement of the study. It is unclear that this increasing regulation has necessarily been brought about by any evidence of significant or widespread failure of self-regulation in organizational research,[1] or a growing incidence of such failure, however. Rather it would seem to represent the extension of practices from the domain of medical research, where they have been established for some decades, perhaps reflecting the general decline of trust in expert authority and its replacement by relationships of accountability (Bond, 2012; O'Neill, 2002).

In most academic settings there are now a whole range of processes and procedures involved with the regulation of research ethics, the differences and relationships between which are not always easy to discern (and may be conflated in the institutional arrangements set up to administer research ethics). In principle, however, it is possible to distinguish between ethical codes, ethical guidance, ethical review and research governance.

Ethical codes seek to establish the principles of what is considered to be ethical research practice and hence, often implicitly, what practices potentially raise ethical concerns. Ethical guidance seeks to translate these principles into advice that researchers may use in the planning of their research, but without necessarily putting in place any mechanism to ensure that this is followed. Ethical review is then the mechanism that assesses whether proposed research meets the relevant ethical standards and grants approval to studies that do so, while research governance (sometimes subsumed under ethical review) is about procedures that are intended to ensure the ethical conduct of research.

---

[1]This is not to say that ethical malpractice does not occur (Wilson, 1997) or that there are not pressures on academic researchers that may lead them to engage in practices that may be ethically questionable.

Ethical codes

A wide range of ethical codes produced by different professional associations, funding bodies and individual institutions may be considered to be applicable to research in organizations. Bell and Bryman (2007), for example, identify nine such codes from academic social research organizations in the UK and USA that they propose may be relevant to management research, including the Academy of Management, British Psychological Association, the American Sociological Association and the Association of Social Anthropologists. Given that it is not just management researchers who conduct research in organizations, other professional codes, such as those of the British Society of Criminology or the American Educational Research Association, or codes of funding bodies such as the Economic and Social Research Council, or the Swedish Research Council, or of Government departments or codes of policy-related organizations, such as the UK Department for Work and Pensions or the Irish National Disability Association may also be considered to apply to such research. A broad selection of Internet links to different ethics codes is available from the Council of European Social Science Data Archives at www.cessda.org/sharing/rights/4/.

Discussions of the history of ethical codes typically trace the origins of ethical regulation of research to the Nuremberg Code on medical experimentation that emerged from the war crimes trial of German medical doctors at the end of the Second World War. Another widely cited influence was the Tuskegee Syphilis Experiment. This was a study carried out between 1932 and 1972, in which 600 impoverished, African-American sharecroppers, 399 of whom had contracted the disease at the start of the research, were excluded from treatment for syphilis (even through this became widely available after the 1940s) in order to study the natural progression of the disease. While these may seem extreme cases in relation to any ethical concerns that may be encountered in research in organizations, the principles that emerged from them inform much current practice. Thus, the analysis by Bell and Bryman (2007) of nine ethical codes of UK and US academic social research associations (see Table 4.1), showed that almost all include some version of the Belmont principles (www.hhs.gov/ohrp/humansubjects/guidance/belmont.html), that were first set out in 1979 by the US National Commission for the Protection of Human Subjects of Biomedical and Behavioural Research in a report citing both Nuremberg and Tuskegee.

The Belmont principles are defined as 'respect for persons', 'beneficence' and 'justice'. The first principle requires that all individuals are treated as autonomous agents and that there is special protection for those, such as children or vulnerable adults, whose autonomy may be diminished. This means that all subjects must enter into research voluntarily and with adequate information, a process generally referred to as informed consent.

Table 4.1 Common principles of ethical codes for social research

Principle	Implications
Respect for persons	Protection of vulnerable participants Voluntary participation Adequate information
Beneficence	Do no harm Maximize benefit, minimize harm
Justice	Fair distribution of costs and benefits of research
Privacy	Respect for participant's privacy
Confidentiality	Protect confidentiality of research data
Anonymity	Protect anonymity of participants
Honesty and transparency	Open and honest communication with all interested parties
Declaration of interests	Clear statement of researchers' funding and affiliations

Beneficence is understood as placing two potentially conflicting obligations on the researcher: to do no harm and to maximize the benefit of research and minimize the harm to subjects. Finally, justice concerns the fair distribution of costs and benefits of research to all potential participants. Most ethics codes also emphasize the need for researchers to respect the privacy, confidentiality and anonymity of research participants, to be honest and transparent in their communication with participants and to declare interests. A smaller number of codes also propose additional principles such as reciprocity (suggesting that research should be of mutual benefit to both the researcher and participants and/or be a collaboration between the two) and misrepresentation (requiring that reporting of research findings should not be false or misleading).

Despite these commonalities (and some variation in detail), codes differ in what Bell and Bryman (2007) refer to as the 'ethical tone' of their wording. Some adopt an imperative tone, implying that the principles constitute absolute standards that should not be violated, while others are more advisory, indicating that deviation from the principles may be allowable if adequately justified. Whether imperative or advisory, however, the extent to which codes have an effect on the conduct of research necessarily depends both on the institutional mechanisms that support them and on how seriously they are taken on board by individual researchers. A code that researchers have no incentive to adhere to or that they consider as a cosmetic exercise is little more than a pious aspiration. Some critics also suggest that codes encourage a tick box mentality (Sin, 2005) that enables researcher to abdicate their individual ethical agency (Bell and Wray-Bliss, 2009). 'Rather than encouraging ethical discussion and deliberation – the development of "ethical mindfulness" – procedural codes and regulations merely serve to undercut the researcher's integrity and judgement', as Pollock (2012: 7) puts it.

Table 4.2 Types of research involving more than minimal risk (ESRC, 2010)

Research involving potentially vulnerable groups or those who lack capacity

Research involving sensitive topics

Research involving groups where permission of a gatekeeper is normally required for initial access to members

Research involving deception or which is conducted without participants' full and informed consent

Research involving access to records of personal or sensitive confidential information

Research which would or might induce psychological stress, anxiety or humiliation, or cause more than minimal pain

Research involving intrusive interventions or data collection methods

Research where the safety of the researcher may be in question

Research undertaken outside of the UK

Research involving respondents through the Internet

Research which may involve data sharing of confidential information beyond the initial consent given

---

www.esrc.ac.uk/about-esrc/information/research-ethics.aspx

Ethical guidance and review

The institutional mechanisms supporting ethics codes may include both ethical guidance and ethical review. The former, as its name suggests, is generally advisory, seeking to translate the ethical principles into practical advice for researchers, that will both sensitize them to potential ethical issues in their research and encourage more ethically reflective practice. Guidance may be accompanied by some process of self-certification in which the researcher registers that they have considered the principles and have identified no potential ethical concerns. Where concerns are identified this may be the prelude to more formal ethical review. Table 4.2 lists types of research that are considered as involving more than minimal ethical risk, as identified by the UK Economic and Social Research Council.

Some institutions, or sometimes particular groupings within institutions, however, may not allow self-certification and may require all research to be formally reviewed. Generally speaking, medical, biological and psychological research is most likely to impose mandatory review. While this might suggest that ethical review may not be a requirement for some forms of research in organizations, studies that fall within the remit of these disciplines may be expected to adhere to their ethical review process whether this is suitable or not. A social researcher carrying out a study in a hospital, for example, may be expected to follow the same procedures that would be applied to the ethical review of a randomized controlled trial of a new drug, even if many of the issues these procedures require them to address may not be applicable to their study. At the very least, the time involved in completing the necessary paperwork may be a serious deterrent to social research in such settings (Pearce, 2002).

Where ethical review is institutionalized, specialist panels – Institutional Review Boards (IRBs), Independent Ethics Committees (IECs) or Research Ethics Committees (RECs) – are typically established to approve, monitor and review research proposals. While these panels provide consistent scrutiny of all research and visible oversight of the ethics of research, critics question their effectiveness in regulating research practice because their primary focus is typically on review and approval of research proposals rather than on monitoring or audit of what researchers actually do. They may therefore be effective in preventing research that has obvious ethical shortcomings from being carried out and in alerting researchers to ethical issues that they may not have foreseen in their research proposals. Whether this is sufficient to ensure that research is ethical, however, depends on the researchers' adherence to the principles that their proposal has been deemed to conform to, in the actual conduct of their research. In the absence of mechanisms to check that this is the case, evidence of non-adherence is likely to depend on complaints by research participants or third parties. Thus ethical review can be seen more as a way of providing an institution with some protection against such complaints than necessarily ensuring that research is ethical (Adler and Adler, 2002; Bledsoe et al., 2007). In focusing ethical scrutiny at the stage of planning of research, rather than its conduct, ethical review is also seen as compartmentalizing ethics, 'shutting them off into a preamble to research' (Shaw, 2008: 403), rather than promoting an ethical reflexivity that runs through the lifetime of a project (Calvey, 2008).

Although it is possible that non-adherence of research practice to ethical principles, whether institutionally reviewed or not, may be due to unscrupulous researchers (who may not have any compunction about misrepresenting their intentions in their research proposal), it may also be an unintended consequence of the contingencies of research practice, as will be discussed in Chapter 5. This may be particularly the case with research adopting flexible designs, which does not assume that all details of a study can be specified in advance. As a consequence, some social scientists have argued that the biomedical model of research ethics adopted in most review processes is unsuitable for use in evaluating qualitative social research (Van den Hoonaard, 2002; Pollock, 2012). This is not just a matter of what are seen to be inappropriate expectations regarding the research process, but also of the expertise of the research ethics committee members to evaluate social research (Schrag, 2011). Furthermore, it is argued (Dingwall, 2006: 51) that the 'risks to human subjects [in biomedical and social research] are not comparable and the power relationship between researcher and researched is so different as to render prior scrutiny irrelevant and inappropriate'.

Social scientists' concerns about ethical review have been reinforced by the broad remit of some ethics procedures which include provisions, for example, that deem research 'which is not of sufficient quality to contribute something useful to existing knowledge' to be unethical (www.dh.gov.uk/en/Publicationsandstatistics/ Publications/PublicationsPolicyAndGuidance/DH_4108962) and evidence that proposals for social research that do not conform to the biomedical model are being rejected on such grounds (Lincoln and Tierney, 2004).

Consequently, critics of ethical review in the social sciences have denounced it as 'censorship' and 'anti-democratic' (Dingwall, 2006), describing the threat that the 'tightening regulatory vice' poses to creativity in social research (Bledsoe et al., 2007: 617). Nor, they argue (Schrag, 2011), is there much evidence that it is effective in protecting research participants.

Other social scientists, however, are less dismissive of ethical review, arguing that the problems identified are neither inevitable nor unavoidable (Bond, 2012) and should be considered as failures of practice rather than principle (Nicholls et al., 2012). Ethical review, they argue, is both necessary to avoid harm to research participants (which critics, they suggest, dismiss too lightly) and potentially beneficial to social researchers. The arguments of writers such as Schrag (2011), moreover, assume an isomorphism in ethical review practice that overlooks the significant variation in different settings, nor do they engage adequately with the available evidence of how ethical review bodies actually work (Hedgecoe, 2008, 2012). Rather than dismissing ethics review of social research as unnecessary and repressive, Bosk (2007) argues, there is a need to understand the circumstances that have given rise to the concerns that it expresses and to develop procedures that can ensure effective protection of both participants' rights and researchers' freedoms.

Even if there are exceptions to the claim of Israel and Hay (2006: 1) that 'social scientists are angry and frustrated' at the constraints and distortions imposed on their work by ethical regulation, however, it is clear that ethical review of social research remains controversial. While some such as Dingwall (2006: 57) may argue that social researchers should 'deprive [ethical review bodies] of the oxygen of legitimacy', there is more commonly an acknowledgement that demands for the exceptional treatment of social research are likely to be ineffective and that a return to self-regulation is institutionally implausible (Bell and Wray-Bliss, 2010). This does not mean that the well-documented failings of certain ethical review procedures do not need to be addressed, or that even those that are not seen to be specifically deficient could not be improved, but that efforts may best be focused on the most effective tactics to achieve this.

Research governance

Research governance can either be taken as broader than just research ethics, including topics such as health and safety, finance and intellectual property, or as those aspects of research ethics concerned with the conduct of research. Within the latter definition it is possible to distinguish between the ethics of research practice and publication ethics. The former consists of the personal ethics of the researcher in relation to matters such as integrity, honesty, openness, fair treatment of others and ethical practice in a research team (which may consist of just a student and a supervisor, or a principal investigator and a research assistant, or a large group of researchers under a senior research leader). Such guidance may also include advice on procedures to prevent and deal with misconduct (see, for example, the code of practice for research at http://www.ukrio.org/). Publication ethics relate to the responsibilities of researchers in the reporting of their research, such as acknowledgement of sources and the avoidance of plagiarism, as well as the responsibilities of journal editors and publishers in ensuring freedom of expression and the integrity of the academic record. While these issues are usually of concern only after research in organizations has been completed, and particularly in the case of the ethics of research conduct, are by no means specific to research in organizations, they may nevertheless be relevant to the reporting of organizational research as is discussed in Chapter 7.

Organizational research ethics

As will be evident from discussion in later chapters, the appropriate ethical stance, the principles and practice of ethical regulation and the ethics of reporting are a continuing focus of debate in the organizational research literature. Consistent with the focus of this book on the practice of research, however, it would not seem appropriate to seek to define a priori inviolable principles that all organizational research must follow or to view ethics as a one-off activity that can be addressed in isolation from the conduct of research. Rather it would seem more important to cultivate reflection on the ethics of research practice and ethical mindfulness in the conduct of research.

EXERCISES

1 What is the relevant ethics code for your field of research?
    • What issues may be encountered in applying this code in organizational research?
2 What process of ethical review applies to organizational research in your institution?
    • What issues may be encountered in applying this process?
3 Rate each of the following statements on a scale from strongly disagree to strongly agree:

	Strongly disagree	Slightly disagree	Slightly agree	Strongly agree
Who needs ethical codes? No serious researcher would ever do anything unethical				
Ethical codes are pious aspirations that are of little use as a guide to research practice				
Ethical codes cannot be absolute so, in the end, it is up to the researcher to make their own judgements				
Even if ethical codes cannot be absolute, researchers should always do their best to follow them as closely as possible				
Research that does not follow the relevant ethical code should not be conducted				

What arguments would you make to justify your position?

Further reading

There is a large and growing literature on research ethics. The following titles provide an introduction and overview of the subject with respect to social sciences in general.

Iphofen, R. (2009) *Ethical Decision Making in Social Research: A Practical Guide*. Basingstoke: Palgrave Macmillan.
   As its title suggests, this provides a practically oriented introduction to research ethics and the process of ethics review.

Wiles, R. (2013) *What Are Qualitative Research Ethics?* London: Bloomsbury Academic.
   An accessible overview of research ethics.

Farrimond, H. (2013) *Doing Ethical Research*. Basingstoke: Palgrave Macmillan.
   Includes discussion of ethical dilemmas in the practice of social research.

Israel, M. and Hay, I. (2006) *Research Ethics for Social Scientists: Between Ethical Conduct and Regulatory Compliance*. London: SAGE.
   An introduction to debates about ethical regulation in the social sciences.

There are also a large number of online sources relating to research ethics. See for example:

www.ethicsguidebook.ac.uk/
Provides guidance on research ethics from a UK perspective, with links to other resources.

www.hhs.gov/ohrp/policy/index.html
Provides information on policy on guidance from the US Office for Human Research Protections (not restricted to social sciences).

References

Adler, P.A. and Adler, P. (2002) 'Do university lawyers and the police define research values', in W.C. Van den Hoonard (ed.), *Walking the Tightrope: Ethical Issues for Qualitative Researchers*. Toronto: University of Toronto Press, pp. 34–42.

Bell, E. and Bryman, A. (2007) 'The ethics of management research: an exploratory content analysis', *British Journal of Management*, 18 (1): 63.

Bell, E. and Wray Bliss, E. (2009) 'Research ethics: regulations and responsibilities', in D.A. Buchanan and A. Bryman (eds), *SAGE Handbook of Organizational Research Methods*. London: SAGE, pp. 78–92.

Bledsoe, C.H., Sherin, B., Galinsky, A.G., Headley, N.M., Heimer, C.A., Keldgaard, E., Lindgren, J., Miller, J.D., Roloff, M.E. and Uttar, D.H. (2007) 'Regulating creativity: research and survival in the IRB iron cage', *Northwestern University Law Review*, 101: 593.

Bond, T. (2012) 'Ethical imperialism or ethical mindfulness? Rethinking ethical review for social sciences', *Research Ethics*, 8 (2): 97–112.

Bosk, C.L. (2007) 'The new bureaucracies of virtue or when form fails to follow function', *PoLAR: Political and Legal Anthropology Review*, 30 (2): 192–209.

Bronfenbrenner, U. (1952) 'Principles of professional ethics: Cornell studies in social growth', *American Psychologist*, 7 (2): 452–5.

Bryman, A. and Bell, E. (2011) *Business Research Methods*, 3rd edn. Oxford: Oxford University Press.

Calvey, D. (2008) 'The art and politics of covert research doing "situated ethics" in the field', *Sociology*, 42 (5): 905–18.

Denzin, N.K. (1968) 'On the ethics of disguised observation', *Social Problems*, 15 (4): 502–04.

Dingwall, R. (2006) 'Confronting the anti-democrats: the unethical nature of ethical regulation in social science', *Medical Sociology Online*, 1: 51–8.

Douglas, J.D. (1976) *Investigative Social Research*. Beverly Hills, CA: SAGE.

Erikson, K.T. (1967) 'A comment on disguised observation in sociology', *Social Problems*, 14 (4): 366–73.

Fletcher, J.F. (1997) *Situation Ethics: The New Morality*. Louisville, KY: Westminster John Knox Press.

Gans, H.J. (1968) 'The participant observer as a human being: observations on the personal aspects of fieldwork', in H.S. Becker, B. Geer, D. Riesman and

R.S. Weiss (eds), *Institutions and the Person*. Chicago, IL: Aldine Publishing Company, pp. 300–17.

Hammersley, M. and Traianou, A. (2012) *Ethics in Qualitative Research: Controversies and Contexts*. London: SAGE.

Hedgecoe, A. (2008) 'Research ethics review and the sociological research relationship', *Sociology*, 42 (5): 873–86.

Hedgecoe, A. (2012) 'The problems of presumed isomorphism and the ethics review of social science: a response to Schrag', *Research Ethics*, 8 (2): 79–86.

Israel, M. and Hay, I. (2006) *Research Ethics for Social Scientists: Between Ethical Conduct and Regulatory Compliance*. London: SAGE.

Lincoln, Y.S. and Tierney, W.G. (2004) 'Qualitative research and institutional review boards', *Qualitative Inquiry*, 10 (2): 219–34.

O'Neill, M. (2002) *A Question of Trust*. Cambridge: Cambridge University Press.

Nicholls, S.G., Brehaut, J. and Saginur, R. (2012) 'Social science and ethics review: a question of practice not principle', *Research Ethics*, 8 (2): 71–8.

Pearce, M. (2002) 'Challenging the system: rethinking ethics review of social research in Britain's National Health Service', in W.C. Van den Hoonard (ed.), *Walking the Tightrope: Ethical Issues for Qualitative Researchers*. Toronto: University of Toronto Press, pp. 43–58.

Pollock, K. (2012) 'Procedure versus process: ethical paradigms and the conduct of qualitative research', *BMC Medical Ethics*, 13 (1): 25–37.

Schrag, Z.M. (2011) 'The case against ethics review in the social sciences', *Research Ethics*, 7 (4): 120–31.

Shaw, I. (2008) 'Ethics and the practice of qualitative research', *Qualitative Social Work*, 7 (4): 400–14.

Sin, C.H. (2005) 'Seeking informed consent: reflections on research practice', *Sociology*, 39 (2): 277–94.

Van den Hoonaard, W.C. (2002) *Walking the Tightrope: Ethical Issues for Qualitative Researchers*. Toronto: University of Toronto Press.

Wilson, D. (1997) 'The insidious erosion of ethics', *Times Higher Educational Supplement*, 16.

5

Getting in: Seeking and Negotiating Access

Chapter objectives

- to identify the activities that may precede organizational fieldwork

  o preparation for fieldwork
  o site selection

- to identify the activities involved in negotiating access to fieldwork sites

  o establishing contact
  o the process of access negotiation
  o confidentiality agreements
  o characteristics associated with successful access negotiations

- to review the debate on covert research in organizations

In the very beginning

As the discussion of the research process in Chapter 3 highlighted, a consider-able amount of work often needs to be undertaken before research in organiza-tions can get under way. At the very least the researcher needs to decide on their area of interest and the specific topic, within this, that they wish to inves-tigate. Approaching an organization without any indication of what is to be studied is unlikely to elicit a positive response, as the organization will be unable to judge what aspects of its activities will be subject to scrutiny, and whether it would be happy to allow this, or the resources, such as staff time, that this may involve. This is not to rule out the possibility that fieldwork might be initiated, perhaps in a small informal organization that has little differentia-tion of responsibilities, with only a vague expression of general interest in studying 'the organization', but this may be considered as simply deferring the need to identify a specific focus, as there is likely to be too much going on for a researcher, or even a team of researchers, to study everything. Some focus will almost certainly be necessary in practice therefore, even if it may not be essential for the commencement of fieldwork in all circumstances.

There may be more debate, however, over whether or not this interest needs to be expressed as specific research questions and a formal design. Researchers employing flexible designs, such as organizational ethnography, might argue that since it is rarely possible to know in advance exactly how their research will proceed, as it seeks to be responsive to local contingencies, it would be misleading to suggest that the focus of the research will be confined solely to pre-specified questions or follow a pre-specified design. Indeed some would suggest that it would be unethical to do so, as it would be deceiving participants about how the research may actually proceed in practice. Pollock (2012: 25), for example, argues that current ethical regulation adopts a procedural framework that is inconsistent with the 'complex and shifting nature of real world settings' and delegitimizes qualitative studies that seek to pursue a more flexible and responsive research process.

Notwithstanding the evidence that the research process in many classics of organizational research, such as *Men Who Manage* (Dalton, 1959) or *Boys in White* (Becker et al., 1961), as well as in more recent studies such as Kunda (1992) or Ho (2009), did not always follow their original plans, organizational researchers who seek to emulate the methods of the natural sciences, even when using qualitative data, e.g. Yin (2003), King et al. (1994), might argue that this is a failing of the authors rather than a necessary adjustment to research practicalities. If unforeseen developments prevent the completion of research as planned, then the study should be abandoned and another developed from scratch, if necessary with a new design and research questions. Changing the research design or questions in midstream, or, even worse, when results do not turn out as planned, would make the study invalid and may even be considered as evidence of research misconduct.

Whether or not a researcher would consider that research questions and design should be specified before commencing a study, however, there may nevertheless be pragmatic reasons for doing so. As will be discussed in more detail below, organizations may expect researchers to provide a clear description of what they hope to do and may doubt the competence of a researcher who is unable to provide this. Indeed the absence of such a description may simply encourage suspicion about the real motivation of the research, which would seem unlikely to be to the researcher's advantage.

A second, pragmatic reason for developing research questions and a research design may be to meet the requirements of funding bodies and ethical review procedures. Despite the complaints of social scientists (as discussed in Chapter 4) that such bodies often assume a biomedical research model that is poorly suited to the characteristics of their work, in many settings it may be impossible to proceed with research without their approval. While there may be some scope for negotiation and flexibility in this process, wholesale rejection of its requirements would seem unlikely to get very far. Therefore researchers will often need to be able to present their study in terms of pre-specified questions and designs, whether or not this is methodologically appropriate or reflective of how the work will be carried out in practice.

Approaching the field

Assuming that it has been possible to establish, with whatever degree of formality, what it is intended that the research will study and how it is planned to study it, there may still be quite a way to go before fieldwork can actually be commenced. Three activities, in particular, may be considered a part of this necessary prelude: theoretical training, practical training and site selection. Each of these will now be considered in turn.

Theoretical training

Broadly speaking, there are two opposing views on whether a researcher should be thoroughly versed in the relevant literature before entering the field, with one school of thought seeing this as essential to any effective fieldwork. Thus, in an article reflecting on his lifetime experience of anthropological fieldwork (now included as an appendix to the abridged edition of his *Witchcraft, Oracles and Magic among the Azande*), the renowned social anthropologist Sir Edward Evan Evans-Pritchard, argued:

> Sometimes people say that anybody can make observations and write a book about a primitive people. Perhaps anybody can, but it may not be a contribution to anthropology. In science, as in life, one finds only what one seeks. One cannot have the answers without knowing what the questions are. Consequently the first imperative is a rigorous training in general theory before attempting field-research so that one may know how and what to observe, what is significant in the light of theory. It is essential to realize that facts are in themselves meaningless. To be meaningful they must have a degree of generality. It is useless going into the field blind. One must know precisely what one wants to know and that can only be acquired by a systematic training in academic social anthropology. (Evans-Pritchard and Gillies, 1976: 240)

Substitute 'organization' for 'primitive people' and organization theory for anthropology, and similar sentiments may be found in literature on research in organizations, particularly among proponents of fixed designs in which the primary objective of fieldwork is gathering (typically quantitative) data to test hypotheses that are logically integrated with prior research. Thus Sekaran and Bougie (2010: 39) argue that a literature review should be conducted prior to fieldwork, to ensure that: important variables that are likely to influence the problem situation are not left out of the study; a clearer idea emerges of what variables will be most important to consider, why they are considered important and how they should be investigated to solve the problem.

Similarly Tharenou et al. (2007: 8) place 'finding the theory' (which they define as 'relationships between constructs') as the second stage in the research process, immediately following the formulation of the initial research question.

Opponents of this view would argue that it is precisely because 'one finds only what one seeks', that 'rigorous training in general theory before attempting field-research' will ensure that one sees only what existing theory expects, or at least that one's view of what one sees will be filtered by prior training (Haynes, 2012). As with those bistable images that can be viewed as either a duck or a rabbit, as either a vase or two people facing each other, or as a young woman or an old lady,[1] being primed with one interpretation can make it hard to see the other (especially if there is no indication that other interpretations are possible). What is more, in treating the field solely as a venue for theory testing, the possibility of deriving new insights is ruled out and the assumptions of existing theory are taken for granted. Thus proponents of grounded theory (e.g. Glaser and Strauss, 1967) seek to bracket preconceptions and to develop theory inductively from their data, for example, while for ethnomethodologists (e.g. Sharrock and Lynch, 2011), the taken-for-grantedness of everyday life is the specific focus of interest.

While there may be grounds for suggesting that approaching fieldwork 'know[ing] precisely what one wants to know' may overly constrain the research process, it may also be argued that it is never possible to approach the field with a wholly open mind. Prior reading will shape what one sees, however much one may try to avoid this. Having seen the two images in the bistable figures it is no longer possible to suppress the awareness of the other image when seeing one of them. Thus Delamont (2004) discusses how access negotiations and initial fieldwork are guided by the researchers' 'foreshadowed problems' that emerge from reading and interaction with colleagues.

As will be discussed in relation to issues of data collection, moreover, the problem in organizational fieldwork, especially where it involves observation, is that there is almost always far more potential 'data' available than it could be feasible to 'collect'. Nor is this surplus of potential data avoided in research that relies solely on interviews as there will generally be more potential interviewees than it would be feasible to talk to and even if the number of interviewees is sufficiently small, there will always be more that they could have been asked about. Some element of selection in what is considered to be relevant

---

[1] See http://www.psy.ritsumei.ac.jp/~akitaoka/reversiblee.html for illustrations.

data to collect and in what it will be feasible to collect is therefore inevitable. This is the case too in experimental and survey research, except that the act of selection takes place before entering the field, but is no less significant. Having some theoretical basis on which that selection is made may thus be considered reasonable (and, in more formal designs, mandatory) even if it may not be the only, and some would argue should not be the primary, principle guiding data collection.

Skills training

Separately from, but potentially in addition to, preparatory theoretical training, it may be considered necessary for researchers to acquire practical skills and/ or knowledge relevant to the practices that are to be studied. If you are planning to study in a school, you should have some experience of teaching, if you are going to study in an IT department, you should have relevant hardware or software knowledge, if you want to study in a surgical operating theatre you should have some understanding of what goes on there. Several reasons are put forward for such training:

- familiarity with the setting and its social norms – enabling the researcher to 'blend in' and avoid drawing attention to their presence
- familiarity with professional language – enabling the researcher to understand what participants are talking about, without (potentially disruptive) translation
- credibility with participants in the setting – enabling the researcher to pass as at least a minimally competent member of the setting rather than as a low-status outsider
- building trust, especially where the participants feel that they are misunderstood by outsiders
- demonstrating the researcher's commitment to the research topic.

For example, before undertaking his study of Wall Street Bond traders, Abolafia (1998) took a course to become a futures trader and passed a national exam to gain certification. He also attended finance courses at his university and kept abreast of financial news. Similarly, Leidner (1993) attended McDonald's Hamburger University before gaining access to a franchise as a crew member.

The argument for researchers acquiring skills relevant to their proposed research setting relates to a further issue in the fieldwork literature, which Lofland and Lofland (1995) refer to as 'starting where you are' or what Riemer (1977) refers to as 'opportunistic research': that is, researchers studying settings which they are already familiar with, either through immediate personal experience or indirectly through 'accidents of remote biography and personal history' (Lofland and Lofland, 1995: 13) or to which some special expertise that they possess facilitates access. In addition to the examples cited by Lofland and Lofland (1995), this is a recurring theme in reports of organizational fieldwork. Orr (1996), for example, had previously worked as a photocopier technician before carrying out his ethnography of Xerox field service technicians, Ram's family were in the clothing business and he had worked in the family firm for many years (Ram, 1994), and Goodwin (2009: 8) had been an anaesthetic and recovery nurse prior to studying the development of anaesthetists' expertise and gained access to clinical areas, including operating theatres, through anaesthetists with whom she had worked previously.

For Lofland and Lofland (1995) the justification for such an approach is in the personal engagement that such linkages create, which they see as necessary to effective fieldwork, although they also acknowledge that it can create methodological and ethical difficulties (as will be discussed further in later chapters). Orr (1996) notes too that familiarity can blunt awareness, making it hard to see phenomena as remarkable and leading to details being omitted from fieldnotes because they appeared obvious in the field, but prove less easy to recall at a distance.

Quite apart from these potential difficulties, not all researchers in organizations are convinced that prior familiarity with a setting is either necessary or desirable. A certain distance and discomfort in the research setting can be of benefit to research (Ybema and Kamsteeg, 2009), not just in making the everyday exotic, and allowing the researcher to adopt roles that permit more questioning of the taken-for-granted (see Chapter 6), but in sustaining the researcher's identity as 'the professional stranger' (Agar, 1980). Thus Hammersley and Atkinson (2007: 90) argue that 'there must always remain some part held back, some social and intellectual distance'. Davis (1973: 335) refers to this stance as that of a Martian, who adopts an attitude of

> intransigent and unremitting doubt toward everything the members of a[n] ... organization ... may tell him, or even show him, concerning their motives, purposes, values, plans for everyday action, and so forth ... [in order to] divest himself completely of the vast array of unwitting cultural assumptions, rules of thumb, modes of sensibility and – were it somehow possible – the very language, which comprise the 'cognitive stuff' of our everyday worlds and beings.

Site selection

For researchers adopting the principle of 'starting where you are', choosing the organization in which to conduct their research will be a product, directly or indirectly, of personal biography – some incident or association in their life provides the motivation for the research and the connection that leads to the fieldwork. While such an approach to site selection may be considered suitable for ethnographic studies it may not be viewed as appropriate for other forms of research in organizations, especially those that look to collect data from multiple sites. Nor would it seem reasonable to assume that all researchers will necessarily be so fortunate as to stumble upon a relevant site (or sites) for their research by chance. How, then, can a researcher go about finding organizations in which to carry out their study?

This question can be seen as having two components: identifying the potential population of target organizations and selecting sites for study within that population. In some domains the target population may be well-known and clearly defined. A researcher studying prisons in the UK, for example, can obtain a list of all institutions and their categories from the Ministry of Justice website. Identifying the population of clothing manufacturers in the West Midlands, on the other hand, may be very difficult. As Ram (1994) describes, not only do such businesses tend to be small and recruit among a closed community, but they are also suspicious of official-dom and not inclined to organize or register themselves collectively. Getting any sense of even the number, let alone the characteristics of such businesses may therefore be a major challenge.

For larger and more formal organizations there may be a number of sources that could be used to establish a list of potential sites:

- Trade directories
- Company databases
- Telephone yellow pages
- Trade Associations
- Chambers of Commerce.

These sources may not necessarily be a complete listing of all organizations in an industry sector or in a region, however, as there may often be no requirement for organizations to be registered and some may be deterred by listing fees or perceptions of the allegedly representative body. They may nevertheless be sufficiently authoritative to be taken as a reasonable proxy for the whole population, even if their coverage is not actually complete. Taking a sample of the organizations listed in a directory or database may therefore be considered 'good enough' as a sampling frame, even if, in practice, such sources are neither necessarily definitive nor representative.

In many cases, however, there may be no central listing of all, or even a plausible subset, of potential target organizations and it is necessary to use more indirect means to locate suitable organizations such as:

- Press stories
- Trade meetings/conferences
- Online search.

Having established by whatever means a list of potential target organizations, the next step is to select among them. There are various ways in which this can be done, depending on the objectives and assumptions of the study.

Table 5.1 Types of sampling methods

Type of sample	Method
Random	Use a random number generator, e.g. spreadsheet RND() function to identify study sites within a numbered list of all potential sites
Systematic	Pick every nth site from the numbered list (where n corresponds to the proportion of the total to be sampled)
Stratified	Divide the total into categories according to some criterion, e.g. size, and select randomly within those strata
Cluster	Divide the total into groups, e.g. by geography, and select all sites within some groups
Quota	Divide the total into categories and select a number of sites from each category according to a specified proportion, e.g. 75% SMEs, 25% large organizations

Where the research aims to collect representative data about the population of organizations, for example by carrying out a survey, some form of statistical sampling is likely to be expected. This may take a variety of forms, as shown in Table 5.1.

More in-depth studies, which, for reasons of practicality, are likely to involve a smaller number of sites, may need to forego statistical representativeness. Some rationale for site selection is still likely to be needed, however. Yin (1993, 2003), in his discussion of the case study method, suggests that sites might be selected for study on the basis that they represent critical, extreme, typical or revelatory cases. Sites selected for their criticality are viewed as test cases for a particular theory or phenomenon. There are several ways in which this might apply. If a theory is supported by evidence from the chosen site, for example, then it suggests that it may be robust to other challenges. Conversely, from a falsificationist perspective, a single negative case can lead to the rejection of a theory. Or a case may provide evidence for comparing competing theories. A critical case need not be solely in relation to a theory, though, but may relate to observation of a particular phenomenon. For example an intervention might be studied on the busiest ward in a hospital or the most difficult class in a school on the grounds that if it is effective there, then there is a good chance that it will also work in less demanding settings.

Selecting sites in terms of their being an extreme case reflects a logic that emphasizes the value of understanding phenomena in exceptional conditions. DeRond (2009, 2012), for example, has studied high-performing teams, such as a boat race crew or military surgeons in a field hospital to understand how teamwork functions in such circumstances.

Typical, or exemplary, sites would be chosen because they are considered to best represent a particular type of organization. Although not statistically representative they are considered as having most, if not all, of the characteristics that are associated with their particular type. The logic of their selection is that findings in this setting will tell us more about the class of organizations to which they belong than would findings from other organizations deemed less typical. There is likely to be some element of circular logic in the selection of such sites, however, as the characteristics associated with what is considered to be a typical site (which is often those that are best known) come to define what is seen as typical of such organizations. McDonald's defines what a fast food company is like, for example, or Goldman Sachs an investment bank.

A revelatory case would be selected because it provides a rare or unique opportunity to gain insight on phenomena deemed otherwise impenetrable. Studies of secretive or normally inaccessible organizations, such as religious cults (Ayella, 1990) or intelligence service organizations (Johnston, 2005; 't Hart, 2007) may be examples of this type.

These logics largely relate to the selection of a single site as a case study. There is a second category of selection criteria in relation to multiple sites. Here, as Yin discusses, there may be two alternative logics: that of replication and that of sampling. In the first situation sites are chosen because it is considered that they provide similar conditions for the testing of theory or observation of phenomena. Such replication may be *literal*, seeking to find similar results, or *theoretical*, seeking to observe contrasting results for theoretically explicable reasons.

Following a sampling logic, on the other hand, sites are selected to explore the effects of various conditions on the phenomenon of interest. In principle a sampling case design should include at least one case of all the possible conditions: a large and a small firm in two different industries, say. In practice, in many studies the potential number of degrees of variation makes it unfeasible to have a case in 'every cell of the matrix'. With just three dimensions of variation, such as size, industry and location, each with just two conditions, such as start-up/established, 16 cases would be needed to cover all combinations and the study would inevitably have to sacrifice analytical depth.

As this suggests, it may not always be possible to find sites that meet the ideal criteria. Notwithstanding the emphasis on 'principles' of site selection, therefore, more pragmatic considerations may apply, as Yin (1993) acknowledges in identifying 'feasibility and access' as a potential selection criterion. As is discussed below, this would appear to have been the operative criterion in many widely cited studies.

For studies focusing on a single site, the selection principle may indeed be reversed. Thus, rather than choosing a site in terms of its qualities relative to the population of potential sites, it may be chosen because of its particular qualities. Lofland and Lofland (1995) propose that potential sites should be evaluated in terms of four criteria: appropriateness, access, ethics, immediate risk and personal consequences. For Lofland and Lofland, appropriateness is primarily about the suitability of a site in terms of the data-gathering methods proposed. Thus it is suggested that participant observation is best suited to phenomena that are 'physically located somewhere, at least temporarily' (Lofland and Lofland, 1995: 20) – intensive interviewing to 'amorphous social experiences' that are unique to individuals, for example – while other data-gathering methods, including quantitative methods, may be appropriate to study other types of phenomena.

Evaluating a site for access, Lofland and Lofland (1995) suggest, is likely to be influenced by several considerations. In particular they mention: by the investigator's relationship to the setting (are they a complete outsider, or do they already have some connection with the site?); by the roles that may be assigned to the researcher by those in the setting (by virtue of, for example, their gender or age); by the size and complexity of the research locale (which may be beyond the scope of a single person to study and require a team of researchers); and by the intrinsic ease or difficulty of gaining entry to particular types of sites (the contrast is made between studying in open public settings or 'observing the day-to-day workings of a segment of the Central Intelligence Agency' [Lofland and Lofland, 1995: 25], although even the latter may be less impenetrable than they imply, as Johnston's study of analytic culture in the US intelligence community [Johnston, 2005] illustrates).

Ethical evaluation of potential sites concerns the likely scale and severity of ethical problems that may be encountered. This may relate to: the morality of the practices to be studied; the risk of harm to those studied; the extent of deception involved; and inequalities between the researcher and their 'subjects'. For Lofland and Lofland (1995) the risks of fieldwork may be not just physical, but also emotional. How distressing may the phenomena studied be and how long does the researcher feel able to sustain their involvement under such circumstances? Finally, personal consequences, in terms, say, of potential responses to reports of the research findings, are considered to be inherently unknowable, but deserving of (necessarily imperfect) forethought.

Establishing contact

Having established which organizations constitute potential sites for the proposed research, the next step is to establish contact with the organization members who are in a position to permit (or refuse) access to potential research participants at these sites. This may not be straightforward, however, even for a questionnaire study. For example, a questionnaire sent to a general job title in an organization, such as 'The Marketing Manager, Acme Corporation', would seem unlikely to reach the intended recipient. Even if the organization does not have a policy of refusing to answer unsolicited correspondence, unless there is just one person whose job title matches that given they may not be willing to devote time to identifying the appropriate recipient, so the questionnaire may simply be binned. Efforts to obtain names and contact details for suitable recipients, therefore, are likely to be rewarded.

Table 5.2 Approaches to gaining contact details for research access

Type of contact	Personalization	Advantages	Disadvantages
Cold calling the organization's published contact number to obtain contact details for individuals	None	Readily accessible Can contact large and representative sample	Public contact point may not be willing to disclose contact details for individuals Contacts may be referred to PR department who may seek to control research access First point of contact may not have knowledge to identify suitable individuals
Identifying relevant individuals from public sources, e.g. web sites, press stories, LinkedIn	None	Publicly accessible	Public sources may not be sufficient to establish contact details Public sources may not be up-to-date Press stories may not be representative Contacts may have to go through a secretary/PA
Meeting relevant individual at public events, e.g. conferences and trade shows and obtaining business cards	Low	Establishes some minimal commitment to interaction	Individuals may 'forget' meeting Contacts may have to go through a secretary/PA Individuals unlikely to be representative
Identifying relevant individuals who have had some contact with your institution, e.g. attending events, giving presentations, alumni	Low	Evidence of some degree of engagement	Individuals may not have access to relevant contact details Risk to future institutional contacts if problems arise Individuals unlikely to be representative
Indirect personal contacts e.g. of colleagues, supervisors	High	Social capital of referrer may encourage response	Risk to social capital of referrer if problems arise Individuals unlikely to be representative
Personal contacts, i.e 'family and friends'	High	Personal social capital may encourage response	Responses may be affected by personal relationship Individuals unlikely to be representative

A similar process of obtaining contact details is also likely to be necessary for more engaged forms of data-gathering, such as interviews and observation. There are various ways in which such data may be obtained, as shown in Table 5.2. In general, the more personalized the approach, the more likely that suitable contacts will be made (and that individuals contacted will agree to participate in research). The coverage of personalized approaches, however, is likely to be lower and more selective and a trade-off will typically have to be made between the representativeness of contacts and their receptivity to the invitation to participate in research. The balance of this trade-off may be tipped towards personalization by the typically low success rate of cold calling, even when armed with individuals' contact details, which can make it a frustrating and dispiriting experience. With the exception of fixed designs, in which representativeness is given high priority, therefore, more personalized forms of contact may be preferred. This is not to say that this is always acknowledged in research reports, but where access procedures are discussed it would seem that many, if not most, relied on direct or indirect personal contacts. Buchanan et al. (1988), for example, gained access to an organization over lunch with a friend, Zaloom (2006) gained access to the Chicago Board of Trade through the son of family friends with whom she was staying, and Morrill's access to business executives was facilitated by a 'a close relative, ... a longtime management consultant and respected member of the local business community chosen for the study' (Morrill, 1995: 233).

First line gatekeepers[2]

In all these approaches to gaining access there will be at least one person who acts as the initial 'gatekeeper', controlling, intentionally or unintentionally, who the researcher is able to contact. This may be: the receptionist who answers the published contact number; the post room staff who decide how to distribute unpersonalized, or incorrectly addressed, mail; the secretary/personal assistant to a senior manager; the individual whose contact details have been obtained; the personal contact who has agreed to facilitate access.

Each of these will have their motives for being helpful or obstructive and may be required to follow organizational rules about the handling of requests (Randall et al., 2007).

---

[2]The literature typically uses the term gatekeeper to refer to individuals who have the power to decide whether to grant access to a group or organization – what are referred to as 'qualified prospects' below. As Randall et al. (2007: 174) observe, however, 'In an organizational context these can include different managerial sections, secretarial staff, "shop floor" workers, and more. In other words, gatekeepers are not always the high-status members of an organization, quite the contrary.'

Table 5.3 Duration of access negotiations in different studies

Study	Focus	Duration of access negotiations
Taylor (1991)	An institution for 'people labelled retarded'	Two days
Buchanan et al. (1988)	New technology and organizational change	One week to 26 months
Randall et al. (2007)	Air Traffic Control	'Many weeks'
Okumus et al. (2007)	Implementation of strategic decisions in a hotel group	4 months
Mollona (2009)	The experience of labour in the steel industry	6 months
Jackall (1988)	Occupational ethics of corporate managers	9 months
Winkler (1987)	Work of company directors	1 year (of a 3-year study)
deRond (2012)	A team of combat surgeons in a field hospital in Afghanistan	18 months
Morrill (1995)	Executive conflict	18 months
Walford (2001)	The City Technology College initiative	19 months

Two implications follow from this. The first that it is always good practice to treat gatekeepers well (as Goldman and Swayze [2012] discuss, a sympathetic administrative assistant can enable access where more formal approaches have been unsuccessful) whatever their formal status in the organization, and secondly that it is important to be sensitive to the rules that they may operate under. This is not to say that first line gatekeepers will have no discretion in the application of these rules, but that the strictness with which they are applied is likely to depend on how the gatekeeper is treated by the researcher and on the researcher's recognition of the favour that is involved in the exercise of that discretion.

For the researcher undertaking a survey, establishing a confirmed contact in the target organization to whom the questionnaire can be sent may be all the access that is needed. For researchers wishing to undertake interviews, or more especially observations, in the target organization, in contrast, this may be just the start of extensive (and frequently protracted) access negotiations (Crabtree et al., 2012). Table 5.3 illustrates the timescale involved in gaining access in a range of different studies.

As Table 5.3 shows, gaining access can take a long time and there is significant variation in the duration of access negotiations. In part, at least, this can be related to the focus of the research. Organizations would seem likely to be more reluctant to agree to a study of potentially sensitive topics, such as executive conflict or commercial decision-making, than a study of routine production

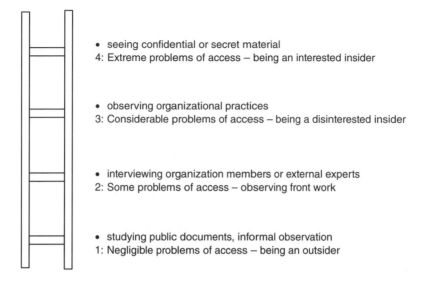

- seeing confidential or secret material
4: Extreme problems of access – being an interested insider

- observing organizational practices
3: Considerable problems of access – being a disinterested insider

- interviewing organization members or external experts
2: Some problems of access – observing front work

- studying public documents, informal observation
1: Negligible problems of access – being an outsider

Figure 5.1   The access ladder

activities (although these too may be considered sensitive in some circumstances). Gray (1980) proposes the metaphor of an 'access ladder' to describe the relative difficulty of access for different types of study, involving different researcher roles.

At the lowest rung of the ladder is access to information that can be obtained from publicly accessible sources, such as libraries or general and specialist media or by informal observation and conversation. Such data, Gray suggests, is likely to involve negligible problems of access, as the researcher remains an outsider. Moving to the second rung of the ladder, however, where the researcher seeks to study the organization's 'front work' (Douglas, 1976) through interviews with primary respondents in the organization or external experts, may encounter 'some problems of access' (Gray, 1980: 311). Greater problems are likely to be encountered in getting to the third rung, where the researcher seeks to play the role of a disinterested insider, by, for example, undertaking passive observation of organizational activities. Finally, access problems may be extreme at the fourth rung, where the researcher seeks to become an interested insider, for example, being able to view secret or confidential material.

As can also be seen from Table 5.3, however, while it may be relatively more difficult to gain access to study sensitive topics than to study organizational 'front work', organizations, and individuals within them, vary in the sensitivity they accord to different topics and in their receptivity to the idea of being the subject of research. A request to study a particular topic in one organization may face many objections, but be granted permission with no hesitation in another. Just because a topic may be at a higher rung on the access ladder, therefore, doesn't necessarily mean that there will be extreme difficulties in gaining access (or conversely that there may not be considerable problems in gaining access to study less sensitive, or more publicly accessible, topics).

While access may, to some extent, be a lottery, and therefore subject to the whims of organizational gatekeepers, there are still techniques that a researcher can adopt that may make a successful outcome more likely. One source of such techniques, Walford (2001) proposes, may be the popular literature on commercial selling. As Walford (2001) notes, many academic researchers would balk at the notion that they were engaged in anything so vulgar as 'selling' their research – although it is not unusual to find access negotiations described in such terms (e.g. Roesch-Marsh et al., 2012 Smith 2010). In practice, as will be discussed below moreover, the two processes of selling and gaining research access have sufficient similarities that the comparison may not be wholly inapt.

Access as selling

Drawing on books such as *Selling to Win* (Denny, 2009), *The American Marketing Association Handbook for Successful Selling* (Kimball, 1994) and *The Perfect Sale: All You Need to Get It Right First Time* (Thornely and Lees, 1994), Walford (2001) suggests that the selling process may be seen as comprising four stages: approach, interest, desire and sale.

Approach

The first stage, 'approach', is about the process of identifying and contacting suitable 'prospects'. That is, people who are likely to want to buy what is being sold. In the research context, this means people who likely to want to be research participants. The selling literature has little to add to Table 5.2, in terms of how to identify prospects, except to advise against cold calling if at all possible.

With a list of prospects identified, however, Walford (2001) emphasizes, it is important to ensure that they are 'qualified', that is, in research terms, in a position to grant access (they are 'gatekeepers' in the conventional use of the term). Denny (2009) refers to this as 'tuning' the prospect list. It can typically be done with a phone call to the organization, ideally without needing to speak to the prospect at all, so as not to take up too much of their time. If contact is made with a qualified prospect, though, it may be necessary to have a 'sales speech' prepared, providing a brief summary of the research and what is being requested from the organization. Unless the prospect is immediately receptive to being involved in the research, the aim should not be to discuss the organization's participation at this stage, especially if there is a risk of this being refused, but to get the prospect's agreement to being sent an access request letter that they will be able to consider in their own time.

Cold calling is something that even professional salespeople loathe, as Denny (2009) acknowledges, but it is likely to be a necessary part of gaining access to many organizations. The selling literature provides tips on such things as getting past switchboards (ask to speak to the contact by name and give your own first name and surname, rather than an explanation of the purpose of your call) how to handle voicemail (avoid it and call later, if at all possible), and how to project a positive telephone manner (smile while you are talking, apparently), but these do little to make it any easier.

To make matters even worse, the initial contact made with an organization may not always be suitable. As Randall et al. (2007: 171) observe,

> Organisations are complex and this is often manifested in the sheer difficulty of finding someone who is able to take responsibility for a decision about access. Here, one often has to take on trust statements of the kind, 'It's not really me who deals with this kind of thing, but I'll pass it on to someone who might know who does'.

Further contact(s) may need to be made, therefore, to reach the right person. This is likely to be facilitated if the initial contact can be prevailed upon to provide the name and contact details for qualified prospects, or, better still, to make the referral themselves ('referred leads', provided by individuals outside the organization, as in the personalized approaches in Table 5.2, may perform a similar role). Otherwise the researcher is likely to find themselves back to square one. All in all, initial contact with an organization, except for the most sociable of people, can be very trying.

Contrary to the common 'vision of top managers as what we called "alpha-wolf" decision-makers who could decide whether or not to guarantee access to all parts of their organizations' (Morrill et al., 1999: 55), moreover, there may often be more than one person, or group, in an organization, whose approval is needed before access can be achieved. Working out who the different gatekeepers are may not always be easy, however. In his study of workplace relations, for example, Gouldner (1955: 255)

> made a 'double-entry' into the plant, coming in almost simultaneously by way of the Company and the Union. But it soon became obvious that we had made a mistake, and that the problem had not been to make a double-entry, but a triple-entry; for we had left out, and failed to make independent contact with a distinct group – the management of that particular plant. In a casual way, we had assumed that main office management also spoke for the local plant management and this, as a moment's reflection might have told us, was not the case. In consequence our relations with local management were never as good as they were with the workers or the main office management.

Table 5.4   Primary gatekeepers in different organizational types (after Morrill et al., 1999)

| | | Authority structure ||
		Centralized	**Decentralized**
Decision-making routines	**Rationalized**	Individual top manager	Multiple top managers
	Politicized	Ruling coalition	Multiple coalitions

Morrill et al. (1999) propose a way of addressing this problem through a typology of gatekeepers that relates them to the decision-making routines of the organization (rationalized or politicized) and the authority structures (centralized or decentralized), as shown in Table 5.4.

Furthermore, in larger organizations, local sites, although supportive of granting access, may feel obliged to seek approval from head office. Similarly, seeking access permission from a functional department may get the PR department involved (Ho, 2009). Reports of such referrals suggest that this can not only add considerable delay, but tends to lead to refusal, often without explanation (Buchanan et al., 1988; Leidner, 1993). It may therefore be best if the locus of access decision-making can be kept, if at all possible, at the level at which contact has been made.

Interest

With a qualified prospect identified the second stage of the sales process is to write to them, engaging the prospect's interest. Compared to a telephone call, a letter has the advantage that the recipient can read it at a time of their choosing (rather than potentially being interrupted by a telephone call), it provides a permanent record of what is proposed (for future reference) and can include more detail than may be easily remembered from a phone call. While email has similar qualities, Denny (2009) suggests that it should be avoided. Even if messages are not weeded out by organizational spam filters, it seems that they have less credibility than a letter, especially if the latter is on headed paper.

Following what Denny (2009: 71) describes as a key principle of selling, that 'you can only sell one thing at a time', the purpose of this initial communication is just to sell (i.e. get) an appointment, not to 'close the deal'. Similarly for a researcher, the letter is about securing a first face-to-face meeting, not permission to undertake more extended fieldwork.

To this end, the communication needs to be clear, brief and engaging. Clarity is important as a demonstration of competence – if a researcher cannot describe their work clearly then others are unlikely to be persuaded of its merits. Brevity of communication has two advantages. The person being contacted is likely to be busy, so if they cannot quickly understand what is being communicated they will not waste their time on it. Secondly, as Walford (2001: 39) observes, 'every additional piece of information gives a chance for an objection or problem to be raised in the mind of the reader'. Keeping it short makes it harder for the prospect to find reasons not to agree to meet.

The initial communication, or spiel (Smith, 2010) should therefore be viewed as a form of what consultants call the 'elevator pitch' (Pincus, 2007) – a concise summary of the reasons why an organization should engage their services that can be delivered to the prospect as the elevator/lift travels between the floors of a building. Finally the initial communication needs to be persuasive so that the prospect is moved to take action on it and agree to the appointment.

Buchanan et al. (1988: 57) advise against the use of the terms 'research', 'interview' and 'publish', in the initial communication with an organization as they argue that they are perceived to be 'threatening and dull'. 'Research', they suggest, evokes the idea of long, tedious questionnaires; 'interview' suggests an interrogation by the police or an inquisitorial journalist; while 'publication', conjures an image of the organization's commercial secrets or insider stories being splashed across the front page of a national newspaper. They therefore recommend telling potential participants 'we want to learn from their experience by talking to them and we will write an account of our work, which they will see'. Similarly, in a survey study of management practices, Bloom and Van Reenen (2010: 208) report that they 'positioned the surveys as a "piece of work on lean manufacturing," never using the word "survey" or "research," as telephone switchboards usually block surveys and market research.' Although euphemistic language of this sort would seem unlikely to deter potential participants, few other authors appear to detect such sensitivities and the necessity of avoiding these terms may therefore be questioned.

While a number of the popular selling books go so far as to provide readers with form letters that they can adapt to their needs, this would not seem appropriate in a research context in which the message to be communicated is likely to be highly specific. It is nevertheless possible to make some general suggestions about the form and content of an initial letter requesting research access.

In total, a request for access should probably be no more than two, well-spaced pages, the first of these being a covering letter and the second a clear, concise description, in non-technical language, of the research that expands on the brief statement in the covering letter. There is no need for this description to go into great details, let alone to discuss the theoretical or methodological relevance of the research, rather the aim is to demonstrate how the organization's participation will help to advance understanding of some important topic.

Hales and Webster (2008) suggest a wide range of different functions that the initial letter should fulfil, as shown in Table 5.5.

Table 5.5   Functions of an initial contact letter (after Hales and Webster, 2008)

1. It identifies the reason for conducting the study
2. It explains how and why the organization has been selected
3. It explains what information is to be collected
4. It suggests what the respondent's role is likely to be
5. It indicates the importance of the research (to the sponsor and 'society')
6. It states how the research will be organized (for example as an interview or observation)
7. It explains the researcher's credentials and relevant background
8. It states how the confidentiality of information will be maintained
9. It provides a means by which the recipient can contact the sender
10. It notes that the organization's participation is voluntary but vital to the value of the research
11. It may offer a procedure to enable respondents to opt out of the research

An illustration of what this might look like is given in Figure 5.2 (numbers in the text relate to the functions identified by Hales and Webster, 2008). This is not intended as a form letter and the more personalized an initial letter can be made, for example by referring to some comments by the contact that are relevant to the topic to illustrate that their views have been recognized as significant, the more likely it will be to receive a positive response. Potential refinements might be:

- to indicate information has already been gathered from other organizations (assuming that it has);
- to provide more details on the research outputs and how they might be of benefit to the target organization;
- to indicate that the letter will be followed up by a phone call to the contact's office perhaps two weeks after the date of the letter 'to check that the letter has been received'. This can be an incentive for the contact to respond (positively or negatively) within that period, but also indicates that they will be contacted if they do not reply (which may be easier for them).

Bearing in mind that, especially with a flexible design, the precise focus of the research may not be known in advance it may be desirable to develop an easily comprehensible statement of what the research is about that offers sufficient latitude to enable various possible avenues to be explored without exceeding its terms. Such a description may also be useful to give to organization members (either verbally, or as a document) when fieldwork is under way. In this latter context, Taylor and Bogdan (1988: 33) propose that such statements should be 'truthful, but vague and imprecise'. Goffman (1989: 127) makes a similar point rather more strongly: 'I like a story such that if they find out what you are doing, the story you presented could not be an absolute lie. If they don't find out what you're doing, the story you presented doesn't get in your way.'

These documents need to be prepared with care to ensure that the first impressions of the research are as favourable as possible and that they give

[Name of Contact]   University of Watermouth
[Name of Organization]   [Department of X]
[Address 1]   [Address 1]
[Address 2]   [Address 2]
[Address 3]   [Address 3]

                                                                              Date

Dear [Contact Name],

I am a [student/researcher/lecturer/professor] at the Department of X at the University of
Watermouth studying [topic of research]. I enclose a summary of my research project (1).
My interest in [topic of research] has developed out of [my experience as a [job role
relevant to the topic of research]/earlier research on [a related research topic]](7). I am
particularly interested in gaining insight on [two or three specific issues relating to the
research topics].

My initial investigations have identified [name of target organization] as one of the leading
organizations in the area of [topic of research] (2) and, as [contact's job role](4) for [target
organization], your views on [the two or three specific issues] (3) would be particularly
valuable for my research. I am therefore writing to ask if I might be able to meet with you to
discuss [topic of research] at [target organization] and to explore the possibility of
gathering further data on [topic of research] at [target organization] in due course(6). Your
views on [specific issues] will enable us to gain a better understanding of [topic of
research] and thus to [address a recognized problem/improve practice/gain insight on this
neglected issue](5).

The meeting should not take more than 45 minutes and could be arranged at a time and a
location to suit you. If you do not consider that you would be the most appropriate person
to talk to on this matter or are unable to meet at this time, I would be grateful if you could
suggest who I might talk to instead(10). Any information gathered at the meeting will be
kept confidential(8) and will be used solely for the purposes of research.

If you have any questions regarding the research, please do not hesitate to contact me at
[University email address] or by phone on [University telephone number](9).

I look forward to hearing from you.

Yours sincerely,

Signature

[Printed name]

Figure 5.2   Sample access letter

an accurate picture of what it will mean for the target organization to be
involved in the research. This does not mean that, with the agreement of the
organization, it may not be possible later to expand the scope of the research
beyond that set out in the initial access request, but that if the research is
limited to the original terms it will be sufficient for the purposes of the study.
Thus if the request is for a 45-minute meeting, it should be possible to con-
clude the business within that time.

If the research is expected to involve a significant commitment of time on the part of the organization, for example a longitudinal study, participant observation for several months, or interviews with a substantial number of organization members, it may be best not to imply that the purpose of the initial meeting is to get agreement to the whole programme of research, but rather to discuss the possibility of conducting research with the organization. It may therefore be helpful to have a phased plan of research that can be implemented progressively depending on how the relationship with the organization develops. An initial meeting, for example, might lead to a request for some preliminary interviews, or some short period of observation, which might then be extended with the agreement of both parties.

The same can apply to the duration of the initial interview itself. If it goes well, it can often overrun the originally allocated time (although the researcher should, of course, draw the organization member's attention when the agreed time has elapsed, even if this rarely leads to the immediate termination of the meeting). Walford (2001: 43), for example, states that he requested a 45-minute meeting with headteachers, 'although none of the meetings was this short and some went on for over two hours'. Asking for less than an hour, however, signals the researcher's awareness of how busy organization members are (or profess themselves to be) and suggests that the meeting will not be too arduous even if it does not go well.

As will be discussed in further detail below, some organizations may insist on a more formal agreement being made, covering such issues as confidentiality, publication rights, and the duration of the study before research is allowed to proceed. In the absence of such a requirement, however, the initial access request may be treated as defining the terms of an implied contract and be circulated to other organization members as a statement of what is involved. It is therefore important that the research can be carried out within the terms that it sets out, as the researcher may be held to them.

Desire

If the initial approach is successful and an appointment is granted then the nature of this second stage will depend on the type of research being conducted. For some studies, typically involving fixed designs with structured data-gathering methods, a single interview with an organization may be sufficient and no further contact with the organization will be required. The focus of the meeting can therefore be solely on data-gathering. More typically, however, the first meeting is both an opportunity to gather some preliminary data, and an exploration of the potential for further contact, whether this is in the form of further interviews with other organization members, permission for observational research, or future follow-up interviews. In terms of the selling literature, therefore, the meeting is the setting for the third stage of the process – establishing the prospect's desire for the product, or, in the research context, the organization's agreement to participate in the research.

According to Walford (2001: 44) there are 'two main aspects to raising the desire to purchase an item or service: overcoming objections and stressing benefits'. In terms of the former, Buchanan et al. (1988) suggest 'the two most common reservations that can block research access concern time and confidentiality'. The time staff spend on answering a questionnaire or being interviewed, for example, may be considered a diversion from more productive activities. Similarly organizations often have reservations about the potential exposure of sensitive data or the reputational risk of adverse findings. In participant observation research there may also be concerns about potential costs, such as the provision of workspace or a computer account, associated with the presence of the researcher 'on-site'. Even if in practice these costs are rarely significant for most organizations, they may nevertheless constitute a real barrier to access.

In order to overcome objections, Buchanan et al. (1988) recommend that the researcher should raise them before they are presented and should indicate how they have been successfully dealt with in other studies (preferably the researcher's own, but if not, in the published literature). This is not to say that it will be necessary, or even possible, to address all potential objections in an initial meeting (indeed it is unlikely to be a good sign for the prospects of a successful research engagement if the meeting focuses on objections rather than benefits). It is probably a good idea before the meeting, however, for the researcher to have given some thought to how they might address key concerns so that they can provide a considered response should the matter be raised, rather than having to come up with a solution on the spot. This would seem particularly the case with confidentiality and publication because if agreements on these are too restrictive, research can be significantly constrained. Given their potential importance, specific attention is paid to these issues below and they will also be returned to in discussions of the reporting of research in organizations in Chapter 7.

If organizations often seem to find it all too easy to identify objections to research, its benefits may prove more elusive. This may be less of an issue for action research and consultancy where the basis of the engagement is specifically geared to addressing an organizational problem. Even here, however, the organization may not perceive themselves as facing the particular problem the researcher wishes to study, or may not consider it as a priority. The challenge in the initial meeting, therefore, may be in persuading the organization that they have a problem that they would benefit from having addressed.

This task would seem likely to be even more challenging for research that is motivated by scholarly, rather than organizational interests. While there may be some organizations, perhaps involved in research themselves, who may be persuaded of the merits of the pursuit of knowledge for its own sake, it may be expected that, more commonly, organizations will want to see some return from their participation (Shenton and Hayter, 2004).

One form of benefit that may be identified for research that involves several comparable organizations is in providing benchmarking data, allowing organizations to assess their practices or performance against others. Providing such data is likely to involve significant confidentiality issues, however, and can only proceed with the agreement of all parties involved. It may be attractive to organizations, though, where commercial benchmarking services are not available or the organization cannot afford their cost.

Similarly, with participant observation research it may be possible to present the participation as a potential benefit to the organization. This may be more persuasive if the researcher has skills that are directly applicable to the activity being observed, for example having programming skills in a study of software development, or copywriting skills in a study of an advertising agency. Even if the researcher does not have specialist skills relevant to the specific activity, there may be a benefit from an 'extra pair of hands' in some support role, but only if the researcher is quickly able to learn the job without taking up too much of the regular staff members' time.

Nor need these benefits always be limited to the immediate research activity. For example there may be activities that the researcher could undertake, perhaps making use of their independence from the organization or specific skills, to offset the 'costs' of their research. Some organizations may expect this as a 'price of entry' and it will be important for the researcher to judge whether the time and resources this may require exceed the value of access. Occasionally the organization's demands may go beyond what might be considered reasonable or ethical. Holliday (1995), for example, reports, being asked to conduct industrial espionage in the course of her fieldwork.

In some circumstances the benefits of research may be sufficiently attractive to the organization that they may be willing to pay for them (indeed for consultancy this is the principle on which the engagement is based). While payment of honoraria or expenses may be seen as less compromising of the researcher's independence, and perhaps more like industrially funded research, they still create some level of expectation of returns to the organization that the researcher may be considered obliged to fulfil. In some cases these returns may be defined in terms of specific 'deliverables' that may be peripheral to the focus of the research. Although payments from the organization may be attractive, therefore, in helping to defray the cost of fieldwork, this will need to be weighed against the potential diversion of effort from more research-productive activities.

In the absence of any such tangible benefits, researchers commonly have to resort to claims about the value to be gained from an independent or objective perspective. As Randall et al. (2007: 175) observe,

> Any ethnographer of organisations quickly recognises an almost universal fact of organisational life, which is that members of any particular unit or department will have little or no idea what goes on in adjacent units or departments. (One of the major values of ethnography is precisely that a view of the whole organisation can be obtained, one which is not available to other organisational members.)

Similarly, Buchanan et al. (1988) suggest that offering prospective organizations a report on the research findings can be effective in gaining access. In themselves, however, neither an independent overview nor a written report of findings would seem likely to be very persuasive, unless the research can be presented as addressing an issue that is already of concern to the organization or that it can be persuaded it should be concerned about. Unless those with whom access is being negotiated have already recognized their lack of a view of the whole organization, or the topic of the research, as a problem, the researcher will need to construct an argument that connects the research with the issues that the organization sees itself as facing.

There are two ways in which it may be possible to identify such issues – by preparatory research on the target organization and by careful listening during the initial meeting. Coming to the meeting well briefed on the organization's situation may enable potential benefits to be identified, but also demonstrates the researcher's interest in the organization and their competence at gathering relevant information. While such preparation may be second nature to researchers, the advice on listening may be more counter-intuitive. This is another area, however, in which, Walford (2001) suggests, researchers may learn from the selling literature. According to Kimball (1994), for example, 'you persuade the prospect by getting them to talk', while Denny (2009) suggests that the most important skill in selling is to ask questions. In a sales presentation therefore, it is the prospect rather than the salesperson who should do more of the talking. Rather than attempting to talk the organization into granting access by giving a detailed presentation that tries to cover all eventualities, it may be more effective to structure the meeting more as a conversation in which the organization's views on the research topic are explored. Listening in this way, Walford (2001: 43) argues, 'gives the salesperson "buying signals" and indicates potential hesitations and objections'. Similarly it can allow a researcher to understand the organization's 'needs and desires' and enable the research to be shaped to meet them better.

While the researcher needs to prepare carefully for the initial meeting, therefore, with plans for how they would respond to the organization's likely concerns, they also need to show flexibility in adjusting to unanticipated problems.

Walford (2001), for example, reports on an initial meeting in which the head-master being interviewed made it clear that his conception of research was very different from the 'open ethnographic approach' that Walford had intended to pursue. As a result, Walford adjusted his presentation to propose a fixed design. On another occasion Walford had asked for six weeks of unstructured access to a school and was offered four, under tightly specified conditions.

Although gaining access is often presented as a process of negotiation, there-fore, from the researcher's perspective it is unfortunately one in which they generally have a weak hand. As Pettigrew (1990: 286) states, 'social scientists have no insuperable right to be granted access to any institution or anyone in it'. Consequently, Ryan and Lewer (2012: 75) argue, 'all researchers of organi-zation and management are more often beggars rather than choosers'. They are seeking something from the organization and may not be able to offer anything very much in return that is recognized to be of value by the organiza-tion. As Irvine (2003: 119) puts it, 'They had control of their gate and were not obliged to let me in. I was eager to please, keen to convince, and willing to compromise in the bargaining stage, aware that if they shut the door in my face, the study was lost.'

Consequently, the researcher may have little they can do if the organization insists that they moderate their position. This may need to be factored into the initial request, for example by asking for more time, facilities or flexibility than is strictly needed for the study, to allow scope for concessions. Thus Walford (2001) speculates on whether, if he had requested eight weeks of access he might have been granted the six that he really wanted, rather than the four that he was offered. This is a delicate judgement, however, as inflating the initial request may simply lead to it being rejected outright.

Before entering into discussion of an access request it may be a good idea too for the researcher to give consideration to the minimum resources that would be compatible with the successful conduct of the research, so that they can decide whether proposed constraints on access are acceptable or not. In prac-tice, this decision is likely to be swayed by the availability, or otherwise, of alternative fieldwork sites. Researchers may be willing to accept less than sat-isfactory access conditions for lack of anything better and in the hope that once initial access has been agreed it may be possible to negotiate some easing of restrictions at a later date.

'Sale'

The final stage of the selling process is 'closing the deal' and making the sale. In research terms this means getting the agreement of the organization to grant research access. This may involve a formal written agreement, but more typically relies on the written, but sometimes simply verbal, consent of a suitably 'qualified' prospect (or prospects) to the original access request sent to the organization. A written letter of permission may be advantageous in providing something to present to others if the researcher's presence is ever questioned, but may not be necessary in all circumstances, especially in smaller organizations.

Although in some organizations once access has been agreed the researcher may be given pretty much carte blanche to pursue the research as they please, more typically, further negotiation is required on the specific terms of the 'bargain' being made between the researcher and the organization (Horwood and Moon, 2003). As with permission for access, this may be settled by informal verbal discussion or involve a written agreement, of various degrees of formality. The possible terms of this agreement are likely to vary with the nature of the research and the character of the organization, but may include items such as:

- who can be interviewed/observed
- the duration of the study
- the use of the findings
- deliverables
- benefits to the organization.

A particularly sensitive item, for both parties, may be confidentiality.

Confidentiality agreements

As was discussed in relation to research ethics in Chapter 4, confidentiality and anonymity are widely promoted as central to good research practice. Researchers are expected to maintain the confidentiality of the data they gather and to preserve the anonymity of those they are reporting on. This may be a particular issue in commercial organizations which may be concerned that their competitors may gain access to sensitive data. As a result they can sometimes seek to insist that researchers sign a commercial non-disclosure agreement (a multi-page legal document normally used with suppliers and business partners). These are rarely well suited to research, however, as they typically require any disclosure whatsoever of information to other parties (which would include academic colleagues) to be subject to formal written agreement from the organization. At the very least this is likely to delay the reporting of findings, and, if it involves departments outside those being studied (and especially the legal department), potentially prevent this altogether (as the onus is likely to be placed on the researcher to prove that disclosure will not cause any harm to the organization, which may be impossible in practice). While confidentiality of research findings is a sound principle, therefore, in practice, formal confidentiality agreements, especially where they have been designed for other purposes, tend to adopt a presumption against publication, which can severely constrain research.

Title of Research Project:

CONFIDENTIALITY AGREEMENT

During the course of my research, I understand that I am likely to discuss and have access to information that [name of organization] and individuals within it regard as confidential. By signing this statement, I am indicating my understanding of my responsibilities to maintain confidentiality and agree to the following:

- I agree not to divulge, publish, or otherwise make known to unauthorized persons or to the public any information obtained in the course of this research project that could identify the persons who participated in the study.

- I will make all reasonable efforts to hold in strict confidence any information that I am told in advance is confidential
    - I will not copy, reveal or disclose such information to any third party
    - I will not use any such information for my own benefit or the benefit of any organization with which I am affiliated now or in the future.

- I will gather information only to the extent and for the purposes necessary for the conduct of my research.

- I will not disclose any information obtained in the course of my research except as, with the agreement of [name of organization], may be necessary for the conduct of my research. Where such disclosure is related to non-commercial, academic publication such agreement shall not be unreasonably withheld.

- This Agreement shall not apply to any information which:
    - at the date of this Agreement are in the public domain or subsequently come into the public domain through no fault of mine;
    - were already known to me on the date of disclosure, provided that such prior knowledge can be substantiated;
    - properly and lawfully become available to me from sources independent of the supplying party;
    - are disclosed pursuant to the requirement or request of a governmental agency provided that in such event I shall inform you of the nature and extent of any disclosure so required.

- I understand that breach of confidentiality may be subject to [penalties].

- This Agreement shall come into effect from the date below and the obligation under the Agreement shall remain in effect for a period of three (3) years.

- This Agreement shall be subject to relevant national law.

Signed   Date

Figure 5.3   Sample confidentiality agreement

Access to some organizations, however, may only be granted if a confidentiality agreement is in place. In which case, research is likely to be facilitated if this can be kept brief and relatively informal and avoid the participation of third parties, such as the PR or legal departments, who are only likely to seek to impose additional restrictions on access. This is not to suggest that the researcher should seek to evade reasonable expectations of confidentiality, but rather that it is better if the agreement can be framed in a way that acknowledges the need for the researcher to share findings with, say, an academic supervisor, other members of a research team, or, potentially, examiners (who may be required to abide by the agreement as a condition of being given access). It is also important that, if at all possible, the agreement recognizes that the researcher may have a legitimate interest in reporting their findings, not least to an academic audience. To this end, it can be helpful if the researcher has a draft confidentiality agreement prepared beforehand, that specifies both the circumstances in which the researcher will be permitted to report their findings as well as the restrictions on the use of data that they will gather, as the basis for negotiation, rather than leaving it to the organization. A sample confidentiality agreement is shown in Figure 5.3.[3]

Point of entry

Gaining access to an organization can be achieved by different routes. A common distinction is made, for example, between top-down and bottom-up access. In the former, access is obtained through contact with senior members of the organizational hierarchy while in the latter, access is gained at lower levels in the hierarchy. Both have advantages and disadvantages.

Establishing contact with senior organizational members may be more difficult than with those of lower status, as they may be shielded from contact by secretaries or PAs, their diaries tend to be fully scheduled a long time ahead, and their time is seen to be very valuable (Thomas, 1993; Leblanc and Schwartz, 2007). They are likely to have the authority, however, to grant permission for access to organization members lower in the hierarchy. For precisely this reason, though, research that has been approved by senior organization members may be viewed with suspicion, if not hostility, by those lower in the hierarchy. It is a common observation of shop-floor studies, for example, that researchers are suspected of being management 'spies', sent to gather information that will be used in ways that will not be to the advantage of lower-level employees (e.g. Blau, 1964; Korczynski, 2011).

Establishing contacts with lower-level employees, in contrast, is likely to be easier, but they may not have the authority to grant access, or, even if they do, their remit may be limited and the scope of research may consequently be restricted. In particular, gaining access to higher levels of the organization may

---

[3]This agreement is a composite of various sources and is intended to illustrate the possible scope of such a document. No claims are made for its legal standing in any jurisdiction.

be difficult having made entry at lower levels. On the other hand, research may be viewed more sympathetically by lower-level employees if access is gained at their level (Johansen, 2008).

At whatever point in the organizational hierarchy entry is made, perceptions of the researcher may be influenced by others' perceptions of the individual or department granting them access. This will be discussed further in terms of the politics of research in organizations in Chapter 6, but may be significant in access planning if there is a choice of potential entry points, or if there is reason to believe that entry by a particular route may affect the attitudes of organization members towards the research, for example by making it easier or more difficult to gather data on particular groups or individuals. It may not be possible to do very much to alter such perceptions, but awareness of them may enable their possible influence to be considered.

As gatekeepers for the research, the individuals granting access may also seek to use this position to influence how it is carried out. Perhaps the most overt way in which they may seek to do this, and potentially the most ethically problematic if the gatekeeper is unaware of the unreasonableness of their request, is as a means to advance their own interests in the organization. A number of studies, for example, report attempts by managers to use the researcher to gain information on the activities and plans of their subordinates (e.g. Beynon, 1988; Walford, 2001; Ferdinand et al., 2007): 'You will be my eyes and ears in this project – you will be our man on the ground,' as one manager put it (Alcadipani and Hodgson, 2009: 135).

Another type of gatekeeper may see the granting of access more as an opportunity to pursue their own research and seek to impose their own objectives and methods on the project. Randall et al. (2007: 171) describe this as the 'reverse gatekeeper' function and advise that 'It is good policy to go along with this, because failure to do so can result in a loss of goodwill, even though this sometimes means time will be wasted.' While causing fewer ethical difficulties this may create significant practical problems for the researcher if their agenda diverges from that of the gatekeeper. Considerable diplomacy may therefore be required to avoid alienating the gatekeeper while pursuing the original research plans.

Even if they do not seek to push the research in a particular direction, the gatekeeper is likely to be seen as the 'sponsor' of the research and its successes or difficulties may reflect back on them. This can be advantageous for the research because the sponsor may be motivated to make efforts to ensure its success, but can cause tensions where research does not progress as planned or where the findings prove unfavourable to the organization. Being aware, at the outset, of the mutual commitment to the research may not ensure that it does not run into any difficulties, but should mean that both parties enter the agreement with a better understanding of what they are letting themselves in for.

Such distinctions between different types of gatekeeper should not be taken to mean that there is necessarily only one gatekeeper for any piece of research. Rather there may be multiple gatekeepers with each of whom access may need to be negotiated at different stages of the research. Burgess (1991), for example, identifies multiple gatekeepers in his study of a school, including the head-teacher, the chair of the school governors, heads of department, teachers and pupils, each controlling access to different areas of school activity.

Gaining access to conduct research in an organization can therefore be a long-winded and sometimes fraught process, involving considerable skills of persuasion and negotiation. While it may not be possible to provide guidance that will ensure a successful outcome to an access request, it is nevertheless possible to make some general observations on the characteristics associated with successful access negotiations.

Preparation

Although there are quite a number of accounts of research access being granted with almost no effort on the researcher's part, careful preparation before making the access request is likely to be needed in many cases. Preparation may relate to a number of areas, such as:

- identifying target organizations and contacts within them
- identifying benefits of research for the organization
- customising the access request letter
- deciding on the minimum conditions necessary for conduct of the research
- consideration of contingency plans if access is restricted or refused.

Credibility

Access would seem likely to be facilitated by evidence of the researcher's credibility as an investigator of the phenomenon under study. This may be acquired from a track record in the relevant research field – Walford (2001) recommends taking along an example of the results of previous research to the initial meeting as a way of demonstrating the researcher's experience in the field and the type of outputs that may be expected. Where the researcher cannot provide this from their own work a somewhat less satisfactory alternative would be the work of someone connected with the researcher, a student's supervisor for example, or a well-recognized article in the field that serves as a model for the study. This advice runs contrary, however, to that in the selling literature which emphasizes that it is better to try to resolve reservations face-to-face, rather than leave the prospect with resources that can provide them with potential reasons for refusal. While it may be beneficial, therefore, to have such materials as back up, if evidence of a track record becomes a sticking point in negotiations it may be better to supply this on request rather than proffering it in advance.

Credibility may also be acquired directly by evidence of non-research experience in the field, having worked in a similar organization for example, or indirectly by the 'brand' of the researcher's institution (hence the use of headed paper in the access letter), or the standing of the individual making a referral (Ortner, 2010). Just as it is important to demonstrate credibility it is just as important not to damage it in interactions with the organization, especially with people in senior positions. Most of this will be obvious things such as the attention paid to the grammar, spelling and layout of the access letter, punctuality in arriving for meetings, appearance (a rule of thumb is to try to be at least as smart as organization members), and efforts to appear well informed about the organization and its activities (Ryan and Lewer, 2012).

Some organizations, particularly those that perceive themselves as subject to critical scrutiny, may also seek to establish that the researcher is sympathetic, or at least not evidently hostile, to their principles. Barker (1984: 15), for example, gained access to the Unification Church because they perceived that 'she had been prepared to listen to their side of the argument and they could not believe that anyone who did that could write anything worse than what was already being published by those who had not come to find out for themselves'. Even in a less contentious area, Walford (2001) reports that when seeking access to undertake a study of a public school, the headmaster's questioning of him was clearly intended to establish whether he was 'one of us' and sought the name of a referee who could provide such assurances.

Persistence

Without an inside track to the organization, gaining research access can be hard work. Even under favourable conditions a success rate of one in four is good going. As a result a researcher will typically need to pursue many more leads than they need and to follow up on organizations that do not respond (positively or negatively), in line with the timescale indicated in the access request. If the follow-up indicates that the organization is hesitant about granting access, Leidner (1993: 235) proposes the advice (attributed to Howard Becker): 'act as though all you can hear is "yes" or "maybe"'. While this would seem consistent with the 'access as selling' argument, it may not come naturally to researchers, who, as Walford (2001) observes, tend to be apologetic about their research and balk at the idea of hard-selling themselves or their work. While being careful not to appear too pushy, however, it can be surprising how dogged a researcher can be in pursuit of access to an organization that is important to their study.

If the initial follow-up suggests that the request is under consideration then a date should be sought by which the decision is expected and the researcher may offer to call again after that date to check on the outcome. In some cases consideration of the request may be repeatedly deferred and the researcher therefore needs to strike a balance between showing a keen interest in gaining access to the organization and pestering the contact. After maybe four or five deferrals with no indication of a decision in sight, it may be diplomatic to consider the request refused in practice, but leave the organization with an invitation to initiate contact if the request is subsequently approved.

While it can be highly frustrating if a request is refused without what would appear to be proper consideration, or if an organization appears to be stringing the researcher along without making a decision, the researcher needs to remain courteous and to accept rejection gracefully. This may be important for future research requests with the same organization and to enable insights to be gained, if possible, on the reasons for refusal so that access requests in other organizations can be modified where necessary.

The slow pace of access approval in many cases (as shown in Table 5.3) means that the researcher may find themselves waiting for extended periods to hear back from organizations (Smith, 2001). Van Maanen (2011) talks of the 'unbearable slowness of ethnography', but similar delays are not uncommon in less engaged forms of research such as interview-based studies and surveys. It is consequently a good idea to initiate access requests as early as possible so that any delay to the research timetable is minimized, and to consider how the waiting time can be productively used. In the way of these things, research access is also often a process of famine and feast. There may be a long period without success and then the first organization to approve access is quickly followed by several others. For the researcher this can create a number of dilemmas. If the number of sites agreeing to access exceeds that envisaged in the research design, for example, then the researcher will need to decide which to pursue.

Before a decision is made not to pursue research in any organization, however, the terms of the initial access request should be fulfilled and at least one preliminary meeting be held with each organization that responds positively to the access request. This is necessary to demonstrate that the claims made in the request regarding the importance of the organization's participation were authentic, but also to provide insurance if access subsequently does not work out with a preferred organization. As will be discussed in the next chapter, access may not be a once and for all decision and initially favourable sites can prove problematic later on. It is not a good idea, therefore, to bet the whole research on the first positive response or to alienate other organizations from whom access has been sought.

With more organizations offering access than expected, or needed, it may be tempting to expand the scope of the study. Assuming that the original design was well thought out, however, the costs and benefits of a larger study need to be given careful consideration. Assuming that research resources are fixed, involving more organizations will mean less depth at each site, for example. Similarly, where the design adopts a sampling logic it may be the case that the organizations responding positively are misaligned with the original criteria – there are too many organizations of one type and not enough of another. It may therefore be necessary to consider whether, if after suitable efforts to remedy the imbalance, the study should proceed with a convenience sample.

Flexibility

As the discussion of giving consideration to adjusting a research design in the light of access opportunities indicates, it may be necessary for the researcher to be flexible in their approach to access. This is not to propose that research plans should be abandoned at the first sign of difficulty, but that research, as Bismarck observed of politics, is an 'art of the possible' (Buchanan et al., 1988). Considered revision of research designs in the face of access difficulties that have survived the best efforts to overcome them would seem preferable to not being able to conduct the research at all. Of course there is no objective measure of intractability or what constitutes best efforts and judgements are likely to be influenced by the time, and perhaps funding, available to pursue matters further. With due acknowledgement of and reflection upon the consequences of such compromises, however, research need not be completely blocked by such difficulties.

Luck

Notwithstanding researchers' attempts to portray their choice of research sites and modes of access as the product of careful and systematic procedures, as Bryman (1988) observes, it would seem that there can often be a significant element of luck, or if you prefer it serendipity, in gaining access to organizations. Thus, Van Maanen and Kolb (1985: 11) argue, 'Most field-workers would probably agree that gaining access to most organizational settings is not a matter to be taken lightly but one that involves some combination of, strategic planning, hard work, and dumb luck.' Buchanan et al.'s chat with a friend over a pub lunch (Buchanan et al., 1988), a colleague's meeting on a tennis court with an executive from the parent company of the target organization (Jackall, 1988) cannot be planned for, but may provide the initial contact from which research access is gained. This does not mean that the researcher should abandon careful preparation, systematic search and attention to presenting a credible appearance, but rather that where the research design allows such flexibility, being alert to opportunities and pursuing them if they arise can be a key factor in achieving effective access.

Coda: covert research

One solution to the problem of gaining access to organizations that has a long, if not always honourable, tradition is that of covert research – gaining access to organizations without informing them that research is being carried out. The ethics of such studies have been hotly debated (Davis, 1961; Douglas, 1976; Erikson, 1967; Lofland, 1961; Homan and Bulmer, 1982) and a number of codes of research ethics explicitly proscribe such an approach (hence their relegation to a coda to this chapter).

Proponents of covert research, however, argue that it is necessary to study certain sorts of organization and certain sorts of organizational practices, especially those that may be socially disapproved (Maravic, 2012) and this is even acknowledged in some ethical codes. The British Sociological Association, for example, states that

> the use of covert methods may be justified in certain circumstances. For example, difficulties arise when research participants change their behaviour because they know they are being studied. Researchers may also face problems when access to spheres of social life is closed to social scientists by powerful or secretive interests. (British Sociological Association, 2002)

In an organizational context this might include the study of secretive organizations such as religious cults (Wallis, 1977), of questionable organizational practices, for example in the police (Holdaway, 1982), or of phenomena likely to be altered by participants' awareness of being observed, such as prescribing or medicines administration errors by hospital clinicians (Taxis and Barber, 2003).

It is also argued by Roth (1962: 283) that secrecy is always present in fieldwork:

> So long as there exists a separation of role between the researchers and those researched upon, the gathering of information will inevitably have some hidden aspects even if one is an openly declared observer ... Therefore, even in those cases where the researcher has made a deliberate effort to explain to his [sic] subjects just what he is going to do, he will frequently find them acting surprised when he actually goes ahead and does it.

Opponents of covert research, on the other hand, see it as 'violating the principle of informed consent, invading subjects' privacy, using deception, and betraying trust, possibly harming the interests of the group studied' (Bulmer, 1982: 252). Furthermore, critics suggest it is not just the research subjects who are affected by covert observation, 'it harms investigators, whose relations with those studied, and indeed their very view of reality, are distorted by their own bad faith' (Cassell, 1980: 35).

Even if not directly proscribed, the controversy surrounding covert research would seem grounds for caution in considering its adoption. While proponents such as Bone (2006), Calvey (2008) and Maravic (2012) argue that restricting covert research risks allowing significant types of organizations to place themselves beyond scrutiny and is likely to preclude the study of certain topics, such views are in the minority. In what would appear to be a climate of increasing regulation, therefore, such research would seem likely, rightly or wrongly, to become ever more marginalized.

EXERCISES

1 For an organization with which you are familiar:

- Who are the first line gatekeepers?

  o In what ways do they control access to the organization?
  o What might make them more (or less) likely to grant access?

- Who has the authority to grant access to the organization?

  o What arguments are likely to persuade them to grant access?

2 You are:

(a) the head of the design team for an innovative product that your company hopes will enable it to enter a highly profitable new market
(b) a sales manager in charge of a number of sales teams with significantly different performance levels
(c) the R&D Director of a small hi-tech start-up that was spun out from your Ph.D. research project

- For each role, prepare a balance sheet of the advantages and disadvantages of allowing a researcher to study your unit/organization.
- What conditions might you wish to place on access?

3 Rate the statement on a scale from strongly disagree to strongly agree.

	Strongly disagree	Slightly disagree	Slightly agree	Strongly agree
Commercial selling is an appropriate model for gaining research access in organizations.				

What arguments would you make to justify your position?

4 Which of the following would you consider to be a reasonable 'price of entry' to enable you to gain research access?

- Analysing data not related to your research
- Carrying out an 'academic' survey that the company hopes will inform its marketing activities
- Gathering data from a competitor organization
- Providing training to staff in the use of a software package with which you are familiar
- Providing the company management with recommendations for action on the topic you are studying

5 Rate each of these statements on a scale from strongly disagree to strongly agree.

	Strongly disagree	Slightly disagree	Slightly agree	Strongly agree
Covert research is unethical and should not be permitted under any circumstances.				
Some legitimate types of organizational research involve deception, so covert research should therefore be permitted (with suitable safeguards).				
Some organizations would never willingly permit research access, so if these organizations are to be studied then covert research is necessary.				
All research involves deception, so there cannot be an objection to covert research in principle (it is just a matter of degree).				

What arguments would you make to justify your position?

Further reading

Sampling

Daniel, J. (2012) *Sampling Essentials: Practical Guidelines for Making Sampling Choices*. London: SAGE.

References

Abolafia, M.Y. (1998) 'Markets as cultures: an ethnographic approach', in M. Callon (ed.), *The Laws of the Markets*. London: Wiley-Blackwell, pp.69–85.

Agar, M.H. (1980) *The Professional Stranger: An Informal Introduction to Ethnography*. London: Academic Press.

Alcadipani, R. and Hodgson, D. (2009) 'By any means necessary? Ethnographic access, ethics and the critical researcher', *TAMARA: Journal of Critical Postmodern Organization Science*, 7 (3/4): 127–46.

Ayella, M. (1990) '"They must be crazy", some of the difficulties in researching cults', *The American Behavioral Scientist*, 33 (5): 562.

Barker, E. (1984) *The Making of a Moonie: Choice or Brainwashing?* Oxford: Basil Blackwell.

Becker, H.S., Geer, B., Hughes, E.C. and Strauss, A.L. (1961) *Boys in White: Student Culture in Medical School*. Chicago, IL: Chicago University Press.

Beynon, H. (1988) 'Regulating research: politics and decision making in industrial organizations', in A. Bryman (ed.), *Doing Research in Organizations*. London: Routledge, pp. 21–33.

Blau, P.M. (1964) 'The research process in the study of the dynamics of bureaucracy', in P.E. Hammond (ed.), *Sociologists at Work*. New York: Basic Books, pp. 16–49.

Bloom, N. and Van Reenen, J. (2010) 'Why do management practices differ across firms and countries?', *The Journal of Economic Perspectives*, 24 (1): 203–24.

Bone, J. (2006) '"The longest day": "flexible"contracts, performance-related pay and risk shifting in the UK direct selling sector', *Work, Employment and Society*, 20 (1): 109–27.

British Sociological Association (2002) *Statement of Ethical Practice for the British Sociological Association*. http://www.britsoc.co.uk/about/equality/statement-of-ethical-practice.aspx

Bryman, A. (1988) 'Introduction', in A. Bryman (ed.), *Doing Research in Organizations*. London: Routledge, pp. 1–20.

Buchanan, D., Boddy, D. and McCalman, J. (1988) 'Getting in, getting on, getting out and getting back', in A. Bryman (ed.), *Doing Research in Organizations*. London: Routledge, pp. 53–67.

Bulmer, M. (1982) 'When is disguise justified? Alternatives to covert participant observation', *Qualitative Sociology*, 5 (4): 251–64.

Burgess, R.G. (1991) 'Sponsors, gatekeepers, members, and friends: access in educational settings', in W.B. Shaffir and R.A. Steffins (eds), *Experiencing Fieldwork: An Inside View of Qualitative Research*. London: SAGE, pp. 43–52.

Calvey, D. (2008) 'The art and politics of covert research: doing "situated ethics" in the field', *Sociology*, 42 (5): 905–18.

Cassell, J. (1980) 'Ethical principles for conducting fieldwork', *American Anthropologist*, 82 (1): 28–41.

Crabtree, A., Rouncefield, M. and Tolmie, P. (2012) *Doing Design Ethnography*. London: Springer-Verlag.

Dalton, M. (1959) *Men Who Manage: Fusions of Feeling and Theory in Administration*. New York: Wiley.

Davis, F. (1961) 'Comment on "Initial interaction of newcomers in Alcoholics Anonymous"', *Social Problems*, 8 (4): 364–5.

Davis, F. (1973) 'The Martian and the convert', *Journal of Contemporary Ethnography*, 2 (3): 333–43.

Delamont, S. (2004) 'Ethnography and participant observation', in C. Seale, G. Gobo, J.F. Gubrium and D. Silverman (eds), *Qualitative Research Practice*. London: SAGE, pp. 217–29.

Denny, R. (2009) *Selling to Win*, 3rd edn. London: Kogan Page.

de Rond, M. (2009) *The Last Amateurs: To Hell and Back with the Cambridge Boat Race Crew*. Thriplow: Icon Books.

de Rond, M. (2012) 'Soldier, surgeon, photographer, fly: fieldwork beyond the comfort zone', *Strategic Organization*, 10 (3): 256–62.

Douglas, J.D. (1976) *Investigative Social Research*. Beverly Hills, CA: SAGE.

Erikson, K.T. (1967) 'A comment on disguised observation in sociology', *Social Problems*, 14 (4): 366–73.

Evans-Pritchard, E.E. and Gillies, E. (1976) *Witchcraft, Oracles and Magic Among the Azande*, abridged edn. Oxford: Oxford University Press.

Ferdinand, J., Pearson, G., Rowe, M. and Worthington, F. (2007) 'A different kind of ethics', *Ethnography*, 8 (4): 519–43.

Glaser, B.G. and Strauss, A.L. (1967) *The Discovery of Grounded Theory: Strategies for Qualitative Research*. Hawthorne, NY: Aldine de Gruyter.

Goffman, E. (1989) 'On fieldwork', *Journal of Contemporary Ethnography*, 18 (2): 123–32.

Goldman, E.F. and Swayze, S. (2012) 'In-depth interviewing with healthcare corporate elites: strategies for entry and engagement', *International Journal of Qualitative Methods*, 11 (3): 230–43.

Goodwin, D. (2009) *Acting in Anaesthesia: Ethnographic Encounters with Patients, Practitioners and Medical Technologies*. Cambridge: Cambridge University Press.

Gouldner, A.W. (1955) *Patterns of Industrial Bureaucracy*. London: Routledge and Kegan Paul.

Gray, P.S. (1980) 'Exchange and access in field work', *Journal of Contemporary Ethnography*, 9 (3): 309–31.

Hales, J. and Webster, S. (2008) *Methodological Review of Research with Large Businesses Paper 2: Making Contact and Response Issues*. London: Her Majesty's Revenue and Customs.

Hammersley, M. and Atkinson, P. (2007) *Ethnography: Principles in Practice*. London: Routledge.

Haynes, K. (2012) 'Reflexivity in qualitative research', in G. Symon and C. Cassell (eds), *Qualitative Organizational Research: Core Methods and Current Challenges*. London: SAGE, pp. 72–89.

Ho, K.Z. (2009) *Liquidated: An Ethnography of Wall Street*. London: Duke University Press Books.

Holdaway, S. (1982) '"An inside job": a case study of covert research on the police', in M. Bulmer (ed.), *Social Research Ethics. An Examination of the Merits of Covert Participant Observation*. London: Macmillan, pp. 59–79.

Holliday, R. (1995) *Investigating Small Firms: Nice Work?* London: Thomson Learning.

Homan, R. and Bulmer, M. (1982) 'On the merits of covert methods: a dialogue', in M. Bulmer (ed.), *Social Research Ethics: An Examination of the Merits of Covert Participant Observation*. London: Macmillan, pp. 105–21.

Horwood, J. and Moon, G. (2003) 'Accessing the research setting: the politics of research and the limits to enquiry', *Area*, 35 (1): 106–9.

Irvine, H. (2003) 'Trust me! A personal account of confidentiality issues in an organisational research project', *Accounting Forum*, 27 (1): 111–31.

Jackall, R. (1988) *Moral Mazes: The World of Corporate Managers*. New York: Oxford University Press.

Johansen, T.R. (2008) '"Blaming oneself": examining the dual accountability role of employees', *Critical Perspectives on Accounting*, 19 (4): 544–71.

Johnston, R. (2005) *Analytic Culture in the U.S. Intelligence Community: An Ethnographic Study*. Washington, DC: Central Intelligence Agency.

Kimball, B. (1994) *AMA Handbook for Successful Selling*. Chicago, IL: American Marketing Association.

King, G., Keohane, R.O. and Verba, S. (1994) *Designing Social Inquiry: Scientific Inference in Qualitative Research*. Princeton, NJ: Princeton University Press.

Kunda, G. (1992) *Engineering Culture: Control and Commitment in a High-tech Corporation*. Philadelphia: Temple University Press.

Korczynski, M. (2011) 'The dialectical sense of humour: routine joking in a Taylorized factory', *Organization Studies*, 32 (10): 1421–39.

Leblanc, R. and Schwartz, M.S. (2007) 'The black box of board process: gaining access to a difficult subject', *Corporate Governance: An International Review*, 15 (5): 843–51.

Leidner, R. (1993) *Fast Food, Fast Talk: Service Work and the Routinization of Everyday Life*. London: University of California Press.

Lofland, J. (1961) 'Reply to Davis', *Social Problems*, 8 (4): 365–7.

Lofland, J. and Lofland, L. (1995) *Analyzing Social Settings: A Guide to Qualitative Observation and Analysis*, 3rd edn. London: Wadsworth.

Maravic, P. von (2012) 'Limits of knowing or the consequences of difficult-access problems for multi-method research and public policy', *Policy Sciences*, 45 (2): 153–68.

Mollona, M. (2009) *Made in Sheffield: An Ethnography of Industrial Work and Politics*. Oxford: Berghahn Books.

Morrill, C. (1995) *The Executive Way*. Chicago, IL: University of Chicago Press.

Morrill, C., Buller, D.B., Buller, M.K. and Larkey, L.L. (1999) 'Toward an organizational perspective on identifying and managing formal gatekeepers', *Qualitative Sociology*, 22 (1): 51–72.

Okumus, F., Altinay, L. and Roper, A. (2007) 'Gaining access for research: reflections from experience', *Annals of Tourism Research*, 34 (1): 7–26.

Orr, J.E. (1996) *Talking about Machines: An Ethnography of a Modern Job*. London: Cornell University Press.

Ortner, S.B. (2010) 'Access: reflections on studying up in Hollywood', *Ethnography*, 11 (2): 211–33.

Pettigrew, A.M. (1990) 'Longitudinal field research on change: theory and practice', *Organization Science*, 1 (3): 267–92.

Pincus, A. (2007) 'The perfect (elevator) pitch', *BusinessWeek: Managing*. Available at: http://www.businessweek.com/careers/content/jun2007/ca20070618_134959.htm

Pollock, K. (2012) 'Procedure versus process: ethical paradigms and the conduct of qualitative research', *BMC Medical Ethics*, 13(1): 25–37.

Ram, M. (1994) *Managing to Survive: Working Lives in Small Firms*. Oxford: Blackwell.

Randall, D., Harper, R. and Rouncefield, M. (2007) *Fieldwork for Design: Theory and Practice*. London: Springer.

Riemer, J.W. (1977) 'Varieties of opportunistic research', *Journal of Contemporary Ethnography*, 5 (4): 467–77.

Roesch-Marsh, A., Gadda, A. and Smith, D. (2012) '"It's a tricky business!": the impact of identity work in negotiating research access', *Qualitative Social Work*, 11 (3): 249–65.

Roth, J.A. (1962) 'Comments on "Secret observation"', *Social Problems*, 9 (3): 283–4.

Ryan, S. and Lewer, J. (2012) 'Getting in and finding out: accessing and interviewing elites in business and work contexts', in L.L.M. Aguiar and C.J. Schneider (eds), *Researching Amongst Elites: Challenges and Opportunities in Studying Up*. Farnham: Ashgate, pp. 71–88.

Sekaran, U. and Bougie, R. (2010) *Research Methods for Business: A Skill-Building Approach*, 5th edn. Hoboken, NJ: Wiley.

Sharrock, W.W. and Lynch, M. (2011) *Ethnomethodology*. Los Angeles, CA: SAGE.

Shenton, A.K. and Hayter, S. (2004) 'Strategies for gaining access to organisations and informants in qualitative studies', *Education for Information*, 22(3–4): 223–231.

Smith, V. (2001) 'Ethnographies of work and the work of ethnographers', in P. Atkinson, A. Coffey, S. Delamont, J. Lofland and L. Lofland (eds), *Handbook of Ethnography*. London: SAGE, pp. 220–33.

Smith, W.R. (2010) 'Field lessons: the whys and hows of interview-based fieldwork', *French Politics*, 8 (1): 101–8.

Taxis, K. and Barber, N. (2003) 'Ethnographic study of incidence and severity of intravenous drug errors', *British Medical Journal*, 326 (7391): 684–7.

Taylor, S.J. (1991) 'Leaving the field: research, relationships, and responsibilities', in W.B. Shaffir and R.A. Stebbins (eds), *Experiencing Fieldwork: An Inside View of Qualitative Research*. London: SAGE, pp. 238–47.

Taylor, S.J. and Bogdan, R. (1988) *Introduction to Qualitative Research Methods: A Guidebook and Resource*, 3rd edn. Chichester: Wiley.

Tharenou, P., Donohue, R. and Cooper, B. (2007) *Management Research Methods*. Port Melbourne, Victoria: Cambridge University Press.

't Hart, P. (2007) 'Spies at the crossroads: observing change in the Dutch Intelligence Service', in R.A.W. Rhodes, P. 't Hart and M. Noordegraaf (eds), *Observing Government Elites: Up Close and Personal*. Basingstoke: Palgrave, pp. 51–77.

Thomas, R.J. (1993) 'Interviewing important people in big companies', *Journal of Contemporary Ethnography*, 22 (1): 80–96.

Thornely, N. and Lees, D. (1994) *The Perfect Sale: All You Need to Get It Right First Time*. London: Arrow Books Ltd.

Van Maanen, J. (2011) 'Ethnography as work: some rules of engagement', *Journal of Management Studies*, 48 (1): 218–34.

Van Maanen, J. and Kolb, D. (1985) 'The professional apprentice: observations on fieldwork role in two organizational settings', *Research in the Sociology of Organizations*, 4: 1–33.

Walford, G. (2001) *Doing Qualitative Educational Research: A Personal Guide to the Research Process*. London: Continuum International Publishing Group.

Wallis, R. (1977) 'The moral career of a research project', in C. Bell and H. Newby (eds), *Doing Sociological Research*. London: Allen and Unwin, pp. 149–67.

Winkler, J. (1987) 'The fly on the wall of the inner sanctum: observing company directors at work', in G. Moyser and M. Wagstaffe (eds), *Research Methods for Elite Studies*. London: Allen and Unwin, pp. 129–46.

Ybema, S. and Kamsteeg, F. (2009) 'Making the familiar strange: a case for disengaged organizational ethnography', in S. Ybema, D. Yanow, H. Wels and F. Kamsteeg (eds), *Organizational Ethnography: Studying the Complexity of Everyday Life*. London: SAGE, pp. 101–19.

Yin, R.K. (1993) *Applications of Case Study Research*. London: SAGE.

Yin, R.K. (2003) *Case Study Research: Design and Methods*, 3rd edn. Thousand Oaks, CA: SAGE.

Zaloom, C. (2006) *Out of the Pits: Traders and Technology from Chicago to London*. London: University of Chicago Press.

6

Getting on: In the Organization

Chapter objectives

- to identify the processes that may be involved in establishing access in an organization
- to consider ethical issues that may arise in establishing access
- to identify issues in gathering data in the field
- to consider threats to the validity and reliability of fieldwork data
- to consider how fieldwork may be affected by organizational politics
- to consider emotional and ethical issues in the conduct of fieldwork

With access permission granted, and the research approved by all the necessary individuals and groups in the organization, the researcher might expect that it will finally be possible to actually get started with the research. In a survey study this may indeed be the case, as, with access to respondents granted, it should then be possible to administer the questionnaire without further constraints. It may be advantageous, though, if respondents are encouraged to participate by somebody (probably in a position of relative authority) within the organization, and it may take some time to find such a sponsor and to gain their endorsement of the research. Some of the aspects of relationship-building discussed below may therefore be necessary, even if the research does not involve direct access to the research site. Similarly, studies involving analysis of pre-existing documents and/or data within an organization, even if they do not require much interaction with organization members, may nevertheless encounter issues such as trust (the granting of access may not be sufficient to persuade individuals to share data), organizational politics (the willingness of individuals to share data may be influenced by who has granted access) and ethics (release of data may harm the interests of certain groups), as discussed below.

Approval of a study involving field experiments, in contrast, may be expected to be the prelude to a considerable amount of work in setting up the conditions for the conduct of the experiments and in carrying them out. This is hardly likely to be possible without authorization from senior organizational levels or extensive cooperation from organization members. Building and sustaining an effective relationship at both levels of the organization is therefore likely to be essential to the setting up and conduct of the experiments. Furthermore, while any individual experiment may involve only relatively brief and limited interaction with research participants, it may be necessary to build trust and rapport with them to ensure their effective engagement.

For research involving more extended interaction with an organization, such as multiple interviews or participant or non-participant observation, however, gaining access can feel like climbing a mountain – no sooner have you reached what you think is the summit, than you discover that there are further peaks still ahead. As Roesch-Marsh et al. (2012: 259) report:

> You have your research access approval signed and you think YES I am in! Then you start to realize that that is in fact just the beginning, now the real process of making contact with respondents begins and that requires a whole new series of negotiations.

Being granted access, which as Reeves (2010) argues is not necessarily the same as gaining entry, to an organization is rarely a one-off event, therefore, but an ongoing process that may need to be renegotiated at every stage of the research and with each new participant. As Bosk (1996: 130) puts it: 'gaining my initial entree was a multi-staged diplomatic problem. Each interaction was a test and access was the result of continual testing and retesting.' Three main features of this process may be identified that apply in all forms of extended fieldwork: fitting in; building trust; and building rapport. In studies involving extended observation in the research site there is likely to be a further need for the researcher to find a role in the setting that will provide a reason for their presence and enable them to gather data.

Fitting in

Although there is a tradition in organizational research of 'insider studies' (Brannick and Coghlan, 2007; Costley et al., 2010; Tietze, 2012), whether visiting an organization to conduct interviews, or commencing a more extensive observational study, the researcher more typically enters the organization as an outsider. This status may often be symbolized by a requirement to enter the organization site only by the main entrance, to sign, or be signed, in, and to wear a badge at all times. The researcher's movement around the organization is also likely to be restricted.

For an interview study this may not be a problem, as it is already an artificial situation (being asked questions by a relative stranger is not usually part of most people's work activities) and access is normally only required to the interviewee's verbal responses, the success in eliciting which is likely to depend on the researcher's interviewing skills as much if not more than the interviewee's familiarity with the setting in which the interview takes place. Observational studies that seek to get 'behind the scenes' of the organization, however, may be difficult if the researcher is always identifiable as an outsider and does not have reasonable freedom of movement. 't Hart (2007), studying the perhaps exceptional setting of the Dutch Secret Service agency, for example, was hampered by not receiving his own security pass until he was about a third of the way into his six-month study. This is not to suggest that researchers should not be expected to make organization members aware of what they are doing or that they should be given unrestricted access to any part of the organization they wish to study, but that observational research is likely to be difficult unless the researcher can shed their outsider status to some degree.

While this may partly be dependent on actions taken by the organization, such as issuing of security passes, or notifying those being observed of the researcher's bona fides, the researcher themselves may also need to take efforts to fit in. The motivations for such efforts, Gans (1968: 306) argues, may be personal as much, if not more, than they are functional (in order to facilitate access). 'Aside from not wanting to alienate the people one is studying, the participant observer also wants to be liked and, in his own marginal way, to feel part of the group.'

There are many aspects to 'fitting in' to an organizational setting. Among the more important of these may be: dress, seeking to follow the norms adopted by organizational members; of language, learning the jargon and acronyms relevant to the research so as to be able to follow what is said without having to ask for clarification; or routine, being seen to be present at the organization site for similar periods of the day as organizational members, and acting in conformity with local behavioural norms.

In terms of dress, both Ryan and Lewer (2012) and Froschauer and Wong (2012) note the importance attached to the wearing of business attire in the conduct of even interview-based organizational research, especially when it involves elite groups. In Ryan's case this was brought home by being reprimanded by a senior manager for not wearing a tie (having misinterpreted the dress code from an earlier visit on a 'casual Friday').

Dress may also be important in enabling unobtrusive observation. Atkinson (1997), for example, discusses how the wearing of a white coat enabled him to blend in with the medical students he was studying, while Van Maanen (1991: 38) reports that for his fieldwork with the police, he 'dressed for the street as I thought plainclothes officers might – heavy and hard-toed shoes, slit or clip-on ties, and loose-fitting jackets that would not make conspicuous the bulge of my revolver'.

Conversely, Marques (2011) describes how, having gained top-down access to a manufacturing plant, she was expected to wear a protective jacket featuring the company's logo when on the shop floor. As she discovered, this 'boss little coat' (as the workers called it) prevented her from being accepted by the shop floor staff. Fitting in, however, need not always mean dressing exactly the same as those being studied. For example Oleson and Whittaker (1967: 277) did not wear a nurses uniform in their study, but 'adopted rather an informal style of student dress ... [that] symbolized an easy, and we hope friendly, approach and relationship with the students'.

Learning the language in specialist settings can be a serious challenge for researchers. Rhodes (2007), for example, describes his request for a list of acronyms used in the private office of a British government minister being answered with a document seven pages long! Zabusky (1995: 44) comments on her difficulties with technical discussions at the European Space Agency, although she notes that many of the scientists, because of their extreme specialization, were equally in the dark when meetings addressed 'the intricacies of others' instruments, software or even research ideas'. Even where the language appears familiar, there may be local meanings. Taylor and Bogdan (1998: 64), therefore, advise that 'Researchers must start with the premise that words and symbols used in their world have different meanings in the world of their subjects.'

Being seen to conform to temporal norms would seem to be particularly important in being accepted in an organizational setting. As Marques (2011: 410) observes:

> keeping an engineer-style daytime working schedule in a 24/7 operating plant, I would stay near machine operators without becoming relationally close to them. Only in a second fieldwork period, after establishing an out-of-factory acquaintance with a shop floor team head and then adjusting my schedule to shift work (always following the same team) ... could I really enter the 'field', become established – instituted – by the operators as an acceptable presence, first, and then as a credible interlocutor.

Thus Perlow (1997) reports her work day studying software engineers in a product development team at a Fortune 500 company as starting between 7 and 9 a.m. and continuing until at least 6 p.m. and often until 8 or 9 p.m. While she rarely conducted research after 4 or 5 p.m., the extra hours were an opportunity for informal interaction and, as she notes, earned her the respect of organization members as someone who also worked hard. Similarly, Randall et al. (2007) observe that

> the simple fact of persistence, spending months observing highly technical and tedious work (from an outsider's point of view), was probably key to the success

of the A[ir]T[raffic]C[ontrol] study in respect of the fact that the ethnographers' willingness to participate in unsocial hours, such as the night shift on Saturday (and stay the full length of the shift) was critical in getting a certain level of respect. In this domain, which had something of an 'us and them' culture, it turned out to be important that the ethnographers could demonstrate that they 'really wanted to know' and they did so by their faithfulness to shift patterns.

Punch (1979: 9), too, comments that 'my willingness to adopt precisely the same work hours as the policemen paid dividends in terms of acceptance'.

Conversely, deviation from temporal norms may threaten assimilation. While undertaking his study of Bishop McGregor Comprehensive School, for example, Burgess (1985) at first wandered around the site when he was not teaching. One day, however, he saw a pupil wandering around the school grounds in the middle of a lesson. When challenged, the pupil responded by questioning what Burgess was doing out of class and observed that he didn't seem to have much teaching to do. Realizing that he was under surveillance, Burgess decided to spend most of his non-teaching time in the staff room from then on to avoid drawing attention to his anomalous position in the school.

In some settings, such as in studies of young children in schools it may be very hard for a researcher to blend in (Thorne, 1993). Epstein (1998) for example, discusses how she sought to adopt a 'least adult role' to observe Year 5 primary school children, where she was clearly too big (and old, as the children pointed out) to be an 'ordinary member of the setting', but wanted to avoid being identified as a teacher or school authority figure.

Even where the researcher is not so obviously dissimilar from those they are observing, blending in may be affected by age, gender and racial differences. In their study of nurse training, for example, Oleson and Whittaker (1967) note the effect of the age gap between researchers and student nurses on the ease of interaction between them. Geer (1964: 328) comments on a similar awareness of age difference in fieldwork with freshmen medical students, commenting that:

> Throughout the time that the undergraduate study was being planned, I was bored by the thought of studying undergraduates. They looked painfully young to me. I considered their concerns childish and unformed. I could not imagine becoming interested in their daily affairs.

On commencing fieldwork, however, she found that empathy developed rapidly, although her references to them as 'kids' suggests that an awareness of age difference remained.

There is an extensive literature on gender in fieldwork (Easterday et al., 1977; Gurney, 1985; Warren, 2001) that discusses such issues as its influence on access, on the researcher's role, and problems of harassment. Female researchers, it is suggested for example, may experience difficulties: in gaining access to predominantly male organizational settings; of being marginalized or not being taken seriously if they do gain access; or of being treated as a mascot, a gofer (expected to run menial errands) or a quasi daughter to be paternalistically protected. As Welch et al. (2002: 622), observe, however, 'the gender gap is a double-edged sword: it may encourage elite interviewees to patronise the female researcher, but it may also make them more willing to devote time to an interview'. Other authors take this further, arguing that 'the female researcher is an active participant in how she is perceived and received by informants, capable of negotiating socially constructed scripts that dominate the field setting to her analytic advantage' (Mazzei and O'Brien, 2009: 358). Purdy, for example, discusses her strategic deployment of a number of the problematic gender roles in order to facilitate fieldwork in the world of elite male rowing (Purdy and Jones, 2013).

In some contexts sexuality may be another dimension of differentiation or similarity. For example Bruni (2006) conducted ethnographic research in the editorial offices of a gay newspaper, while Parker (2001) studied a genito-urinary medicine (sexually transmitted diseases or 'clap') clinic with a specialist HIV unit. Issues of race in ethnographic fieldwork have received considerable attention, in particular regarding the historical tradition of European and North American anthropologists studying social groups in Africa, South America and Oceania, raising the 'basic question of whether or not Euro-Americans can penetrate the intersubjectivities of people of color, and, if so, what strategies they should follow to minimize the inevitable biases flowing from having been raised in a different, dominant racial or ethnic population' (Stanfield, 1993: 9). The topic would appear to have received limited attention in the literature on research in organizations, however, only being mentioned in passing by authors such as Ram (1994) and Altinay and Wang (2009), commenting on the advantages conferred by their racial identity in securing access to ethnic minority firms. The limited evidence available would also seem to be inconclusive on whether ethnic similarity is helpful or unhelpful in building rapport (Froschauer and Wong, 2012).

Fitting in is not just about appearances, however, but may also be about identity. Johnson (1975) discusses his efforts at what he describes as 'identity spoilage' to overcome organization members' perceptions of him as a detached academic. This involved the recounting of personal stories that revealed him to be a fallible person whose best laid plans often went awry. Johnson (1975: 95) describes this as an effort to 'construct a front of humility, to appear as a humble person who would be a regular guy and do no one any dirt'. Similarly Punch (1979: 9) reports that his voicing of disparaging remarks about intellectuals and sociologists proved to be a reliably effective way 'to puncture the initial defences of new acquaintances within the police'.

Building trust

One of the reasons why organizations may seek to constrain the researcher's access may be concerns about their trustworthiness. This may relate to continuing worries about confidentiality and it may take some time for these to be allayed, during which organization members may go to great lengths to prevent the researcher gaining access to, or even awareness of, particular activities. For example, Punch (1989: 184) comments that 'to a large extent I never actually witnessed the phenomenon I was studying – [police] "corruption"' and it was only in his second phase of fieldwork that he began to learn of its existence, but still only in relation to past cases rather than to the continuing corruption at the time of the study.

The researcher's trustworthiness may be an issue not just in relation to keeping information about the organization confidential from external third parties, but also within the organization. As was noted in Chapter 5, having been granted access to the organization by those senior in the hierarchy, lower-level employees may suspect the researcher of being a management spy, or, in a school, that the researcher will report student behaviour to the headteacher. Access may therefore be restricted until it is evident that confidentiality is being maintained. Thus Fine (2009: 234) observes:

> Because these spaces are not public arenas, access is provided through management; as a consequence, researchers will have, even in the most optimal circumstances, a burden of trust to overcome ... As a result, who I *really* represented was an issue, although one that became muted when it grew clear that I was not reporting to management.

Such trustworthiness may be acquired fortuitously, as when potentially inappropriate behaviour is overseen. Measor and Woods (1991), for example, identify a critical step in the development of trust between them and students they were studying as being an incident in a classroom in which the researcher said nothing when a pupil misbehaved behind the teacher's back, but in full view of the researcher and the other children. Similarly Ryan (2009) reports that the fact that he did not 'dob in' a cleaning supervisor who brought his niece and nephew to work in contravention of company policy, helped to transform the supervisor's initial hostility such that they became one of his most invaluable informants. As Epstein (1998: 34) observes, however, the researcher's failure to conform to expected norms can create role ambiguity for the organization members – as one of the pupils she was studying put it: 'are you a girl or a teacher?'

Alternatively, organization members may deliberately orchestrate deviancy to see how the researcher responds or may set up 'membership tests' in which the researcher is required to participate in deviant behaviour. While conducting fieldwork in a psychiatric hospital, for example, Taylor (1987: 290) was

'drinking beer on the night shift, pitching nickels, betting, and smoking ciga-
rettes in areas where this was prohibited' within the first few visits. For organization members, such tests have the dual benefit of both providing evidence
of the researcher's confidentiality and making them complicit in the deviancy
(and therefore vulnerable to exposure themselves).

Tracking the researcher's acceptance by organization members can become
something of an obsession during early stages of fieldwork when feelings of
marginality can be a source of considerable anxiety. In the early days of his
study of social workers, for example, Johnson (1975: 93) attempted to construct
an 'index of trust' to assess how he was 'getting along' with different participants. Did they ask him to join them for coffee, for example, or take him along
on 'other stops unrelated to the job'. Every two weeks he would review his
fieldnotes to rate where he was on the index with each of the social workers.
He subsequently realized the naivety of this idea, however, when a worker
with whom he considered he had a trusting relationship from the beginning
revealed that he had only been taking him on 'safe' visits where nothing significant was happening.

In particular, observation of 'deviant' behaviour (such as children violating
school rules [Thorne, 1993]), or being told 'strategic secrets' (Goffman, 1989),
may be viewed as an indication that the researcher is indeed sufficiently
trusted that, as Bogdan and Taylor (1975: 45) put it, 'events that occur during
their observations do not differ significantly from those which occur in their
absence'. Unfortunately (or perhaps better, realistically) the researcher may
never know whether this has been achieved. As Randall et al. (2007: 170) comment, 'even if entry is successful, some areas might be regarded as "sacred" and
off limits to the observer'. Punch (1979: 13), for example, reports, towards the
end of his first observational study with the Amsterdam police in which he had
accompanied patrolmen on shifts at all times of the day and night for several
months, observing, and occasionally assisting, in a wide variety of 'incidents',
he attended a celebration party at the flat of one of the officers whom he considered had been most open with him during the fieldwork. At the party,
'thanks to the liberating effects of alcohol', several policemen started to talk
about corruption, revealing a 'subterranean culture that had largely escaped
me'. As his key informant explained: 'we only let you see what we wanted you
to see ... We showed you only half of the story.'

While it may be impossible for a researcher to judge whether they are fully
trusted (Laverick, 2010), and of course organization members may not trust each
other either, Johnson (1975: 94) nevertheless proposes some 'practical procedures
[that may be] used for developing trust'. One such tactic he describes as 'reconstruction of one's biography'. This involved a number of ways in which he sought
to manage organization members' views of him. In the early days of the research,
for example he sought to highlight aspects of his personal history that would

connect with those of organization members he was interacting with. When he was talking to someone who had grown up on a farm he would talk about his own childhood on a farm, while with someone who had grown up in the city he would refer to his own experiences as a child in the city. Sometimes, in what were termed 'bull sessions', when the social workers tired of their routine and the 'prevailing bureaucratization of spirit', these 'reconstructions' could take flight into complete fabrications. Although a colleague referred to this as 'trading whoppers', Johnson suggests that this was not meant as a challenge, but as an acknowledgement of their mutual awareness of the game they were playing. This is not to advocate misrepresentation of the researcher's experience, particularly where this could arouse suspicions of inconsistency or deceit, but to recognize that perceptions of similarity and shared experience between researcher and organization member may facilitate the development of trust. It is also to recognize the temptation to exaggerate in such reconstruction and the need to contain this to settings where expectations of consistency and veracity are relaxed.

A second procedure for developing trust that Johnson (1975: 101) describes is what he calls 'normalising social research'. He proposes that two important ways in which this can be done are: '(1) to normalise perceived deviance and (2) to instruct members of the observed group in how to manage a social researcher'. The first of these is a more active version of the non-reporting of deviance mentioned earlier, in which the researcher reassures members that their 'deviant' behaviour, such as leaving work early or picking up some shopping on the way back from visiting a client, is unexceptional. The second involves inviting members to manage the presence of the observer in whatever way is least disruptive to their work. In this way, Johnson argues he was able to demonstrate his concern to be unobtrusive and, by ceding control to the social worker, to reduce any threat he was perceived as posing.

Building rapport

Biographical reconstruction may not only contribute to building trust with organization members, it may also help to establish the rapport necessary for members to be willing to allow the researcher access to their world. A sense of common feeling and understanding is not something that can be easily simulated and may take some time to grow sufficiently. Pettigrew (1973), for example, reports that it took him two-and-a-half months before he felt that he was fully accepted.

The development of rapport between the researcher and organization members may be viewed as a process of mutual construction of their respective roles in the research activity. Olesen and Whittaker (1967: 274) suggest that this process involves four phases:

1. surface encounter – the initial contacts, often between total strangers;
2. proffering and inviting – the reciprocal definitions of self by self and others;
3. selecting and modifying – the mutual selection of meaningful and viable portions of research roles;
4. stabilizing and sustaining – the achievement of a tentative balance between researcher and informants.

In the first phase, the researcher and organization members encounter each other as strangers, judging the other party in terms of broad categories that they are seen to occupy. With sustained interaction, these stereotypes may quite quickly give way to more differentiated roles through the proffering and inviting of definitions of what each party is up to. Organization members may question researchers about the reasons for their presence and their expectations of members. In this process, members may also 'coach' researchers in the behaviour they expect of them. As these exchanges proceed, particular understandings of each party's role may begin to be selected, perhaps modifying prior assumptions, and in time these may become, at least provisionally, stabilized.

While the establishment of rapport may be important in extended observational fieldwork, it may be even more critical in interview-based research, where researchers may have minutes rather than months in which to build mutual understanding with participants. This has led to ethical concerns about the 'commodification of rapport and the faking of friendship' (Duncombe and Jessop, 2012) in order to encourage interviewees to open up to the researcher, especially among feminist scholars who place a high value on empathy and friendship in research interactions. Other authors, however, seem less concerned about viewing rapport in such instrumental terms. Carmel (2011: 552), for example, argues that

> it is, to be blunt, in the researcher's interest to develop and maintain friendly relations, even where the researcher may not actually *like* fieldwork participants. Although we are 'interested in people' and their social relations, the interest we have is as social scientists: fundamentally, we are interested in people only for the data they can provide.

Finding a role

For research that involves more than a one-off visit it is likely to be important that the researcher establishes a suitable role in the research setting that will facilitate their observation. Where the researcher undertakes participant observation, this role may be determined by the particular job that they take on. Unless the researcher has relevant skills, such jobs, as Watson (2011) observes, are likely to be at the lower end of the organizational hierarchy. Burawoy (1979), for example, worked as a machine operator at the engine division of a multinational company for 10 months, Ryan (2009) worked as a cleaner and Plankey-Videla (2012) worked on the shop floor of a garment factory. Although such jobs may be effective in gaining insight on organizational work life, their practical demands may limit the scope of observation and make it difficult to maintain systematic fieldnotes. Marques (2011: 415), for example, describes the working conditions in a glass factory:

> During 8-hour shifts (minus a 30-minute meal break), machine operators carry out their tasks in a noisy, hot, poorly ventilated, uncomfortable working place, where ear plugs and protective footwear, gloves and eyeglasses must be worn. The machine demands their continuous attention: if an operator is to take a break, a colleague must replace him. Operators usually remain standing and alternate between the two sides of the machine ... as well as the output monitor ... an early inspection station and a few more spots, all inside a circle of 2–3 metres.

The situation may be somewhat easier (and note-taking less conspicuous) in clerical roles, as Hawkins (2008: 422) observes of her study in a recruitment consultancy: 'since all the consultants were often seen writing at their desks, I was able to write brief fieldnotes in the office without attracting undue attention'.

In observational studies in which the researcher does not have a specific job to perform in the organization there may nevertheless be an advantage in them taking on a role in the research setting, if only to avoid standing out as someone with apparently nothing to do in a setting where everybody else is hard at work. This may not only arouse resentment from organization members, making them uncooperative with the research, but may be stressful for the researcher, who feels that their presence is intrusive and unwelcome. It may therefore be in both parties' interests for the researcher to be doing something at least vaguely productive for the organization. Ideally, too, this should facilitate, or at least not get too much in the way of, their observation.

In practice, this can mean the researcher taking on a variety of tasks that are useful to organization members, while also providing the researcher with a justification for being present and an opportunity to observe. Thus Bosk (1996: 131) acted as an 'extra pair of hands' and a 'gofer' for the surgeons he was studying, becoming 'very proficient in opening packages of bandages, retrieving charts and fetching items from the supply room'. The more menial these tasks the more effective they may be from a research perspective: by accepting a low status role the researcher may become less visible to others, just as, in the normal course of events, people tend not to pay attention to cleaners or waiters going about their work. For example, Johnson (1975: 107) reports that:

> During the course of the research investigations I served as a driver, reader, luggage porter, baby-sitter, moneylender, ticket taker at a local conference, note taker, phone answerer when business was heavy, book reader, book lender, adviser on the

purchase of used automobiles, manager of arrangements for going away parties, bodyguard for a female worker assigned to investigate a situation where a woman was waving a gun around, letter writer, messenger and other things.

While this may, as Johnson argues, be considered under the heading of research reciprocities (Wax, 1952), the quid pro quo for providing access, such a transactional view neglects the benefits to the researcher from having something to do (and being recognized as useful to have around) in the research setting. As Gans (1968: 306) observes: 'The external pressure to become involved is much weaker than the internal pressure – and desire – to become involved.'

It may be even more helpful for the researcher if these tasks provide a pretext for note-taking, such as acting as a secretary for a meeting, or as a personal assistant for a high-status individual. Where appropriate it may also be possible for the researcher to volunteer for tasks that may directly benefit their research, for example by offering to keep a record of organizational activities for archival purposes, or perhaps for a later 'lessons learned' or 'experience review' activity. This may provide an opportunity to conduct interviews that are useful for both the organization and the research.

Whether or not they take on tasks useful to the organization, the researcher is likely to acquire an informal social role. In some settings this may be quite high status. A number of authors, for example, refer to themselves as having being given nicknames such as 'the boffin', the 'egghead' or 'the professor' (e.g. Collinson, 1992). While perhaps flattering, such titles may be unhelpful because they draw attention to the researcher's outsider position and their social distance from organization members, making it harder for the researcher to establish rapport. Furthermore, as Hammersley and Atkinson (2007: 72) note, there may be a 'common resentment on the part of some occupational practitioners, and especially teachers, of detached, often invisible "experts"'.

Similarly, for some organization members, outside experts may be equated with management consultants, whose agenda is often seen as cost-cutting and downsizing. The researcher may therefore be seen as a threat and cooperation with them as potentially harmful to the members' interests. As Zabusky (1995: 45) reports:

> some staff members remained uncomfortable with my presence at meetings and mealtimes, fearing that I was there at the behest of 'management' to conduct some sort of 'time and motion' study … On occasion, people asked me, jokingly yet nervously, whether I was 'keeping track' of who was attending meetings, of how long people stayed at lunch and so on.

Seeing the researcher as an expert, organization members may also assume that they possess an 'expertise' they may not have (but find it difficult to disown). For example they may not explain their jargon or what they are doing, as they assume that the researcher is familiar with it ('of course you will know all about this'), and would be disconcerted if the researcher's ignorance was revealed (especially if they had not admitted it at the first opportunity). The researcher's initial understanding may therefore be inadequate and it may take some time before they are able to recognize what they have missed or misunderstood (if they ever do). Daniels (1983), for example, picked up an expression from a remark by one military psychiatrist that she discovered, only after having used it in a conversation with another officer in an attempt to discover its meaning, was highly pejorative.

Of course researchers may actually possess 'expertise'. O'Neill (2001), for example, had worked in the ambulance service he studied for seven years and found himself switching from observer to participant in an emergency, arguing that he could not be expected to stand back in a situation where he could have helped out and would have been resented by his erstwhile colleagues (and the patient) if he had just stood by observing. This expertise need not necessarily be directly related to the domain under study, however, for it to be useful in the research setting. As an 'educated person', for example, Ram (1994) found himself providing advice to employees (and employers) in the small clothing manufacturers he was studying on matters such as social security, housing, immigration and the education of their children. Similarly the experienced researchers interviewed by Clark (2010) on the reasons why people engaged with their research reported offering advice on university courses, acting as a sounding board for relationship difficulties, and providing practical assistance such as transport.

More often, researchers acquire, and may sometimes actively encourage, a role as a 'socially acceptable incompetent' (Lofland and Lofland, 1995) or fool (Wax, 1971; Ybema and Kamsteeg, 2009). That is, as someone who may be well-meaning and able in other respects, but has no idea how to do what any normal person in the organization does. They are therefore, as Randall et al. (2007: 182) argue, 'licensed to ask naive, even stupid, questions and thus explore much of what is tacit to the experienced member', for example why the clock in the air traffic control centre was 'wrong' (because it was always set to GMT).

For organization members the researcher's incompetence, especially in settings involving skilled manual work, may help to offset anxieties about differences in educational attainment and social status. Dundon and Ryan (2010), for example, discuss how the public failure of one of them at glass-blowing on a factory tour facilitated the development of rapport with union convenors. In other settings age differences may have a similar effect. Thus Parker (2000: 237) notes that 'For my older interviewees my age often forced me into being a novice – a "lad" or "son" who needed to be reminded of his lack of knowledge.' While this may encourage organizational members to provide advice and assistance to the researcher that may both facilitate access and be a rich source of insight on the members' under-standing of the organization, it can sometimes be at the cost, as Parker (2000) warns, of being the subject of 'gentle, or not so gentle, ridicule'. Such humiliation, moreover, needs to be accepted, Wax (1971: 370) argues, 'not because [the researcher] is saintly in nature, but because making fun of improper or incorrect behavior is an ancient if painful method of pedagogy'.

It would seem that incompetence may be more acceptable in lower-status settings in which it is effective in inverting conventional hierarchies. With elites, used to being deferred to, on the other hand, it may be perceived, Lofland and Lofland (1995) note, as a lack of seriousness in preparation, not meriting more than formulaic responses. As Braithwaite (1984: 388) puts it, 'unless knowledge and sophistication concerning the subject matter is established early in the interview, the [elite] respondent will regard the interview as a Pub-lic Relations exercise'. If adroitly played, however, there may be a place in elite settings for a role akin to that of court jester – an incompetent whose presence may be a source of controlled diversion from serious matters, but who is also able to ask penetrating questions under the guise of their foolishness (Kets de Vries, 1990).

First days in the field

Although the process of gaining access may extend much beyond the initial entree to the field, particular significance is often attributed to the first days of fieldwork. Geer's account of the preliminary phase of her study of medical students in training (Geer, 1964), for example, emphasizes how initial research plans were revised in the face of fieldwork contingencies and how early deci-sions, sometimes inadvertent, were a powerful influence on the subsequent course of the study. For Goffman (1989: 130), in contrast, the first encounter with the field is critical because: 'There is a freshness cycle when moving into the field. The first day you'll see more than you'll ever see again. And you'll see things that you won't see again. So, the first day you should take notes all the time.'

Other authors, however, report their initial experiences in the field as being much less productive. Wax (1971:17), for example, comments:

> Usually a beginner arrives in the field ready and eager to begin 'gathering data'. Then for weeks, and sometimes for months, he [sic] gropes and wanders about trying to involve himself in the various kinds of social relationships that he needs, not only in order to accomplish his work, but also because he is a human being.

In her own study of an internment camp for Japanese-Americans during the Second World War she reports that it took four months to develop any kind of social relationship. While the type of general sociological research and the particular setting may make this an extreme case, it may not be unusual for it to take some time for a researcher to find their feet in an organization – a period that can become increasingly frustrating and anxious the longer it goes on.

Another common feeling in the early stages of observational fieldwork is that of confusion and data overload. On entering a research setting there is just so much that could potentially be relevant to the research, far more than it would be feasible for any person to capture, that it can be difficult to choose what to record. Like William James's description of a newborn child's perception of the world, all appears 'as one great blooming, buzzing confusion' (James, 1890: 462). Thus Parker (2000: 238–9) comments,

> All the way through the fieldwork I observed and made notes on everything that might be relevant. Hence for the first few visits I wrote about room plans, smells, clothing, furniture, noises, office decoration and much more ... The intensity of the first view visits was tiring[, however]. I had immersed myself in a mass of largely incoherent impressions and saw no way of ordering the huge quantity of ideas I had generated.

Similarly Charmaz and Mitchell (2001: 161) observe:

> A potential problem with ethnographic studies is seeing data everywhere and nowhere, gathering everything and nothing. The studied world seems so interesting (and probably is) that an ethnographer tries to master knowing it all. Mountains of unconnected data grow but they don't say much.

These initial stages of observational fieldwork can also be highly stressful as the researcher seeks to establish themselves in the setting. There is not just the discomfort of making one's way in a new social context, but there may be active hostility and suspicion towards the researcher (Fielding, 2004). However much the researcher is convinced of the benevolence of their intentions, these suspicions may be hard to dispel and may be unwittingly confirmed by the researcher's actions. For example, Blau (1964) spent the first two weeks of his fieldwork in a private office reading the rules and regulations that governed the operations of the agency he was studying and being introduced to the supervisors of the various departments. While this was helpful in orienting his research it raised suspicions amongst the clerical workers who he subsequently sought to observe. Indeed Johnson (1975) underwent what organization members described as a 'crucifixion' at an open meeting organized by the social work managers to introduce him to the teams he would be studying, during which he was directly accused of clandestine operations, and was only, as he reports, saved from immediate ejection by his obvious lack of composure under fire and the personal connections of his wife.

The ethics of access

The ultimate indicator of successful access is often described in terms of 'becoming part of the furniture' (Collinson, 1992; Punch, 1979; Randall et al., 2007), where organization members become so used to the presence of the researcher that they forget they are there. In principle, this is the ideal situation for an observational researcher, because if organization members are genuinely unaware of the researcher's presence (and of course, their protestations to this effect do not necessarily make it so, indeed potentially the opposite), events should, as Bogdan and Taylor (1975: 45) put it, 'not significantly differ from those which occur in [the researcher's] absence'. This can pose an ethical dilemma for researchers however, as organization members may not always wish the researcher to be aware of their unguarded behaviour. 'It would be a rash investigator', though, as Cassell (1980) argues, 'who, at a critical or confidential moment, said: "Wait a minute – don't forget you're being studied!"'

While such unintended disclosure may be dealt with retrospectively by requesting that the behaviour should be considered 'off the record' ('forget you ever saw that'), this may be considered to be simply deferring the dilemma to the stage of reporting the research (as will be discussed in Chapter 7). A further issue of more immediate significance, however, may be that of 'guilty knowledge' (Fetterman, 1983) and the researcher's rights or duties to report it. While, as Johnson (1975) argued, the normalization of some degree of deviancy may be a tactic in building trust with organization members, there is considerable debate over how far the researcher should take this.

On the one hand, the emphasis placed in many ethical codes on the avoidance of harm could be seen to imply that researchers should report anything that might cause harm to others (Burr and Reynolds, 2010) – a duty that, Bell and Bryman (2007) suggest, might be argued to extend to possible harm to organizations being studied. Furthermore, in some cases reporting may even be a legal requirement (Wiles et al., 2008). To do so, however, would be to risk harm to research participants, break the confidentiality of research findings and almost certainly ensure the termination of the fieldwork. Consequently a number of authors report their reluctance, sometimes despite severe misgivings, to jeopardize their research, generally by invoking the confidentiality guarantees they had offered to organization members as a condition of access. Randall et al. (2007), for example, report that racist and sexist jokes were commonplace, while Alcadipani and Hodgson (2009: 137) 'routinely witnessed incidents of sabotage, racism and bullying' in their fieldwork, and Taylor (1987: 289) observed mistreatment of patients on a 'ward for the mentally retarded'.

A corollary of 'turning a blind eye' to such behaviour, though, may be that silence will be taken to imply consent. Even if the researcher does not come across clearly unethical or illicit behaviour, in many, perhaps most, fieldwork settings the researcher is likely to encounters views or behaviours that they are not in sympathy with. As Abolafia (1998: 82) observes in relation to his study of the US bond market:

> But the market-makers themselves are suspicious of [any questioning of their views]. They want you to share their assumption that their world is as it should or must be. They want you to believe in the importance and rationality of what they do from the start and not to question it. A critical stance would present me as an outsider not to be trusted. This puts the researcher in a difficult position. I decided that my stance would be that I was open to anything. That was hard to do because some of the things I heard from bond traders were shocking. But I learned to keep a dispassionate 'straight' face, shaking my head and taking it in.

Similarly, Walford (2001: 138) reports his discomfort in not challenging the views of an interviewee whose 'crude bigoted' views he found 'abhorrent', and Pacholok (2012) discusses her feelings that she was 'selling out' in not challenging the sexist and homophobic remarks of her firefighter interviewees.

While it may be the case that such 'horrific' (Walford, 2001) views are common currency in the particular research setting and that exposure to them may be considered a positive, if distressing, indicator of the researcher having been accepted by organization members, they may also be used as a further test, which the observational researcher, by their passivity and neutrality, may be considered as inviting. There may therefore be instances of provocation and hostility from organization members. In the early days of his research, for example, Pettigrew (1973: 57) reports, 'Ray Ashton, the senior systems analyst took every opportunity to belittle me publicly ... [and] Reilly was equally obnoxious'. In the face of such challenges, Gans (1968: 306) argues, 'most often one can keep one's cool enough not to offer foolishly to participate, but the urge to argue remains, and must be suppressed constantly'. While it is of course possible that such antagonism may be personal, relations generally tend to improve with time, but can be distressing while they last.

In the field

Having achieved some degree of acceptance in the field, the researcher then faces the task of gathering data, whether by observation, interviews or through the accumulation of documentation and artefacts. From accounts in many methods textbooks it might seem that this is a straightforward process of 'recording' data as they present themselves to the researcher. In practice, however, this process may pose a variety of challenges.

What are data?

As was noted in relation to the early days in the field, it can be difficult to decide what constitutes data in the research setting. Definitions of qualitative research may place the emphasis on 'people's own written or spoken words and observable behaviour' (Taylor and Bogdan, 1998: 7), but what about how things are said, other sounds, the physical character of the setting or, Fine (1993: 279) suggests, smells, touch and taste? As Sandelowski (2002: 108) argues: 'we tend to forget that observation is not confined to looking but, rather, encompasses all of a researcher's senses'.

This would seem likely to be most apparent in observational research, but there may also be much that an interviewer may be exposed to in the research setting that could potentially be relevant in interpreting what is said, although little of this is likely to be registered in an audio recording of the interview, say. On the other hand, given the impossibility for any individual to pay attention to all potential forms of data simultaneously, some selectivity of focus will be necessary. How, then, should the researcher choose what to exclude?

In practice, such decisions are likely to be influenced by conventions of the research literature that tend to privilege words, as these can be readily presented on the page, and by broader cultural conventions favouring the visual mode, whether in textual descriptions of settings and behaviours or photographs. Technology too may play a part in shaping what data are collected, as the recording, analysis and presentation of video becomes more widely accepted. As this suggests, what is taken to be data may be more a reflection of what can be recorded and what is conventionally accepted as such, rather than any considered assessment of what may provide insight on the phenomena of interest.

Recording data

Where data are 'gathered' remotely by questionnaires, whether postal or online, the questionnaire itself provides the data recording medium. Similarly the procedures for recording interview data, whether as handwritten notes, or, with the permission of interviewees, as audio recordings, are well established. Observational researchers, however, may have more trouble in 'capturing' their data. Part of the problem relates to the number of potential types of data to be recorded, but also to the difficulties of recording them.

Some of these difficulties may be a product of the practical contingencies of fieldwork. Undertaking participant observation, for example, the researcher may not have the opportunity to record data systematically due to the demands of their participant role. For the researcher this can mean that they need to spend a lot of time 'after hours' recording their data. Johnson (1975: 189), for example, reports that during his first weeks in the social welfare office, in his efforts to record 'everything that happened' each day, he was spending 'nine to ten hours per day in the field plus almost the same amount of time recording field notes'. Although his pace slowed somewhat over the course of the research, he was aware of being driven by the 'ideal' of 'the field worker's sixteen hour work day' (Blau, 1964: 289), and feeling guilty at not achieving it, even as his experience made him realise that it was a practical impossibility.

Accepting that it is not possible to record everything, however, does not necessarily alleviate the difficulties of data recording in observational fieldwork, as much of data is ephemeral and cannot be 'captured' in the normal course of work in organizations. Within the limits of what they are able to observe and within their abilities to record this, therefore, the field researcher still needs to select what to record. Which of the conversations they engage in during a day, for example, or even what parts of them, should they try to 'capture'? Or how do they record the mood of a meeting, or the effect of an announcement on different organization members' morale? Even if continuous video recording could be arranged it would only provide a limited snapshot of what happened in one particular setting at one time, as Garton Ash (2002) argues, and would still not solve the problem of choosing what data are relevant within that recording.

The quality of data collection is also likely to vary over time. As Johnson (1975: 187) describes, this may reflect the researcher's emerging understanding of the setting, but 'the quantity and quality of observational records may [also] vary with the field worker's feelings of restedness, or exhaustion, reactions to particular events, relations to others, consumption of alcoholic beverages, the number of discrete observations, and so forth'. This should not be considered to be a problem that is unique to observational research, moreover, as Johnson (1975: 121) also notes. During the period of his field investigations he 'witnessed bits and pieces of about a dozen other social research projects' and observed that responses to these surveys and interviews reflected the practicalities of the response situation (such as the time available for the response, the amount of space provided on written forms, the temporal coordination of this activity with others); how respondents were feeling at the particular moment; and their judgements about how the research information would be used. Observational studies, as Becker and Geer (1957) argued, therefore offer the researcher insight on the problems that may affect the data recorded in other forms of research in organizations.

Fieldnotes

The usual form in which observational data are recorded is through fieldnotes and the literature includes a wealth of advice on how these may best be written (Emerson et al., 2011; Lofland and Lofland, 1995; Taylor and Bogdan, 1998). This addresses topics such as how and when to write them (as fully and as promptly as possible), what to include:

descriptions of events, people, things heard and overheard, conversations among people, conversations with people ... each new physical setting and person encountered ... changes in the physical setting or people (Lofland and Lofland, 1995: 93)

and techniques to help recall data, such as noting key words and the first and last remarks in a conversation, not discussing observations until they have been recorded, and drawing plans of settings and the researcher's movements around them (Taylor and Bogdan, 1998).

There is also discussion of some of the practical problems of writing notes in the field. Thus Lofland and Lofland (1995: 90) emphasize the need to jot inconspicuously, unless the researcher's participant role makes note-taking legitimate. 'Rather', they advise, 'jot notes at moments of withdrawal and when shielded.' This may be easier said than done, however, unless the researcher, following the advice of Taylor and Bogdan (1998: 69) to 'leave the setting as soon as you have observed as much as you remember', wishes to acquire a reputation for incontinence by retreating to the lavatory to write up their notes every five minutes (Bone, 2006).

If observed taking notes, as Blau (1964) describes, it may be better to be open about what is being recorded, rather than encourage suspicions that the research has a covert agenda. Lofland and Lofland(1995) also stress that the emphasis in fieldnotes should be on the richness of data rather than literary style. In consequence, as Lofland (1971) observes, they often have a 'Warhol' quality, being 'mundane, uneventful and dull'. Their completion can nevertheless become something of a compulsion for the field researcher as they strive to construct as thorough a record of their observations as possible.

The quantity of documentation that this can yield can be quite daunting. John Lofland is reported as recommending that a good fieldworker should expect to accumulate 15 pages of notes for every hour of fieldwork (Punch, 1986), although Johnson (1975) suggests that such productivity is unfeasible and unsustainable in practice. Perhaps more realistically, Wieland (2010) reports producing 700 pages of fieldnotes from 700 hours of participant observation over the course of 6 months and Goffman (1989: 131) suggests that a researcher may get 500 to 1,000 single-spaced pages of notes in a year of fieldwork (although even this he describes as 'too much to read more than once or twice in your lifetime', and consequently advises against 'taking *too* many notes').

Validity and reliability

McCall and Simmons (1969: 78) identify three types of threats to the validity and reliability of field research data:

1. reactive effects of the observer's presence or activities on the phenomena being observed;
2. distorting effects of selective perception and interpretation on the observer's part; and
3. limitations on the observer's ability to witness all relevant aspects of the phenomena in question.

There may be fairly little that a researcher can do about the last of these, which reflects the fact that an individual can only be in one place at one time. Even with a team of researchers there may be aspects of the phenomenon that are not witnessed. Of course this is true of any form of data collection, but awareness that important things are going on elsewhere may be heightened in observational fieldwork where the researcher seeks to gain rich insight on naturally occurring phenomena in context, rather than focusing on specific variables, and is therefore brought up against the limits of their ability to view, let alone record, all the complexity they encounter.

Reactive effects of the observer's presence or activities are sometimes associated predominantly with the organization members' attempts to hide deviancy from the researcher and to present a front that conforms to particular norms of behaviour. For example, Leidner (1993) suggests that, as a result of her presence, insurance agents may have avoided any unethical sales practices and worked more diligently. Similarly Johnson (1975) was aware that he was routinely excluded from certain types of situations, such as when social workers sanctioned clients, and that certain practices, such as sexual liaisons with clients or the manipulation of agency rules for personal financial gain were going on, although he never actually witnessed them.

As has already been noted, while it may be impossible to know even when deviancy is observed whether organization members are acting differently in response to the observer's presence, either playing up or playing down certain behaviours, there may also be more subtle effects. Fine (2009: 237), for example, comments that organization members may have

> a strong desire to allow, or demand, the observer to participate in all aspects of the scene: in part from a desire to help make the experience transparent and in part to cope with the frustration of seeing the researcher standing around, watching, 'doing nothing'.

One way of understanding these effects is in terms of individual and organizational incentives for participation in research. While these may be most apparent in relation to individuals' willingness to answer a questionnaire or be interviewed, they may also influence organization members' interactions with observational researchers.

From an individual perspective, there may be a range of motives for organization members to participate (Goldman and Swayze, 2012). A simple explanation may be in terms of altruism, a desire to be helpful to the researcher. This is not necessarily as advantageous as it may seem, however, as Delamont (2004: 224) observes: 'one of the biggest problems is that informants often want to help the researchers by showing and telling what they think investigators want to see and hear'. Similarly Rod (2011) expressed concern that 'what I was being told in these interviews was the official "party line" organizational perspective, i.e. I was getting a rehearsed, politically correct "I'll give you an idealized what you want to hear" response.'

A personal relationship with the researcher may be another reason for some organization members to participate. This may be the result of prior association, or have been built up during access negotiations. Gatekeepers and sponsors, for example, may be more inclined to participate than those who have had no contact with the researcher.

Some organization members may also be inspired to participate through a commitment to research. As Walford (2001) notes, organization members who have experience of conducting their own research may be more sympathetic to the researcher's plight. In some situations, however, as Walford (2001) and Bosk (1996) observe, such individuals may have their own views on what the researcher should be studying and how they should go about this, and may seek to impose this on the researcher. Johnson (1975) refers to this as the 'inside dopester'. As Welch et al. (2002) observe, this may be a particular issue with elite participants. A variant of this desire to influence research may be the phenomenon observed by Collinson (1992: 235) in which he 'became aware of a competition to see who would be defined as the "most interesting case"'.

In addition to such high-minded motives, individuals may be encouraged to participate in research for more mundane reasons. In some circumstances, for example, there may be financial incentives for participation – entry in a prize draw for completing a survey, say, or direct payment for the time taken up. Other incentives may be more intangible, however. Hutchinson et al. (1994), for example, discuss a range of sometimes unanticipated benefits that participants report themselves as gaining from their involvement in intensive interviews, especially where these involve vulnerable populations or address sensitive issues. Their preliminary analysis identifies these as catharsis, sense of purpose, self-awareness, empowerment, healing and providing a voice for the disenfranchised. There may also be more prosaic reasons for participation in research, such as the alleviation of boredom – talking to the researcher is more interesting than whatever else they might be doing. As Gans (1968: 310) observes 'almost everyone will admit the researcher, for people enjoy being studied. It provides variety in their lives and the attention of the researcher is flattering.'

Researchers can therefore find themselves as recipients for a wide range of commentary from organization members, not all of which may necessarily be related to the ostensive topic of the research. Parker (2000) refers to this role as researcher as confidante, but others (e.g. Bosk, 1996; Morrill, 1995) view it in more psychoanalytic terms, positioning the researcher as a form of therapist, to whom organization members may unburden their thoughts, complaints and concerns. While the relevance of all that is being said may not always be apparent, therefore, the content of such interactions may be informative. That particular matters are mentioned, for example, may indicate that they are of concern to the organization member, but that they may not otherwise have the opportunity to express them. It may also not be just in what is said, but also how it is said that insight may be gained, as the research exchange becomes the conduit for normally suppressed emotions. Similarly, as Wax (1952: 37) notes, 'equally instructive are those occasions when an informant will evade or refuse to discuss some question'. While not suggesting that the researcher should treat research interactions as psychotherapeutic encounters, sensitivity to their unspoken content may be valuable in understanding an organization.

In participating in research, it may not just be the researcher whom organization members are trying to communicate with (Wolcott, 1995). Especially if the topic of the research is seen as being related to matters of contention in the organization, speaking to the researcher may be perceived as a way of getting one's voice heard (all the more so if it is thought that research findings may be presented to those with influence on the matter). In such situations the incentive for participation is likely to be greatest for those with the strongest views on the matter, or those who feel themselves to be otherwise excluded from formal discussions.

Some organization members may seek to use interaction with the researcher strategically, for example to claim credit (or divert blame) for particular events, to gain influence over others (through their views influencing recommendations that may emerge from the research) or to advance a particular position (Sandelowski, 2002). This is not to say that everything the researcher hears should be assumed to have ulterior motives, but that it may be helpful to consider the interests served by particular claims.

A further, and disconcertingly common reason for members to participate in research may be because they are told to by someone in authority, e.g. Plankey-Videla (2012) or, even if not directly instructed to do so, because they believe that participation will be viewed positively, or non-participation will be viewed negatively, by those in authority. It is not unusual when undertaking fieldwork, therefore, for the first part of an interview or meeting to be taken up with explaining to the organization member(s) why it is that they are there, or sometimes correcting misunderstandings about the research that have been conveyed to them by other organization members (Collinson, 1992; Randall et al., 2007).

In addition to incentives to participate, individuals may also face a variety of disincentives to participation. Perhaps the most common of these is workload. It is a perennial observation of researchers in organizations that they experience difficulties in interacting with organization members because members are too busy. Of course this may be a polite or indirect way of rejecting the researcher's request or it may be a front, carefully maintained by the member to disguise their actual idleness (Johnson, 1975: 128). Given the economic pressures in many organizations, however, it would be unwise to assume that it is not a real constraint on organization members' participation and efforts to accommodate this by offering to meet at times that may be convenient for the organization member (if not for the researcher) may be necessary.

Other disincentives may relate to the perception of the research (and the researcher) within the organization. Just as individuals may participate in order to advance particular interests, they may refuse to participate precisely because the research is seen to be aligned with particular interests, of management say, or some other group in the organization. Indeed it may be a deliberate tactic not to participate in the research in order to be able to argue subsequently that the findings are biased. Alternatively, where the research addresses a sensitive topic in the organization, participation may be seen as aligning the organization member with a particular position and therefore an unwise move for the politically astute.

Just as some organization members may be favourably predisposed towards research, however, others may be unsupportive, or may regard participation as a waste of time. While it may be hard to dispel these assumptions, it is important that the researcher makes all reasonable efforts to overcome them, even if they are not ultimately successful, or it may be difficult for them to refute criticisms of their findings as being unrepresentative and distorted.

The remaining threat to validity identified by McCall and Simmons (1969) comes from the selective perception and interpretation of the researcher themselves. Various influences may encourage such selectivity, but also various measure may be taken to overcome it.

One influence that may be a particular issue in extended observational research is that of the relationship between the researcher and organization members. As Gans (1968) observes:

> Participant Observation means frequent contact with specific people, and the field worker, no different from anybody else, forms likes and dislikes. He likes some of the people he is studying better than others, because they share his values, are easier to talk with, are more open in interview situations, or are just friendlier.

Such individuals may have a significant role in research studies, acting as 'key informants'. As a number of researchers (such as Beech et al., 2009; Burgess, 1991; Newby, 1977; Plankey-Videla, 2012; Stebbins, 1991) report, such interactions may sometimes develop into friendships (and occasionally more), that may continue after the completion of the research. While this may be personally supportive for the researcher in an occasionally difficult situation, it can also pose problems for research. Three consequences, in particular, are widely warned against: bias, over-identification and marginality.

Bias may arise in three ways from the close identification of the researcher with particular individuals (Glesne, 1989). The first of these is an exacerbation of the limitations on the ability to observe all relevant aspects of the phenomenon that McCall and Simmons (1969) refer to. By their differential association with particular individuals, the researcher's understanding of the situation becomes more circumscribed. As Gans (1968) puts it:

> If one gravitates towards people one likes and is at ease with, the pleasures of Participant Observation increase significantly, but the sampling of people and situations – always in danger of being skewed because there is only so much a single participant observer can do – may become badly distorted.

Second may be the tendency to place greater weight on the reports of those with whom the researcher is sympathetic, or with whom they have chosen to associate themselves (Ybema and Kamsteeg, 2009) and lastly may be the perceived partiality of any accounts offered by the researcher, despite whatever measures they may take to try to avoid this.

Over-identification may occur with any individuals with whom the researcher has a close connection, but may be a particular issue, Gans (1968) argues, in studies of low-status groups, where feelings of guilt or perceptions of unjust treatment may incline the researcher to ignore behaviour that they consider undesirable or unethical. In the extreme case it can lead the researcher to abandon their independence and 'go native'.

While in principle the researcher may establish a close relationship with any members of the research setting, concerns about marginality reflect the perception that, as Pettigrew (1973) argues, 'the observer's marginal position may attract him to marginal men [sic] in the social structure he is studying'. For example, Blau (1964: 30), noted that:

> It is my impression that the best informants in the early weeks tended to be officials who occupied marginal positions in the work group or the organization. Being not fully integrated among colleagues or somewhat alienated from the bureaucratic system may have made these officials more critical of their social environment, less restrained by feelings of loyalty from sharing their criticism with an outsider, and more interested in the approval of the observer than were those who received much social support and approval within the organization.

Price and Townsend (2009: 83) make a similar point, albeit emphasizing the benefits it may offer in providing 'stories that contradict the "management" or "organisational" position', in their discussion of smokers as research subjects in settings where workplace smoking regulations position them (literally) as social outcasts.

Just as a researcher may form good relations with particular individuals, there may be others in the same setting with whom they may find it hard, or even impossible, to establish any rapport. These individuals may refuse to have anything to do with the research, as is their right under the principle of informed consent. While such 'freeze outs' (Johnson, 1975) may feel like a personal failure and will be an inevitable source of bias in the findings, they need not significantly derail the research. In some situations, however, individuals may actively agitate against the research, for example seeking to discourage their colleagues' participation, making the situation untenable, however sympathetic other organization members may be.

In order to avoid selective perception and interpretation Lofland and Lofland recommend the cultivation of multiple informants and the avoidance of gullibility(!). In practice this is may mean that the researcher will have to interact with individuals with widely differing views, not all of which they may necessarily be sympathetic to. Although this may be possible by adopting a position of studied neutrality, a number of researchers (e.g. Delbridge, 1998; Johnson, 1975) comment on the need to possess a chameleon quality, able to appear accepting (if not necessarily supportive) of each individual's views. This may be considered deceptive, however, if probably necessary (Cassell, 1980).

Although multiple informants may broaden the range of perspectives a researcher is exposed to, this does not address their own biases of perception and interpretation. Wax (1971) suggests that this may be addressed by the scrupulous recording and critical review of fieldnotes. Others (e.g. Becker, 1967) are less sanguine about the possibility of overcoming biases, however, and recommend that they can only be acknowledged and, to the extent possible, made allowance for.

There may be a fourth type of threat to validity and reliability in research in organizations that is not mentioned by McCall and Simmons (1969), and that is the circumstances under which observation or interviews take place. Given the existence of potentially hierarchical relationships and espoused common principles, organization members' behaviour may be influenced by the presence of others. In particular, as Buchanan et al. (1988) report, in some situations managers or others in a position of authority in an organization may demand to sit in on meetings with other organization members, with potentially significant effects on the freedom with which members are likely to express their views. In other situations, interviews may have to be conducted in semi-public settings, for example due to concerns for the researcher's safety in prison research (Laverick, 2010), potentially limiting the candour of interviewees' responses.

The politics of fieldwork

A particular source of difficulty for the researcher in avoiding bias and obtaining a broad range of views is organizational politics – different groups and individuals within the organization may be (or some would argue are necessarily) in conflict with each other. For Randall et al. (2007) this as an 'inescapable fact of organizational life', and one in which, Parker (2000) argues, researchers are unavoidably complicit. This may affect what is told to the researcher, who they are able to speak to and the reception of their findings.

As was mentioned in relation to motives for organization members' participation, the researcher may be seen as a means to advance particular interests and interactions with the researcher may acquire a strategic orientation. If detected (or suspected), this need not in itself be a major problem for the research, as the efforts made to advance interests and the interests themselves may be relevant data. More problematic, however, may be the researcher's perceived alignment with a particular faction. This may be inadvertent, and in some cases unavoidable, for example where the researcher's access to the organization is facilitated by that faction. Such alignment may be in relation to conflict within the organizational hierarchy, between divisions, departments or teams within an organization, or between informal groupings based on individual or collective interests.

If the researcher becomes aware of efforts to co-opt their work in support of particular interests, they would seem to have two options: to permit this alignment (and accept the possible consequences in terms of bias and selective perception), or to attempt to distance themselves from the conflict, by demonstrating their independence and impartiality, maintaining strict confidentiality regarding each party's position. It may be necessary, as part of this process, to address misconceptions of the researcher's position that may be advanced by organization members. There is a danger, of course, that this may lead the researcher to be spurned by both 'sides', although both may equally appreciate the efforts of an honest broker.

Emotions and fieldwork

Fine (1993: 281) proposes that one of the myths of ethnography (and of fieldwork more generally) is that the researcher is a dispassionate observer of the setting. On the contrary, he argues, 'we can never be a cipher'; fieldwork evokes, and is shaped by, emotions (and not just for the researcher, but for organization members too). Among the more widely discussed of these emotions for the researcher are anxiety, boredom and empathy (Kleinman and Copp, 1993).

On anxiety, Gans (1968: 311ff.) observes, gaining access can be 'nerve-wracking', with constant fear of rejection and this may not abate, even after entry is gained. He also identifies further anxieties in the management of the research, such as worries about how the research is progressing, whether the right things are being observed, how to make sense of the data and the tensions in the researcher's dual role as observer and participant. 'Emotionally speaking', Gans argues therefore, 'participant-observation is ... strenuous and tense work.'

At the same time, however, it can also become 'just another job, with a routine which must be followed if the study is to be at all systematic' (Gans, 1968: 309). Given the marginality of the researcher, moreover, this can involve a lot of waiting around for people to be free to meet or for activities over which they have no control to commence. Boredom can therefore be something of an occupational hazard. Thus, Woods (1986: 58) writes, 'the requirement to observe things "as they happen" and to be "unobtrusive", particularly if associated with problems of negotiating access, can mean long periods of boredom'. As Randall et al. (2007: 182) also observe: 'organisational life is frequently boring' and the researcher therefore faces the challenge of 'steering between a feigned interest in the minutiae of mundane work practices (perhaps viewed or reported for the umpteenth time) and prejudging what is of interest or not'. Similarly Fine and Shulman (2009: 181) comment:

> Successful emotional labour and play-acting help earn the confidences of informants. We must be friendly, patient and not too explicit about our intentions. We must act interested when bored and encourage informants to provide richer details. We must nod our heads with polite eyes but bored ears at verbose informants and wait for chances to redirect the conversation.

While over-identification is seen as a threat to research validity (Miller, 1952), it is recognized that extended interaction with organization members is likely to lead to empathy with their situation (sometimes even when studying organizations that the researcher would normally be opposed to). For example, Daniels (1983) talks of becoming 'infatuated' with charismatic key informants among the military psychiatrists and upper-class women volunteers she studied and of the difficulties she had in achieving distance when initially analysing and reporting her work. As Down et al. (2006), Fine and Shulman (2009) and Kleinman and Copp (1993) also note, however, there may be individuals and settings that the researcher never gets to like, to the extent that for some researchers the fieldwork experience can be a continuous struggle against the desire to escape.

Ethics in practice

If fieldwork can be emotionally demanding at times, it can also be ethically testing. As a number of authors discuss, the ethical principles that the researcher might wish to subscribe to may be hard to apply in practice. A number of areas in particular are identified as potentially problematic: informed consent, voluntary participation, confidentiality, beneficence and honesty and transparency.

The principle of informed consent implies that all organization members need to give their individual consent to participation in the research. As Grugulis (2011) reports, some ethics committees may take this literally, insisting, initially at least, that an ethnography of a computer games company ('No under-18s, no members of vulnerable groups, no illegal activities') should obtain:

> full written consent from every worker in the offices (about 250), every delivery person and – on the occasions I went off for a chat with informants – every barrista who served us coffee and waitress who brought us pizzas.

Even if this were feasible, however, as Corrigan (2003) discusses, obtaining written consent does not necessarily mean that research participants are making a free and informed choice. If this is the case with clinical drug trials where what participation involves is clearly defined and the potential risks reasonably well known, then the situation would seem yet more complex in flexible designs, where the nature of participation and its possible effects may not be known in advance. As Laverick observes,

> Ultimately, measures taken by researchers to adhere to research responsibilities set out in professional codes of ethics comprises an element of risk, a subjective assessment and a degree of uncertainty which needs to be weighed up against the potential benefits of conducting the research in the first place. This calculation, while distasteful (and often unarticulated) remains implicit to any research encounter. (2010: 76)

Permission may also be seen as potentially needing to be renewed at every instance of interaction between the researcher and organization members (Thorne, 1980). As Alcadipani and Hodgson (2009: 136) report, however,

> In practice, this proved very difficult to achieve in any meaningful way; securing informed consent from 35 people on a construction site, or from 10 busy managers at the outset of each meeting, posed a range of difficulties. After a few weeks in the field, a customary response to requests for consent was 'F*ck off mate, you always ask this sh*t. Of course I agree, pal'. When I attempted on one occasion to ask the same question to everyone present in a meeting, I was politely told to shut up.

As has been noted previously, while participation in research is supposed to be voluntary (and withdrawal always possible without need for an explanation and with no sanction) it is not unusual to find that organization members present themselves to be interviewed or permit the researcher to observe their work because they are instructed to do so by those in authority in the organization (Plankey-Videla, 2012). Even if their participation is ostensibly voluntary, therefore, it may be influenced by consideration of how it may be perceived by those in authority (or of how non-participation would be viewed).

Non-participation or withdrawal may also be problematic in many organizational settings, where the researcher may interact with a large number of people who are not directly involved in the research, but whose behaviour may be observable by the researcher, across an open-plan office say, or in a general meeting that the research participants are attending. It might be argued that such issues may be avoided by suitable publication of the fact that research is being carried out, allowing those who do not wish to participate to opt out. As a number of authors report (e.g. Collinson, 1992; Randall et al., 2007) however, such messages often do not get through (or, if they do, do not get noticed or understood) even by those directly involved in the research, such that the researcher frequently encounters the reaction of 'this is the first I have heard about this'. It would also mean that, in principle, the research should be terminated, even if there was an objection from just one person who may be not be involved in the research at all, but might possibly be observed in some peripheral way at some point during the course of the study, such as the person making a delivery to the computer games company that Grugulis (2011) refers to.

Just as, over time, organization members may come to forget the researcher's outsider status and allow them access 'behind the scenes', extended interaction between the researcher and organization members, especially where this leads to good informal relationships, may make it hard for the researcher to ensure that they do not inadvertently break any confidences. This may be particularly the case where the researcher may have access to more than one party in the research setting, such as both management and workers or both sides of a commercial partnership, and where there may be a risk of inadvertent disclosure of information that is perhaps not even recognized as confidential from the other side. Pettigrew (1973: 60), for example, describes how he developed good relations with the computer salesman supplying one of the companies he was studying. The salesman would entertain him to 'expensive hotel lunches' that were 'conversationally like a war of nerves. Each of us was trying to generate as much information as possible, while giving away as little as possible.' Similarly, Alcadipani comments that in his conversations with the production director of one company, who had acted as his gatekeeper for research access, he made careful attempts to preserve the confidentiality of the other party in the commercial partnership he was studying, but 'there is nonetheless the possibility that he elicited from me information he would not be able to get otherwise' (Alcadipani and Hodgson, 2009: 136).

It is not just with other participants in the research setting, however, that confidentiality needs to be maintained, but also, as indicated in the confidentiality agreement in Chapter 5, with third parties. Particular care will need to be taken, therefore, to avoid inadvertent disclosure when discussing the research whether formally, such as in a presentation or article, or informally, such as in discussion with friends or colleagues (Wiles et al., 2008).

At the same time, though, confidentiality should not be an excuse for secrecy about the data. It is a reasonable expectation of academic research, for example, that an academic supervisor should have access to a student's data to assess their quality and to check the claims being made from them, and that data used in writing a dissertation or article should, in principle, be available for inspection by examiners or journal reviewers (even if this is rarely invoked). Measures such as anonymization, redaction of sensitive material or employment of secondary confidentiality agreements may therefore be necessary, should such circumstances arise.

As was discussed in Chapter 4, ethical principles suggest that the researcher should seek to do no harm to those they are studying, but, as was discussed earlier, they may find themselves in a difficult position if they observe harm (such as bullying) committed by one organization member against another and do not report it. Similarly it may be difficult for the researcher to know how their findings may be used by the organization, perhaps against the interests of those they have studied (Alcadipani and Hodgson, 2009). Although this may not be particular to organizational research, the authority and capability for certain organization members to act against others may be more clearly defined than in other settings.

Lastly, ethical guidelines generally advocate honesty and transparency. As Gans (1968: 314) argues, however, deception is inherent to participant observation.

> Once the field worker has gained entry, people tend to forget he [sic] is there and let down their guard, but he [sic] does not; however much he seems to participate, he is really there to observe and even to watch what happens when people let down their guard. He is involved in personal situations in which he is, emotionally speaking, always taking and never giving, for he is there to learn, and thus to take from the people he studies, whereas they are always giving information, and are rarely being given anything.

Similarly, Cassell (1980: 35) observes

> field-workers who use friendships to obtain information without continually reminding informants what they are doing are, in a certain sense, deceiving them. So are researchers who agree with, or at least do not contradict, informants' remarks that they find unacceptable.

Yet, as has been discussed, both are recognized features of research in organizations, and as Cassell (1980: 35) concedes, 'such "deceit" is probably necessary in fieldwork and in social life'. Similarly Punch (1986: 39) observes 'in normal social intercourse a person who is totally honest is unbearable and socially immature. To a certain extent, he, or she, *has* to dissemble to protect his or her autonomy and to lubricate relations with others.'

Nor is deception necessarily confined to participant observation. As Roth (1962: 283) argues, 'all research is secret in some ways and to some degree we never tell the subjects [sic] "everything"'. He identifies three reasons for this: in a flexible design the focus of the research may change over time and the organization members might not have agreed to the new line of investigation had they been informed about it at the outset; the researcher may not want the behaviour of organization members to be influenced by knowledge of what they are studying; or organization members may not understand the explanation of the research they are given in the same way that the researcher does. A questionnaire may include questions to test a respondent's consistency or veracity, for example, or interview questions may have a subtext that is not disclosed to the organization member.

As was evident from the discussion of the ethics of covert research in Chapter 4, broadly speaking three different ethical stances on fieldwork may be found among researchers. On the one hand there are those, such as Erikson (1967) and Bulmer (1982), who argue for an absolute prohibition on what they would consider to be unethical research practices that would involve anything other than complete openness. Counter to this would be proponents of conflict methodology (e.g. Douglas, 1976) who argue that society is inherently conflictual and that deception and impression management are pervasive in social life, so researchers are justified in any actions they take in the pursuit of scientific truth, whatever harm this may cause to those they study. Such an argument has arguably become less influential as its claims that social research is motivated by the pursuit of scientific truth have been increasingly questioned. Thus, in 1968 Gans (1968: 314) was already arguing:

> I am not convinced by the assumption that science is disinterested, or that being a scientist allows the researcher to assume a noblesse oblige relationship to those he [sic] studies, for then he is both judge and jury in determining that his activities are for their own good. The social scientist does his work for the same personal motives as any one else, including the hope of a higher income and career advancement, and even if his choice of a research topic is not based on overt ideological concerns, the research itself, once published, may have political consequences which cannot be explained away by the appeal to scientific objectivity.

Opponents of ethical absolutism in organizational research are now more likely to argue for a situational approach to research ethics (Ferdinand et al., 2007) that recognizes the researcher's own ethical judgement. Punch (1986: 80) in particular argues against rigid codes that would 'restrain innocuous research', while being too vague to provide operational guidelines and lacking sufficient consensus to be enforceable. Similarly, Alcadipani and Hodgson (2009: 128) argue for 'more open and honest debate about the pragmatic realities of critical, organizational ethnographic research'. As they note:

During fieldwork, situations were much more complex and fluid than any code or principle could predict ... Indeed, in many situations ethical guidelines provided an excuse to withhold information in order to keep good field relations and maintain my research access, and provided a rationale for disregarding both personal moral misgivings and critical research commitments. (Alcadipani and Hodgson, 2009: 138)

That there are difficulties and dilemmas in applying ethical codes in fieldwork practice, however, does not mean that research ethics can, or should be, disregarded. Rather, as Bell and Wray-Bliss (2009) argue, ethical issues are pervasive in all forms of research and across the whole research process. Nor does ethical formalization absolve individual organizational researchers of responsibility for their relationships with research participants, the organizations they study, other researchers, institutions that support their research or the audiences who may read and apply it. Rather it may be an opportunity for reflection on these responsibilities.

EXERCISES

1
  - Identify four forms of evidence that might indicate that you had been successful in gaining the trust of organization members.
  - How might you assess how reliable this evidence is?

2
  - Identify the measures that you would take to minimize threats to the validity and reliability of what you are told by organization members.
  - What might you consider as evidence of the success of these measures?
  - What might be the limitations of this evidence?

3
  - Describe **three** arguments that might be made **in support of** Bronfenbrenner's claim that 'the only safe way to avoid violating principles of professional ethics is to refrain from doing social research altogether' (Bronfenbrenner, 1952: 453).
  - Describe **three** arguments that might be made **against** Bronfenbrenner's claim that 'the only safe way to avoid violating principles of professional ethics is to refrain from doing social research altogether' (Bronfenbrenner, 1952: 453).

Further reading

There is limited systematic discussion in the literature of the issues involved in 'getting on' in organizations, rather particular issues tend to be referred to in passing in accounts of organizational fieldwork. In addition to the sources cited in the chapter, the following include accounts that provide further insight on the conduct of fieldwork.

Delamont, S. (2002) *Fieldwork in Educational Settings: Methods, Pitfalls and Perspectives*, 2nd edn. London: Routledge.

Hargittai, E. (2009) *Research Confidential: Solutions to Problems most Social Scientists Pretend They Never Have*. Ann Arbor, MI: University of Michigan Press.

Hobbs, D. and May, T. (1993) *Interpreting the Field*. Oxford: Clarendon Press.

Hobbs, D. and Wright, R. (2006) *The SAGE Handbook of Fieldwork*. London: SAGE.

Robben, A.C.G.M. and Sluka, J.A. (2012) *Ethnographic Fieldwork: An Anthropological Reader*, 2nd edn. Malden, MA: Wiley–Blackwell.

Ethics in practice

deLaine, M. (2000) *Fieldwork, Participation and Practice: Ethics and Dilemmas in Qualitative Research*. London: SAGE.

Hammersley, M. and Traianou, A. (2012) *Ethics in Qualitative Research: Controversies and Contexts*. London: SAGE.

Wiles, R. (2013) *What Are Qualitative Research Ethics?* London: Bloomsbury Academic.

References

Abolafia, M.Y. (1998) 'Markets as cultures: an ethnographic approach', in M. Callon (ed.), *The Laws of the Markets*. Oxford: Blackwell, pp. 69–85.

Alcadipani, R. and Hodgson, D. (2009) 'By any means necessary? Ethnographic access, ethics and the critical researcher', *TAMARA: Journal of Critical Postmodern Organization Science*, 7 (3/4): 127–46.

Altinay, L. and Wang, C.L. (2009) 'Facilitating and maintaining research access into ethnic minority firms', *Qualitative Market Research: An International Journal*, 12 (4): 367–90.

Atkinson, P. (1997) *The Clinical Experience: The Construction and Reconstruction of Medical Reality*, 2nd edn. Aldershot: Ashgate.

Becker, H.S. (1967) 'Whose side are we on?', *Social Problems*, 14 (3): 239–47.

Becker, H.S. and Geer, B. (1957) 'Participant observation and interviewing: a comparison', *Human Organization*, 16 (3): 28–32.

Beech, N., Hibbert, P., MacIntosh, R. and McInnes, P. (2009) '"But I thought we were friends?" Life cycles and research relationships', in S. Ybema, D. Yanow, H. Wels and F. Kamsteeg (eds), *Organizational Ethnography: Studying the Complexities of Everyday Organizational Life*. London: SAGE, pp. 196–214.

Bell, E. and Bryman, A. (2007) 'The ethics of management research: an exploratory content analysis', *British Journal of Management*, 18 (1): 63.

Bell, E. and Wray Bliss, E. (2009) 'Research ethics: regulations and responsibilities', in D.A. Buchanan and A. Bryman (eds), *SAGE Handbook of Organizational Research Methods*. London: SAGE, pp. 78–92.

Blau, P.M. (1964) 'The research process in the study of the dynamics of bureaucracy', in P.E. Hammond (ed.), *Sociologists at Work*. New York: Basic Books, pp. 16–49.

Bogdan, R. and Taylor, S. (1975) *Introduction to Qualitative Research Methods: A Phenomenological Approach to the Social Sciences*. New York: Wiley.

Bone, J. (2006) '"The longest day": "flexible" contracts, performance-related pay and risk shifting in the UK direct selling sector', *Work, Employment and Society*, 20 (1): 109–27.

Bosk, C. (1996) 'The fieldworker and the surgeon', in C.D. Smith and W. Kornblum (eds), *In the Field: Readings on the Field Research Experience*. Westport, CT: Praeger, pp. 129–38.

Braithwaite, J. (1984) *Corporate Crime in the Pharmaceutical Industry*. London: Routledge and Kegan Paul.

Brannick, T. and Coghlan, D. (2007) 'In defense of being "native": the case for insider academic research', *Organizational Research Methods*, 10 (1): 59–74.

Bronfenbrenner, U. (1952) 'Principles of professional ethics: Cornell studies in social growth', *American Psychologist*, 7 (2): 452–5.

Bruni, A. (2006) 'Have you got a boyfriend or are you single? On the importance of being straight in organizational research', *Gender, Work and Organization*, 13 (3): 299–316.

Buchanan, D., Boddy, D. and McCalman, J. (1988) 'Getting in, getting on, getting out and getting back', in A. Bryman (ed.), *Doing Research in Organizations*. London: Routledge, pp. 53–67.

Bulmer, M. (1982) 'When is disguise justified? Alternatives to covert participant observation', *Qualitative Sociology*, 5 (4): 251–64.

Burawoy, M. (1979) *Manufacturing Consent: Changes in the Labor Process Under Monopoly Capitalism*. London: University of Chicago Press.

Burgess, R.G. (1985) 'The whole truth? Some ethical problems of research in a comprehensive school', in R.G. Burgess (ed.), *Field Methods in the Study of Education*. London: Falmer Press, pp. 139–62.

Burgess, R.G. (1991) 'Sponsors, gatekeepers, members, and friends: access in educational settings', in W. Shaffir and R.A. Stebbins (eds), *Experiencing Fieldwork: An Inside View of Qualitative Research*. Newbury Park, CA: SAGE, pp. 43–52.

Burr, J. and Reynolds, P. (2010) 'The wrong paradigm? Social research and the predicates of ethical scrutiny', *Research Ethics Review*, 6 (4): 128–33.

Carmel, S. (2011) 'Social access in the workplace: are ethnographers gossips?', *Work, Employment and Society*, 25 (3): 551–60.

Cassell, J. (1980) 'Ethical principles for conducting fieldwork', *American Anthropologist*, 82 (1): 28–41.

Charmaz, K. and Mitchell, R.G. (2001) 'Grounded theory in ethnography', in P. Atkinson, A. Coffey, S. Delamont, J. Lofland and L. Lofland (eds), *Handbook of Ethnography*. London: SAGE, pp. 160–74.

Clark, T. (2010) 'On "being researched": why do people engage with qualitative research?', *Qualitative Research*, 10 (4): 399–419.

Collinson, D. (1992) *Managing the Shopfloor: Subjectivity, Masculinity, and Workplace Culture*. Berlin: Walter de Gruyter.

Corrigan, O. (2003) 'Empty ethics: the problem with informed consent', *Sociology of Health & Illness*, 25(7): 768–92.

Costley, C., Elliott, G.C. and Gibbs, P. (2010) *Doing Work Based Research: Approaches to Enquiry for Insider-researchers*. London: SAGE.

Daniels, A.K. (1983) 'Self-deception and self-discovery in fieldwork', *Qualitative Sociology*, 6 (3): 195–214.

Delamont, S. (2004) 'Ethnography and participant observation' in C. Seale, G. Gobo, J.F. Gubrium and D. Silverman (eds), *Qualitative Research Practice*. London: SAGE, pp. 217–29.

Delbridge, R. (1998) *Life on the Line in Contemporary Manufacturing: The Workplace Experience of Lean Production and the 'Japanese' Model*. Oxford: Oxford University Press.

Douglas, J.D. (1976) *Investigative Social Research*. Beverly Hills, CA: SAGE.

Down, S., Garrety, K and Badham, R. (2006) 'Fear and loathing in the field: emotional dissonance and identity work in ethnographic research', *M@n@gement*, 9 (3): 95–115.

Duncombe, J. and Jessop, J. (2012) '"Doing rapport" and the ethics of "faking friendship"', in M. Mauthner, M. Birch, J. Jessop and T. Miller (eds), *Ethics in Qualitative Research*. London: SAGE, pp. 107–22.

Dundon, T. and Ryan, P. (2010) 'Interviewing reluctant respondents: strikes, henchmen, and Gaelic games', *Organizational Research Methods*, 13 (3): 562–81.

Easterday, L., Papademas, D., Schorr, L. and Valentine, C. (1977) 'The making of a female researcher: role problems in field work', *Urban Life*, 6 (3): 333–48.

Emerson, R.M., Fretz, R.I. and Shaw, L.L. (2011) *Writing Ethnographic Fieldnotes*. London: University of Chicago Press.

Epstein, D. (1998) 'Are you a girl or are you a teacher? The "least adult" role in research about gender and sexuality in a primary school', in G. Walford (ed.), *Doing Research About Education*. London: Falmer Press, pp. 27–41.

Erikson, K.T. (1967) 'A comment on disguised observation in sociology', *Social Problems*, 14 (4): 366–73.

Ferdinand, J., Pearson, G., Rowe, M and Worthington, F. (2007) 'A different kind of ethics', *Ethnography*, 8 (4): 519–43.

Fetterman, D.M. (1983) 'Guilty knowledge, dirty hands, and other ethical dilemmas: the hazards of contract research', *Human Organization*, 42 (3): 214–24.

Fielding, N. (2004) 'Working in hostile environments', in C. Seale, G. Gobo, J.F. Gubrium and D. Silverman (eds), *Qualitative Research Practice*. London: SAGE, pp. 248–60.

Fine, G.A. (1993) 'Ten lies of ethnography: moral dilemmas of field research', *Journal of Contemporary Ethnography*, 22 (3): 267.

Fine, G.A. (2009) *Kitchens: The Culture of Restaurant Work*. London: University of California Press.

Fine, G.A. and Shulman, D. (2009) 'Lies from the field: ethical issues in organizational ethnography', in S. Ybema, D. Yanow, H. Wels and F.H. Kamsteeg (eds), *Organizational Ethnography: Studying the Complexities of Everyday Life*. London: SAGE, pp. 177–95.

Froschauer, K. and Wong, L.L. (2012) 'Studying immigrant entrepreneurs: from ordinary to big players in the transnational capitalist class', in L.L.M. Aguiar and C.J. Schneider (eds), *Researching Amongst Elites: Challenges and Opportunities in Studying Up*. Farnham: Ashgate, pp. 150–78.

Gans, H.J. (1968) 'The participant observer as a human being: observations on the personal aspects of fieldwork', in H.S. Becker, B. Geer, D. Riesman and R.S. Weiss (eds), *Institutions and the Person*. Chicago, IL: Aldine Publishing Company, pp. 300–17.

Garton Ash, T. (2002) 'Truth is another country', *The Guardian*, 16 November, available at www.guardian.co.uk/books/2002/nov/16/fiction.society

Geer, B. (1964) 'First days in the field', in P.E. Hammond (ed.), *Sociologists at Work*. London: Basic Books, pp. 322–44.

Glesne, C. (1989) 'Rapport and friendship in ethnographic research', *International Journal of Qualitative Studies in Education*, 2 (1): 45–54.

Goffman, E. (1989) 'On fieldwork', *Journal of Contemporary Ethnography*, 18 (2): 123–32.

Goldman, E.F. and Swayze, S. (2012) 'In-depth interviewing with healthcare corporate elites: strategies for entry and engagement', *International Journal of Qualitative Methods*, 11 (3): 230–43.

Grugulis, I. (2011) *Research Ethics and James Bond*, available at www.social sciencespace.com/2011/01/research-ethics-and-james-bond/

Gurney, J.N. (1985) 'Not one of the guys: the female researcher in a male-dominated setting', *Qualitative Sociology*, 8 (1): 42–62.

Hammersley, M. and Atkinson, P. (2007) *Ethnography: Principles in Practice*. London: Routledge.

Hawkins, B. (2008) 'Double agents: gendered organizational culture, control and resistance', *Sociology*, 42 (3): 418–35.

Hutchinson, S.A., Wilson, M.E. and Wilson, H.S. (1994) 'Benefits of participating in research interviews', *Journal of Nursing Scholarship*, 26 (2): 161–6.

James, W. (1890) *Principles of Psychology*. London: Macmillan.

Johnson, J.M. (1975) *Doing Field Research*. New York: Free Press.

Kets de Vries, M.F.R. (1990) 'The organizational fool: balancing a leader's hubris', *Human Relations*, 43 (8): 751–70.

Kleinman, S. and Copp, M.A. (1993) *Emotions and Fieldwork*. Newbury Park, CA: SAGE.

Laverick, W. (2010) 'Accessing inside: ethical dilemmas and pragmatic compromises', in J. Scott Jones and S. Watt (eds), *Ethnography in Social Science Practice*. London: Routledge, pp. 73–88.

Leidner, R. (1993) *Fast Food, Fast Talk: Service Work and the Routinization of Everyday Life*. London: University of California Press.

Lofland, J. (1971) *Analyzing Social Settings: A Guide to Qualitative Observation and Analysis*. Belmont, CA: Wadsworth Publishing Co.

Lofland, J. and Lofland, L. (1995) *Analyzing Social Settings: A Guide to Qualitative Observation and Analysis*, 3rd edn. London: Wadsworth.

Marques, E.M. (2011) 'Instituting, de-instituting and under-instituting the complexities of production: struggles on the shop floor', *Social Anthropology*, 19 (4): 409–22.

Mazzei, J. and O'Brien, E.E. (2009) 'You got it, so when do you flaunt it? Building rapport, intersectionality, and the strategic deployment of gender in the field', *Journal of Contemporary Ethnography*, 38 (3): 358–83.

McCall, G.J. and Simmons, J.L. (1969) *Issues in Participant Observation: A Text and Reader*. Reading, MA: Addison-Wesley.

Measor, L. and Woods, P. (1991) 'Breakthroughs and blockages in ethnographic research: contrasting experiences during the "changing schools" project', in G. Walford (ed.), *Doing Educational Research*. London: Routledge, pp. 59–81.

Miller, S.M. (1952) 'The participant observer and "over-rapport"', *American Sociological Review*, 17 (1): 97–9.

Morrill, C. (1995) *The Executive Way*. London: University of Chicago Press.

Newby, H. (1977) 'In the field: reflections on the study of Suffolk farm workers', in C. Bell and H. Newby (eds), *Doing Sociological Research*. London: Allen and Unwin, pp. 108–29.

Olesen, V.L. and Whittaker, E.W. (1967) 'Role-making in participant observation: processes in the researcher–actor relationship', *Human Organization*, 26 (4): 273–81.

O'Neill, M. (2001) 'Participation or observation? Some practical and ethical dilemmas', in D. Gellner and E. Hirsch (eds), *Inside Organisations: Anthropologists at Work*. Oxford: Berg Publications, pp. 223–30.

Pacholok, S. (2012) 'Interviewing elite men: feminist reflections on studying "up" and selling out', in L.L.N. Aguiar and C.J. Schneider (eds), *Researching Amongst Elites: Challenges and Opportunities in Studying Up*. Farnham: Ashgate, pp. 199–215.

Parker, M. (2000) *Organizational Culture and Identity: Unity and Division at Work*. London: SAGE.

Parker, M. (2001) 'Stuck in GUM: an ethnography of a clap clinic', in D. Gellner and E. Hirsch (eds), *Inside Organizations: Anthropologists at Work*. Oxford: Berg, pp. 137–56.

Perlow, L.A. (1997) *Finding Time: How Corporations, Individuals and Families Can Benefit from New Work Practices*. Ithaca, NY: Cornell University Press.

Pettigrew, A.M. (1973) *The Politics of Organizational Decision-Making*. London: Tavistock.

Plankey-Videla, N. (2012) 'Informed consent as process: problematizing informed consent in organizational ethnographies', *Qualitative Sociology*, 35 (1): 1–21.

Price, R. and Townsend, K. (2009) 'Looking through the haze of discontent: smokers as a data source', in K. Townsend and J. Burgess (eds), *Method in the Madness: Research Stories You Won't Read in Textbooks*. Oxford: Chandos Publishing, pp. 83–93.

Punch, M. (1979) *Policing the Inner City: A Study of Amsterdam's Warmoesstraat*. London: Palgrave Macmillan.

Punch, M. (1986) *The Politics and Ethics of Fieldwork*. London: SAGE.

Punch, M. (1989) 'Researching police deviance: a personal encounter with the limitations and liabilities of field-work', *The British Journal of Sociology*, 40(2): 177–204.

Purdy, L. and Jones, R. (2013) 'Changing personas and evolving identities: the contestation and renegotiation of researcher roles in fieldwork', *Sport, Education and Society*, 18 (3): 292–310.

Ram, M. (1994) *Managing to Survive: Working Lives in Small Firms*. Oxford: Blackwell.

Randall, D., Harper, R. and Rouncefield, M. (2007) *Fieldwork for Design: Theory and Practice*. London: Springer.

Reeves, C.L. (2010) 'A difficult negotiation: fieldwork relations with gatekeepers', *Qualitative Research*, 10 (3): 315–31.

Rhodes, R.A.W. (2007) 'The everyday life of a minister: a confessional and impressionist tale', in R.A.W. Rhodes, P. 't Hart and M. Noordegraaf (eds), *Observing Government Elites: Up Close and Personal*. Basingstoke: Palgrave Macmillan, pp. 21–50.

Rod, M. (2011) 'Subjective personal introspection in action-oriented research', *Qualitative Research in Organizations and Management: An International Journal*, 6 (1): 6–25.

Roesch-Marsh, A., Gadda, A. and Smith, D. (20120 '"It's a tricky business!": the impact of identity work in negotiating research access', *Qualitative Social Work*, 11 (3): 249–65.

Roth, J.A. (1962) 'Comments on "Secret observation"', *Social Problems*, 9 (3): 283–4.

Ryan, S. (2009) '"On the mop-floor": researching employment relations in the hidden world of commercial cleaning', in K. Townsend and J. Burgess (eds), *Method in the Madness: Research Stories You Won't Read in Textbooks*. Oxford: Chandos Publishing, pp. 27–38.

Ryan, S. and Lewer, J. (2012) 'Getting in and finding out: accessing and interviewing elites in business and work contexts', in L.L.N. Aguiar and C.J. Schneider (eds), *Researching Amongst Elites: Challenges and Opportunities in Studying Up*. Farnham: Ashgate, pp.71–88.

Sandelowski, M. (2002) 'Reembodying qualitative inquiry', *Qualitative Health Research*, 12 (1): 104–15.

Stanfield, J.H. (1993) 'Methodological reflections: an introduction', in J.H. Stanfield and R.M. Dennis (eds), *Race and Ethnicity in Research Methods*. London: SAGE, pp. 3–15.

Stebbins, R.A. (1991) 'Do we ever leave the field? Notes on secondary fieldwork involvements', in W.B. Shaffir and R.A. Stebbins (eds), *Experiencing Fieldwork: An Inside View of Qualitative Research*. Newbury Park, CA: SAGE, pp.248–55.

Taylor, S.J. (1987) 'Observing abuse: professional ethics and personal morality in field research', *Qualitative Sociology*, 10 (3): 288–302.

Taylor, S.J. and Bogdan, R. (1998) *Introduction to Qualitative Research Methods: The Search for Meanings*, 3rd edn. Chichester: John Wiley and Sons.

't Hart, P. (2007) 'Spies at the crossroads: observing change in the Dutch Intelligence Service', in R.A.W. Rhodes, P. 't Hart and M. Noordegraaf (eds),

Observing Government Elites: Up Close and Personal. Basingstoke: Palgrave, pp. 51–77.

Thorne, B. (1980) '"You still takin' notes?" Fieldwork and problems of informed consent', *Social Problems*, 27 (3): 284–97.

Thorne, B. (1993) *Gender Play: Girls and Boys in School.* Buckingham: Open University Press.

Tietze, S. (2012) 'Researching your own organization', in G. Symon and C. Cassell (eds), *Qualitative Organizational Research: Core Methods and Current Challenges.* London: SAGE, pp. 53–71.

Van Maanen, J. (1991) 'Playing back the tape: early days in the field', in W.B. Shaffir and R.A. Stebbins (eds), *Experiencing Fieldwork: An Inside View of Qualitative Research.* Newbury Park, CA: SAGE, pp. 31–42.

Walford, G. (2001) *Doing Qualitative Educational Research: A Personal Guide to the Research Process.* London: Continuum International Publishing Group.

Warren, C.A.B. (2001) 'Gender and fieldwork relations', in R.M. Emerson (ed.), *Contemporary Field Research: Perspectives and Formulations.* Prospect Heights, IL: Waveland Press, pp. 203–23.

Watson, T.J. (2011) 'Ethnography, reality, and truth: the vital need for studies of "how things work" in organizations and management', *Journal of Management Studies*, 48 (1): 202–17.

Wax, R.H. (1952) 'Field methods and techniques: reciprocity as a field technique', *Human Organization*, 11 (3): 34–7.

Wax, R.H. (1971) *Doing Fieldwork: Warnings and Advice.* London: University of Chicago Press.

Welch, C., Marschan-Piekkari, R., Penntinen, H. and Tahvanainen, M. (2002) 'Corporate elites as informants in qualitative international business research', *International Business Review*, 11 (5): 611–28.

Wieland, S.M.B. (2010) 'Ideal selves as resources for the situated practice of identity', *Management Communication Quarterly*, 24 (4): 503–28.

Wiles, R., Crow, G., Heath, S. and Charles, V. (2008) 'The management of confidentiality and anonymity in social research', *International Journal of Social Research Methodology*, 11 (5): 417–28.

Wolcott, H.F. (1995) *The Art of Fieldwork.* London: SAGE.

Woods, P. (1986) *Inside Schools: Ethnography in Educational Research.* London: Routledge and Kegan Paul.

Ybema, S. and Kamsteeg, F. (2009) 'Making the familiar strange: a case for disengaged organizational ethnography', in S. Ybema, D. Yanow, H. Wels and D.H. Kamsteeg (eds), *Organizational Ethnography: Studying the Complexity of Everyday Life.* London: SAGE, pp. 101–19.

Zabusky, S.E. (1995) *Launching Europe: An Ethnography of European Cooperation in Space Science.* London: Princeton University Press.

7

Getting out: Leaving the Field and Reporting Research in Organizations

Chapter objectives

- to identify issues in bringing fieldwork in organizations to a close

  - when to go
  - premature termination
  - preparing for departure

- to identify issues in reporting organizational research

  - reporting back to the organization

    - types of report to the organization
    - ethics of reporting

  - a right to publish?
  - reporting to an academic audience

For some forms of organizational research involving fieldwork, such as administering an on-site questionnaire or undertaking one-off interviews, the process of leaving the field may be straightforward and unremarkable. The researcher thanks the respondent/interviewee for their time, explains what will be done with the findings and what form of report will be provided to them, says goodbye, checks in their visitor's pass at reception and walks out of the door (possibly never to return again). Other forms of organizational fieldwork, in contrast, especially those involving participant observation, but also extended and repeated interviews, can make 'getting out' of the research setting a more sensitive, protracted, and sometimes problematic, process (Brannen and Oultram, 2012).

As Snow (1980) observed, however, it is a process that has been relatively neglected in the literature and, Iversen (2009) suggests, continues to be so. Matters are exacerbated, Morrison et al. (2012) suggest, by the proliferation of terminology to describe this stage of the research process, including 'getting out', 'leaving the field', 'disengagement', 'closure', 'ending', 'good-bye' and 'exit'. This has led to considerable variation in researchers' views of its scope and implications, while also obscuring the commonalities between studies.

A major source of the complexities in drawing intensive fieldwork to a close arise from the relationships and commitments developed during the course of the field-work that make it hard for the researcher to simply walk away from the setting (Ortiz, 2004). In participant observation studies in particular, but also in longitudinal interview studies, having devoted considerable time and effort to developing rapport with organization members, awareness of the researcher's impending disengagement from the setting is likely to lead to a profound change in their status.

Thus, Janes (1961) discussing participant-observation studies of communities such as his own study of 'Riverville', a small mid-Western town in the lower Ohio valley, identifies the role of the researcher as passing through a number of phases over the course of the fieldwork (see Table 7.1).

In the first instance, Janes argues, the researcher is a newcomer, and their initial interactions with community (or organization) members will be focused on assessing their potential compatibility (What sort of person is the researcher? How do they fit in?). As the researcher becomes involved in the setting, participating in activities, they are provisionally assigned to some category of community membership. As Pettigrew (1973: 59) writes of his initial experiences: 'I became identified as an intellectual and found it difficult to reach informants in the footballer section.' This assignment is likely to be maintained so long as the researcher's behaviour remains consistent with it. As organization members get to know the researcher better, the understanding of their role may become more personalized – not just 'an intellectual', but an intellectual with particular interests and character. At some point in the study, however, awareness of the finite duration of the researcher's engagement with the setting will, perhaps unintentionally, be triggered and their status 'literally overnight' (Janes, 1961: 449) becomes that of the 'imminent migrant'.

Table 7.1   Phases of the participant-observer role (Janes, 1961)

Role
Newcomer
Provisional member
Categorical member
Personalized member
Imminent migrant

Given that this final role is likely to be inimical to continuing research, because the researcher, like an employee serving their notice, will be considered as already on their way out and no longer a full member of the community, it is in their interests to try to manage the onset of this phase. How, then, can this be done, and when is the best time? Although in some senses it is impossible to give definitive answers to these questions, as they will depend on the particular circumstances of the research setting, some general guidance may still be offered.

The first consideration in managing departure from the field can be seen as whether to set a deadline or not. As Iversen (2009: 13), observes, professional practice in some disciplines, such as social work, may include 'definitive ending practices which are based on boundaries and endpoints that are specified from the onset of research contact, frequent reminders of the timetable during fieldwork, and referrals, if needed, upon disengagement', that may be drawn on by researchers. In other disciplines, however, perhaps with less direct linkage to a particular profession, there may be no such practices to guide their withdrawal from the field.

In such circumstances researchers may be tempted to avoid the time pressures associated with having a deadline for the completion of fieldwork and may also see this as an opportunity to trace phenomena as they happen at their own pace, rather than to be driven by an external timetable. This means, however, that there may be no clear cut-off point for the researcher's engagement with the organization, which can create uncertainty for organization members about the researcher's status and risks the researcher outstaying their welcome (Iversen, 2009; Morrison et al., 2012).

A fixed deadline while providing clarity, however, may mean that some activities that a researcher had planned to study may not have taken place, or processes may not have been completed. Since it is often difficult to judge in advance when events will happen or how long a process may take (especially as organizations may have a tendency to be over-optimistic about their targets) there is therefore a risk that the deadline may prevent significant phenomena from being observed. If field relations are good, however, some flexibility is often possible, or the researcher may be allowed to return at a later time to collect more data. On balance, it is usually suggested that it is better to set a deadline (Morrison et al., 2012) and this may, in any case, be imposed by constraints on funding, requirements to submit end-of-grant reports to funding bodies, or the researcher's travel arrangements or other commitments (Buchanan et al., 1988; Iversen, 2009).

In some cases, as was suggested in Chapter 5 in relation to access negotiations, the expected duration of fieldwork may be written into the initial 'bargain' struck with the organization. Any extension will therefore need to be by special request, rather than assumed as of right. As with an interview therefore, if, when approaching the end of the agreed period, it is evident that more time is likely to be needed to complete the research as planned, the researcher will need to broach the possibility of the fieldwork being extended. Such negotiations will need to be opened in sufficient time before the original deadline, so that the researcher does not appear to be forcing the organization's hand. The duration of initial access negotiations may be used to indicate a suitable timescale for the submission of such a request (although it might be hoped that the researcher's insider status would allow matters to proceed rather more swiftly than an initial access request).

An extension request should include an explanation of the reasons for the failure to meet the original deadline and clearly it is desirable that this should be shown to be due to circumstances beyond the researcher's control, rather than their lack of diligence. Moreover, rather than requesting an indefinite extension until some particular activity is completed it may be better to propose a modest extension and to make plans for how the research will proceed if the activity has not finished. In summary, it is better (and more likely to be acceptable to the organization) if the research retains a clear cut-off point.

When to go

One answer to the question of when to go, is 'not too soon'. Different authors, however, have different views on the minimum period necessary for observational fieldwork. The 'quick and dirty' ethnography of Hughes et al. (1994), for example, involves periods of perhaps a few weeks in the field, albeit perhaps repeated over several iterations, although this may be justified by its focus on delivering specific insights for design. For more conventional observational fieldwork Taylor and Bogdan (1998) recommend that researchers should spend at least several months in a setting, although in Taylor (1991: 243) the same author states that 'a year seems like the minimum amount of time to collect data'. Goffman (1989: 130) argues similarly that 'you should spend at least a year in the field. Otherwise you don't get the random sample, you don't get a range of unexpected events, you don't get deep familiarity.'

Without an initial agreement on how long the study will last or any immediate pressure for the research to be completed, there can be the potential for drift. Despite the claim of Denzin (1970: 256) that the fieldworker 'must be prepared to leave the field at the proper time and must have a theoretical grasp of the data so that the exit time is easily discernible', things may not always be so obvious in practice (Snow, 1980). In any organizational research setting at any particular time there is always likely to be something more of interest that could possibly be observed so it can be difficult to draw a clear line. Kleinmann and Copp (1993) and Ortiz (2004), for example, talk of 'compulsive data collection', while Wax (1971: 45) suggests that the urge to gather more data can be 'almost irresistible' (especially if the alternative is the 'grim task of organising and reporting on the data').

Even if the researcher plans for the fieldwork to end when enough data have been collected, it can be hard to judge when this has happened. Should it be a certain number of interviews, for example, or as many interviews as necessary until certain issues have been addressed? In the latter case, moreover, it may not be possible to know whether these are sufficient until analysis takes place, possibly after the fieldwork has been completed.

One of the things that can make it hard for the researcher to decide to end fieldwork may be a sense that they have failed to get behind the scenes and have been observing a somehow atypical picture of organizational life. As Feldman (1989: 31) observes, however, 'it is possible that there is no such thing as a normal time' (in some types of organization at least) and the desire to see how things 'normally' go on may be continually frustrated.

If, therefore, as Randall et al. (2007) argue, there are 'no self-evident completeness rules' for fieldwork, it may nevertheless be possible to identify some indicators by which the researcher can judge whether their fieldwork may be nearing its close. Randall et al. (2007) propose two such rules of thumb: the flattening of the learning curve and knowing what you haven't seen, while Snow (1980), identifies taken-for-grantedness, theoretical saturation and heightened confidence.

Premature termination

If the researcher considers that they have a clear, and agreed, deadline by which they will leave the field, this does not mean that fieldwork may not be terminated before then. Often this will be due to circumstances beyond the researcher's control, such as changes in the organization that make the continuation of the research untenable. While organizations, particularly large ones, when viewed from the outside tend to appear stable, this can mask surprisingly rapid and frequent internal change: an administrative restructuring, for example, can eliminate the research setting as divisions are sold off, departments closed down or functions outsourced; sponsors may be promoted, moved, or leave the organization; the organization itself may be bought out or closed down. Although it is not impossible for the research bargain to survive such upheavals, they are likely, at least, to cause considerable disruption and delay to the research timetable. More often, however, the bargain may not be recognized by the new 'powers that be' and the researcher may find themselves having to renegotiate access from scratch (assuming that they are even given that opportunity).

Another threat to the continuation of fieldwork may arise when research gets caught in organizational politics. Sometimes this may occur because the researcher becomes aligned with a particular faction in a turf war and making things difficult for the researcher may be a relatively easy way for the opposing faction to get at the researcher's associates without threatening them directly. In other cases the researcher, despite their attempts to be neutral, may simply be collateral damage as support for research becomes subordinated to organizational power struggles.

If there may be little that the researcher can do to prevent such problems, other, perhaps, than to ensure that their relationship with organizational members is as good as possible so that they are not abandoned at the first sign of trouble (although this may itself bring dangers of, perhaps inadvertent, alignment in organizational politics) researchers may sometimes bring the problems upon themselves. This may come about through acts of commission, such as breaches of confidentiality (perhaps in circumstances in which the researcher was unaware that it would get back to the organization) or misbehaviour. Walford (2001), for example, describes his 'dis invitation' from a right wing educational policy discussion group after having voiced opinions that were critical of the group's stance. It may also come about through acts of omission, for example where organization members find out that the aim of the research is not quite what they understood it to be (perhaps because this would have affected their behaviour in ways that would have made it difficult to observe the phenomenon of interest), or that the researcher had presented themselves differently to different people in order to develop better rapport with them. Johnson (1975: 98), for example, reports a delicate moment in his fieldwork in which one of the social workers, who he got on particularly well with, confronted him with statements he had made to other social workers that indicated that his politics were the opposite of those he had presented to the trusted intimate. Although Johnson was able to explain the discrepancy in terms of his efforts to gain a rounded picture of the social workers' views, not just of those with whom he was politically sympathetic (a response that surprised the intimate who had not expected an 'academic pussy' to be so shrewd), he was aware that the incident could have escalated into a fieldwork crisis.

The rhythm of fieldwork

Although it is possible, and may be administratively convenient, to set the end of the fieldwork by a particular calendar date, a number of studies describe research projects as following a particular rhythm that may, or may not, fit the deadlines set. Randall et al. (2007), for example, characterize this in terms of the following statements representing the researcher's responses at each stage of the project:

1. 'Everything's really interesting. I don't think I'll ever understand this.'
2. 'Ah . . . right.'
3. 'This is really boring.'
4. 'I've not seen that before.'

Thus, in the initial stage the researcher struggles to make sense of the flood of new experiences they encounter. In time they begin to discern some patterns, that in due course become wearily familiar. Interest may subsequently be reignited if exceptions to these patterns are detected.

Parker (2000: 239) describes a similar trajectory of responses to the first three of Randall et al. (2007).

> The intensity of the first few visits was tiring. I had immersed myself in a mass of largely incoherent impressions and saw no way of ordering the huge quantity of ideas I had generated. Later visits were less exhausting, I assume because I was beginning to develop a framework to catalogue and classify my ideas. Feelings of exhilaration were then more common, especially when I had observed something that seemed to confirm an idea or make a half-conscious connection explicit. Towards the end of each of the cases boredom was a more common emotion – interviews and observations simply repeated things that I already felt I knew but had to pretend to be interested in despite the fact I had heard them many times before.

Taylor (1991: 243) also cites boredom as a 'personal barometer' by which the approach of the end of a study may be judged – 'When I begin to lose the excitement of fieldwork and find most of my observer's comments relate to confirming themes and hunches, I begin to think seriously about wrapping up.' Although the validity of a researcher's boredom as a reliable measure of research completion may seem debatable, therefore, it may be an indicator of some form of empirical saturation, and a sign that planning for withdrawal from the field should commence.

Preparing to go

Lofland and Lofland (1995: 63) suggest that the etiquette of leaving the field is not unlike that in everyday life:

- inform people of your plans ahead of time and try to avoid leaving or appearing to leave abruptly
- explain why and where you are going
- say your goodbyes personally
- promise to keep in touch
- where appropriate, keep in touch.

That there may have been an initial agreement that the research would end on a particular date does not mean that organization members will necessarily have been informed of this or that they will remember that they were. The researcher's announcement of their departure may therefore come out of the blue for some people and careful groundwork may be necessary to ensure that they do not feel let down by the researcher (Iversen, 2009; Morrison et al., 2012). For example an organization member may have assumed the researcher's participation in the completion of some activity beyond the planned end date of the study. Even without expectations or commitments, however, organization members may experience feelings of resentment and betrayal as the contingent and temporary nature of their relationship with the researcher is exposed. 'Thanks for using me, asshole', was the reaction of one participant reported by Morrison et al. (2012: 418), when asked 'how would you feel if the researcher was gone today'. Similarly the title of Beech et al.'s discussion of the relationship between engaged researchers and practitioners is 'but I thought we were friends' (Beech et al., 2009: 196). Managing expectations and reactions and balancing the reasonable forewarning of organization members against the restrictions on research that being perceived as an 'imminent migrant' (Janes, 1961) may bring, can thus be a delicate task.

Once it is known that the researcher will be leaving they are likely to enter into a new mode of work focused on smoothing their exit from the research setting. This may involve a range of practical tasks, such as completion of agreed work assignments, arranging final interviews and administrative housekeeping (for example returning keys and equipment), but also valedictory social occasions – leaving meals or parties, and farewell meetings with key informants, gatekeepers and friends in the research setting (Morrison et al., 2012). Whether as Evans-Pritchard (1973) claims 'an anthropologist has failed unless, when he says goodbye to the natives, there is on both sides the sorrow of parting', or, like Reeves (2010), the researcher was grateful for an excuse to end her fieldwork early as she had 'started to feel "trapped" in the [research setting]; only undertaking the fieldwork out of a sense of duty and habit', or like Punch (1989) they reach a state of fatigue and disillusionment with their research, departure from the field can be an emotional experience.

Fulfilling the bargain

The choice of how and when to leave the field may not be solely at the researcher's discretion, as they may be under an explicit or implicit commitment to fulfil the terms of the 'bargain' (or sometimes bargains) agreed in gaining access to the research setting. Some of these commitments, such as making a presentation of (initial) findings, may need to be carried out before departure from the field and can add to the stress of 'getting out'. It may also take longer to complete agreed tasks than initially expected, so it may be helpful to allow for some over-run when scheduling the departure date if this cannot be easily altered. It is likely to be better to have a few days spare at the end of fieldwork than to be working to the last minute or to have to reschedule travel arrangements.

Other commitments, such as the production of transcripts or reports, may extend beyond the completion of fieldwork and it can prove difficult, once away from the setting, to maintain the momentum of research, especially if returning to a work context with its own demands and pressures (O'Hare, 2009). While it may be hard once away from the field to ensure that dead-lines do not slip, therefore, it is important to ensure that as far as possible, deliverables are supplied as agreed, and that organization members are kept informed of reasons for any delay. This may apply not just to observational fieldwork, but also to more distant research methods, such as surveys or interviews, where some report of findings is offered as an incentive for participation.

Once the researcher has gathered their data and has left the field, however, the pressures to fulfil the bargain are largely moral, as, unless there was some contractual agreement between the researcher and the organization, the organ-ization has little direct recourse against a researcher who fails to deliver. In practice, moreover, the pace of change in many organizations can mean that the organization members who were party to the original bargain may not be in the same position at the end of the study. Thus Leidner (1993: 236) reports

> [The manager] gave me permission to go ahead with the interviews on the condi-tion that he would have the opportunity to respond to transcripts of the interviews from which all identifying details had been removed and to read my writing before publication. As it happened, by the time I completed the interviewing and tran-scription the manager had been transferred to another part of the company and no one else in the office expressed interest when I offered to send the interview transcripts.

Other authors (e.g. Collinson, 1992; Parker, 2000) note a similar loss of interest in the outcome of research when key gatekeepers moved on.

That there may be no evident demand from the organization for the bargain to be fulfilled, and the consequences of non-compliance may be negligible, does not absolve the researcher of their responsibilities. Even if there is little or no personal cost to a 'cut and run' researcher who takes what they want from the field, but does not give even what they have agreed (whether formally or infor-mally) to supply in return, their behaviour may have consequences for future research. One area in which such commitments may be significant is in the reporting of research.

Reporting research in organizations

Writing up of research is not necessarily a discrete activity that occurs only once fieldwork is complete. Rather, especially in an extended study, writing up may run in parallel with data collection. It may be argued, moreover, that, in some ways, the writing of fieldnotes is already a form of writing up (Emerson et al., 2007), since they will involve decisions about how and what to record. It may be unwise, however, to place too much emphasis on this conception of fieldnotes lest it make the researcher too self-conscious. As Lofland and Lofland (1995: 95) argue, fieldnotes are personal documents that should 'flow' and not be inhibited by considerations of style or their reception by others. As a consequence, Emerson et al. (2007: 356) note, 'most fieldnote accounts are literally incomprehensible to others ... [and] most fieldnote entries often have an opaque, idiosyncratic and reader-unfriendly quality'.

Even if fieldnotes can be considered a form of writing up of research, however, then they are still a long way from the sorts of final outputs, such as reports to the organization(s) studied, academic dissertations, academic journal articles, research monographs, newspaper, magazine and trade press articles, that are the typical objectives of organizational research. Just as with interview transcripts or quantitative data, some process of analysis will necessarily intervene between fieldnotes and final reports, if only to condense them to a length suitable for the chosen form of reporting.

The techniques for the analysis of the sorts of qualitative data, such as coding, memoing and diagramming, or statistical methods for quantitative data are already well covered in research methods textbooks collectively, if not always comprehensively in most individual textbooks (as discussed in Chapter 3). Similarly, a number of methods textbooks, e.g. Lofland and Lofland (1995) and Taylor and Bogdan (1998) offer advice on academic writing, covering topics such as how to get started, how to structure writing and how to get finished (additional specialist texts on writing are listed in the further reading at the end of this chapter). Although not always consistent in their advice, for example on the desirability, or otherwise, of careful preparation of first drafts, they nevertheless offer practical recommendations, some of which, at least, are likely to be helpful to novice authors of research reports.

What these books generally lack, however, is much discussion of the practical issues of reporting of research outputs to the organization being studied, or the particular issues that may be encountered in the wider reporting of research in organizations. These topics will therefore be the main focus of this chapter.

Reporting back to the organization

Although researchers may report back to communities or informal social groups on the fieldwork they have undertaken, there is likely to be a greater expectation on researchers studying organizations that they will provide some form of report to the organization itself, perhaps prior, and in addition to, any publication for a wider audience. There may be a number of reasons for this. Thus, access to organizations is more likely to be formally negotiated than access to less well-defined social groups and the organization may insist on a right of approval of findings as a condition of access. Part of the bargain offered in exchange for access may also be to provide a report of the findings to the organization (Crabtree et al., 2012). Indeed, Buchanan et al. (1988: 65) specifically recommend this, both as a way of improving the odds of access being granted, as was discussed in Chapter 5, but also because such reports are 'valuable, because they are useful to both the researcher and the respondent [to the extent that] they are seen to be adequate, appropriate, competent accounts of the organization, from the point of view of the respondents'.

Compared with other groups, the formal structuring of organizations also means that particular individuals or roles (typically senior management, but sometimes also public relations or legal departments) are likely to be assigned responsibility for receipt and approval of reports. For the researcher this can be an advantage as it is clear to whom the report should be submitted and who is able to speak on behalf of the organization in granting (or refusing) permission for the further use of research findings. It can also mean, however, that the approval process is slower, more bureaucratic and more likely to be influenced by interests beyond those of immediate research participants (such as concerns for the broader reputation of the organization).

Similarly, in contrast to traditional ethnographies in which, historically at least, it tended to be assumed that their 'subjects' would neither be able to understand nor be interested in what was written about them, organizations are likely to be aware of, and concerned about, how they are represented publicly. They may therefore expect to be given the opportunity to vet research outputs before these are disseminated more widely and may have the resources to be able to take action if they are unhappy with what is reported about them. Such efforts to control reporting may be legally enforceable where confidentiality/non-disclosure agreements are in place and, in the UK, may be backed by the threat of libel action.

Even if the researcher is not obliged to report back to the organization, however, they may still wish to do so in recognition of the access and assistance they have received. This commitment may particularly be felt to apply to those directly involved in the research, but who may not be officially designated as recipients of reports, such as interviewees, or those observed, especially where these have low status in the organization. It may also be considered appropriate to report back to those responsible for the research being able to be conducted, such as sponsor(s) and gatekeeper(s).

Researchers may also choose voluntarily to share their research outputs with organization members not directly involved in research. For example, they may wish to influence organizational practices in the light of their findings and may therefore target their reports to relevant constituencies in the organization, such as the managers of those involved in the research or senior management. Alternatively, they may wish to inform the wider organization about their work (perhaps as a prelude to attempts to pursue further studies in the same organization) or to give publicity to the achievements of those they have studied.

Reporting back to those involved in the research, or responsible for it, typically has several aims: to check the accuracy of reports (and to get them corrected if necessary), to show and acknowledge the organization members' contribution; to demonstrate the transparency of the research process; and to obtain the organization members' consent to the use of these outputs in wider reporting of the research. With respect to reporting to wider audiences it is desirable (from the researcher's perspective, but also in terms of the demands on the time of organization members) if this approval is granted for all uses of the particular research output, so once a transcript or case description has been approved there is no need to gain permission for subsequent uses of these data. In some situations, however, the organization may seek to retain control over every report, requiring each output (such as a revised case description, or new paper) from the research to be independently approved. It is also possible that, as with requests for access (Chapter 5), approval of the use of research outputs may be escalated to senior organization levels, or PR and/or legal departments may become involved. Again, this is rarely a good sign and may lead to highly drawn out negotiations that tend to start with a presumption against approval, with the researcher having to prove that the proposed use of the outputs will not cause the organization any harm.

In vetting research outputs, the organization is likely to have a number of concerns. Perhaps the most obvious of these is the accuracy of data. This may have a number of aspects. The first is that the account offered in research reports corresponds closely, if not exactly, to data that the researcher has collected. It may therefore be advisable not to 'tidy up' transcripts or quotations that need to be approved too much, even at the cost of comprehensibility. Simply showing that fieldnotes or interview transcripts contain the relevant data, however, may be insufficient to refute accusations of inaccuracy, since the argument may be that the data themselves are not an accurate portrayal of the organization – because they predominantly reflect the views or behaviours of certain groups or individuals, for example (who may perhaps be considered as occupying a marginal position in the organization), because they are a snapshot of a particular point in time, or are otherwise 'unrepresentative'. It may also be argued that the data simply cannot be accurate since they run counter to what the person approving the report knows to be true. Reports may therefore be criticized for being partial, in both senses of the word, i.e. incomplete and biased.

An organization may still have concerns about a research report even if it is accurate, for example if it contains information that is considered commercially confidential. If the research touches on matters that are seen to relate to products or processes that are critical to the organization's current or future competitiveness they may be remarkably sensitive to any disclosure, however obscure the reference or the publication venue. Organizations are also often, perhaps not surprisingly, sensitive to anything that could be seen to present them, or (particularly senior) organization members, in a bad light. While this may be understandable where the 'revelations' might make the organization or members of it subject to legal action, or significantly affect its reputation, organizations may also be concerned even when what is described is neither especially serious nor exceptional, but simply runs counter to what the organization would like to believe about itself. Things may be yet more difficult if the organization does not even acknowledge such problems exist. Thus, as Becker (1964: 275) comments:

> Unless the scientist deliberately restricts himself to research on the ideologies and beliefs of the people studied and does not touch on the behavior of the members of the community or organization, he must in some way deal with the disparity between reality and ideal, with the discrepancy between the number of crimes committed and the number of criminals apprehended. A study that purports to deal with social structure thus inevitably will reveal that the organization or community is not all it claims to be, not all it would like to be able to feel itself to be. A good study, therefore, will make somebody angry.

While for researchers studying communities (e.g. Ellis, 1995) or informal social groups, such as an outlaw motorcycle club (Wolf, 1991), this anger may be forcefully (and perhaps threateningly) expressed if the researcher re-establishes contact with the research participants after having left the field, researchers studying more formal organizations may be called to account (especially where the provision of a report or presentation has been offered as part of the access negotiations). Parker (2000: 238), for example, reports a two-hour meeting in which three directors of a company denied the accuracy of his findings 'with a ferocity that was both humiliating and very revealing'.

Types of report to the organization

Whether researchers report back to the organization as a condition of access having been granted, because they feel an obligation to do so, or because they believe their reports can make a positive contribution to the organization, as Table 7.2 shows, there can be considerable variation in what is reported. Broadly speaking it is possible to distinguish three types of potential report to the organization. At one end of the spectrum is source data, such as interview transcripts or a summary of fieldnotes (the original field-notes, which, as was noted in Chapter 6, might run to hundreds or even thousands of pages and potentially include personal commentary, would seem too much to be reasonably reviewed, but might be made available on request). In the middle would be partially processed data, such as analytic themes from a qualitative data analysis, or a summary case description, which might be expected to be more easily comprehensible than source data, but does not offer any overt interpretation of the findings. At the other end of the spectrum would be some form of final output, providing a commentary on the analysis, or even, in an action research or consultancy study, specific actionable recommendations arising from the findings. In some circumstance the organization might also be provided with full drafts of academic articles or book manuscripts for approval.

Moving across this spectrum involves a shift in the relationship between the researcher and the organization with respect to the research outputs. Where source data are shared, the researcher is likely to be looking to the organization primarily for confirmation of the accuracy of transcripts, notes or observation, and for approval of the use of these outputs in data analysis and their dissemination (in whole, or in part) in publications for external audiences. Although researchers may encounter some problems when seeking approval of transcripts or notes, especially if organization members have been discussing sensitive matters and wish to 'correct' what they may have said in the heat of the interview, more often researchers report this as a valuable opportunity for reflection by organization members on their understandings (which may lead to new insights), but also for the researcher on what was said and their original understanding of it.

Table 7.2 Types of output that may be shared with the organization

Type of output	Examples
Source data	Interview transcripts or notes
	Summary of fieldnotes
	Collated survey responses
Outputs from data analysis	Analytic themes – proposed topics to be developed in publications
	Key findings – a summary of notable (statistically significant/frequently mentioned/strongly endorsed/unexpected) findings
	'Case description' – a narrative summary of the data
Final outputs	Report to the organization
	Recommendations
	Drafts of publications for other audiences

Where only source data are shared it is assumed that the analysis of the data made by the researcher is not something in which the organization need have a say. If the data are accepted as an accurate record and the organization is happy for them to be used in publications, then the researcher is free to conduct any analysis they see fit and to advance any claims on the basis of this analysis that they consider the data are able to sustain, even if the organization might disagree with the claims. Provided that they follow valid procedures and can show that their claims are supported by the data then the conclusions are solely the responsibility of the researcher, however unflattering they may be to the organization. Such a position may be advanced by critical management scholars who seek to question dominant managerial discourses (cf. Alvesson and Deetz, 2000), but may also be advocated on the principle of academic autonomy (Newson and Polster, 2001).

Sharing interim outputs such as analytic themes and case descriptions potentially gives the organization more influence over how findings are presented, as approval is now being sought for the researcher's preliminary interpretations of the data as well as the data themselves. Although, in practice, these interim outputs may be distinguished from source data more by their brevity than by the extent to which they reveal the researcher's analytical stance, the fact that they are more readily comprehensible and may indicate the general direction, if not the endpoint, of the researcher's analysis may make them subject to greater scrutiny by the organization. The organization member faced with a few pages of relatively coherent summary may be more inclined to give them their detailed attention than if they receive dozens of pages of verbatim transcript.

Presenting the organization with a report, recommendations or draft publications, assuming that this is not just a matter of courtesy and that the organization has some actual power of veto over the wider dissemination of outputs, means that the organization can control not just what data are used, but the conclusions drawn from them. In itself, this could be considered to be simply the consistent application of the ethical principles of beneficence and reciprocity (Bell and Bryman, 2007). As authors such as Bell and Wray-Bliss (2009) argue, however, who benefits and who may be harmed by sharing of outputs from research in organizations may not be straightforward, nor, as Ferdinand et al. (2007), suggest may the principle of reciprocity be unproblematic. Benefits for some groups in the organization may harm others, nor can it be assumed that relationships between the organization and the researcher are always collaborative and based on mutual trust. As will be discussed in more detail below, organizations may have the power to suppress research reports that they consider to be counter to their interests, however carefully the researcher has abided by ethical principles.

The ethics of reporting

A particular challenge in reporting most types of output back to the organization is that of ensuring confidentiality. Those working in an organization are
likely to have a good idea of who was involved in the study and may therefore
be able to identify which particular individuals said or did something. Even
if it may not be evident, or even of interest, to anybody outside the organization, individuals' verbal mannerisms and biographies may be sufficiently
distinctive that organizational insiders will be able to work out who they are.
Tolich (2004) proposes that researchers therefore need to be sensitive to what
he terms as this 'internal confidentiality' with respect to organizational insiders, as much as to traditional 'external confidentiality' with respect to organizational outsiders.

It is therefore important before outputs are shared, even with others in the
same organization, to get the research participant's consent to this. While this
may seem straightforward (send them a transcript and get them to indicate
their consent), as Irvine (2003) describes there may be considerable difficulty
in achieving and maintaining confidentiality in practice. This can sometimes be
addressed in the process of data collection, for example by seeking the verbal
agreement of the research participant (at the start and/or end of an interview
or period of observation) to the use of the data, perhaps with an explanation of
how it may be used and the measures that will be employed to maintain confidentiality. Interviewees may also be offered the chance to indicate, during the
course of an interview, if anything they say should be considered 'off the
record', with recording or note-taking being suspended. This cannot guarantee,
of course, that individuals may not say things that they subsequently would not
wish to be shared. As Lofland (1971: 108) observes, 'it happens that participants everywhere do and say things they would prefer to forget or prefer not
to have known, or at least widely known'. It may therefore also be considered
necessary to seek more formal, preferably written, approval of interview transcripts or observation summaries.

From the researcher's perspective, however much they may respect the
autonomy of participants and believe in the principle of informed consent,
seeking such approval is likely to be in the hope that it will be granted, as any
refusal of permission necessarily narrows the data corpus and may make it
hard, or impossible, to substantiate certain claims. A refusal of permission is
therefore likely to be the prelude to extensive negotiations to see if it is possible
to devise a way of using sensitive data, such that it does not cause problems for
the participant(s).

The usual advice in such situations is to employ pseudonyms to disguise
individual's identities, although it should be recognized that this can never be
entirely foolproof (Burgess, 1984). As Daniels (1983: 208) reports, for example:

> I can remember once explaining a theory I had about military psychiatrists where I used metaphors to describe social types of professionals I had encountered … But the disguises I used were too thin and a young resident, knowing where my studies were conducted, [recognized the individuals involved].

Further disguise may be achieved by changing distinguishing attributes, such as gender, of the participants, although this may have the effect of distorting or concealing other potential findings. Thus Bosk (1979) changed the gender of the one surgical resident he was studying who was regarded as a complete failure, because, as the only woman, she would have been immediately identifiable. In doing so, however, he precluded discussion of gender issues in surgical training.

There may be some situations, though, such as where malpractice or criminal behaviour is identified, in which no amount of negotiation or anonymization is likely to succeed in persuading research participants to approve reporting of interviews or observations. As this sort of behaviour is unlikely to be disclosed in an audio recorded interview, moreover, there is unlikely to be any independent evidence to corroborate the researcher's notes, making it impossible to prove their accuracy in the face of an organization member's subsequent denial of such practices. For this reason, Braithwaite (1985) recommends the use of two interviewers in corporate crime research, although it is unclear that this necessarily solves the problem if the organization persists in its denials and has the resources to challenge the researchers' account. Two people's word against one may seem more persuasive, and provide some correction for individual bias, but would seem open to the same refutation as a single researcher's account. This does not mean that, as the White House Tapes and the email evidence presented to the Leveson Inquiry into Press Ethics in the UK illustrate, an independent record of illicit practices does not necessarily exist, but it would seem unlikely to be within the resources of most researchers to gain access to them. Suppression of contested evidence would therefore seem likely to prevail.

Organization members need not be doing anything illicit for them to be concerned about their practices or views being disclosed in a way that would allow them to be identified. It may be enough that they do not endorse dominant organizational discourses with sufficient enthusiasm or engage in practices that are disapproved. Nor is it even necessary that individuals are identifiable for organization members to be worried that reports to the organization may have negative consequences for them. As Alcadipani and Hodgson (2009: 139) observe:

> providing feedback to managers … is driven by a clear instrumental rationality assumption and is underlined by the idea of providing information primarily to improve company productivity. Moreover, such feedback sessions may create harm to people working for the company where problems relate to particular individuals, or where the feedback reveals gaps in management control regimes. Thus

this process runs the risk of disclosing information that would not otherwise be available to senior managers and enabling them to tighten control and increase application of punishment mechanisms.

In organizations characterized by high levels of conflict and mistrust it can therefore be quite a challenge to obtain agreement to the use of research outputs.

Individual organization members' concerns about being identified in research reports also reflect a broader ethical tension in reporting organizational research, regarding who the researcher should be considered to be responsible to. Is it the organization or the individual participants? While the answer may be influenced by whether the research is considered to have been conducted in, with or for the organization (as discussed in Chapter 2), whether or not the organization has commissioned (and perhaps paid for) the research, the researcher could still be considered to have a duty to avoid harm to individual participants and to respect any commitments made to them in gaining their consent to participate in the study. On the other hand, it could be considered that the researcher has a duty to the organization to report any findings to it that might be a cause of potential harm. As with the dilemma of whether to report bullying, discussed in Chapter 6, the researcher may find themselves torn between competing ethical responsibilities.

While the use of anonymity to protect research participants' confidentiality is generally the norm in reporting organizational research (Wiles et al., 2008), there can be circumstances, such as where the findings reflect positively on participants, in which individuals or organizations actually want to be identified. Although this may make matters more straightforward in some respects, it can cause problems if the identification of particular individuals or organizations would threaten the anonymity of other participants (who the findings may depict in a less favourable light). Unless all parties agree, therefore, it may be necessary to maintain anonymity.

A right to publish?

If there is general agreement that the researcher should normally share some form(s) of output with the organization, there is considerable debate about what form(s) the researcher should be expected to share and the extent of the organization's ability to control what is reported about them. On the one hand, some authors such as Buchanan et al. (1988) are happy to offer a report to management as a bargaining chip in access negotiations and to give the organization a right of veto over any publication. On the other, authors such as Bulmer (1988: 156) argue that Buchanan et al. are 'too glib' about the risks to research this may pose, and propose that the 'investigator should retain the right to publish the results independently of the organization, subject to suitable confidentiality safeguards as to the identity and locale of the study'.

For Bulmer this 'right' extends to situations in which the research is sponsored by an organization for a study on itself, so long as it is not considered to be consultancy. Even if there were no problem in distinguishing between research and consultancy, however, it might be argued that, in accepting the organization's funding, some rights are conceded – he who pays the piper calls the tune, and an organization sponsoring research might be considered to have some say in what is reported about it. Nor may a researcher be perceived as being capable of complete independence from an organization that funds them.

This might be countered by arguing that any influence should only be proportionate to the funding provided. So a researcher fully sponsored by the organization might be considered to have less rights than one who receives only expenses and both would have a weaker claim to independence than a researcher who has no financial ties with the organization. From the organization's perspective, moreover, even the granting of access, enabling the researcher to observe phenomena or interview people not otherwise accessible to them, may be considered to evoke some reciprocal commitment on the part of the researcher.

The concern for authors such as Bulmer, however, is that organizations may seek to prevent the dissemination of findings that they consider to be counter to their interests (even if these findings can be shown to be an accurate portrayal). *Causes célèbres*, such as the difficulties experienced by Punch in getting his study of Dartington School published (Punch, 1986), the attempts by Scientologists to discredit Wallis (1977) and to prevent the publication of his research and the pressure applied by the National Coal Board to stop the article by Berry et al. (1985) from being published, indicate that this concern is not entirely without foundation.

That the organization, or individuals within it, may be unhappy with the way they are portrayed need not imply any intent on the part of the researcher to cause harm, but rather it may reflect the 'inauthenticity, dissimilitude, and potential, perhaps inevitable betrayal, [that] are inherent in fieldwork method', as Stacey (1988: 23) argues, in which the 'lives, loves and tragedies that fieldwork informants share with a researcher are ultimately data, grist for the ethnographic mill'. Miles and Huberman (1994: 265) similarly argue that 'it is probably true that, fundamentally, field research is an act of betrayal, no matter how well intentioned or well integrated the researcher. One makes public the private and leaves the locals to take the consequences.' The moment of writing is therefore the one in which the inequalities of the researcher/informant relationship are laid bare (Glesne, 1989; Punch, 1989) and this may provoke negative reactions, particularly if the organization member encounters comments or behaviours that they would prefer not to be reminded of.

It is not always the case, however, that the organization's objections to the findings are simply about their reluctance to face the 'truth', as revealed by the researcher. As Becker (1967) argues, research reports are perhaps inevitably biased, more typically on the side of subordinate groups. Some sources of this bias, such as identification with those being studied, the tendency to associate with marginal individuals and groups, were discussed in Chapter 6, but for some researchers there may also be a more or less explicit political agenda. Punch (1986: 79), for example, recounts the advice of a radical criminologist that he should capitalize on the trust he had developed with the Amsterdam Police 'to gather secretly incriminating documents and to publish these with the intention of causing maximum embarrassment to the police organisation'. Critical research that 'aims to disrupt ongoing social reality for the sake of providing impulses to the liberation from or resistance to what dominates and leads to constraints in human decision-making' (Alvesson and Deetz, 2000: 1), would also seem likely to be sceptical of dominant organizational discourses and sympathetic to the condition of subordinate groups. Whether or not any particular researcher identifies with such positions, their existence means that an organization's concern about the possible harm that may be caused by publication of findings and their interest in vetting any outputs may also have some foundation.

In practice, as authors such as were noted earlier have found, even where a researcher has made a commitment to report findings, the organization may show little interest in receiving them. In part this may be due to personnel changes, which mean that the original gatekeeper for the research is no longer in the same position and their successor in the role does not take the same interest in the research, but also perhaps to the trust developed by the researcher during the course of their fieldwork. It may be easy for the organization to foresee the risks associated with the publication of findings when approached by an unknown researcher proposing to conduct some form of research that the gatekeeper is unfamiliar with, but these concerns may be allayed over time as familiarity with the researcher and their interests demonstrates they are, as Johnson (1975: 95) puts it, 'a humble person who would be a regular guy and do no one any dirt'. While it may be better, as Bulmer (1988) and Punch (1986) argue, not to allow the organization to control what can be reported about it, therefore, that such a concession is made may not always be a significant barrier to publication.

Faced with a refusal by the organization to allow publication of research, sometimes, but not always, after extensive negotiations to seek compromise, some authors have nevertheless sought to proceed with publication. Indeed one of the sources of problems in cases such as Punch and Dartington School (Punch, 1986), Cohen and Taylor and the Prison Service (Cohen and Taylor, 1977) and Wallis and the Scientologists (Wallis, 1977), is that the authors had published magazine articles on the research without consulting the organization.

A number of considerations, however, argue against such a 'publish and be damned' approach. The first, cited by Punch (1986), is that of 'spoiling the field' for others. As Punch (1986: 47) acknowledges, however,

> given that replications are rare in social science, that fieldworkers continually seek new and more esoteric settings and that institutions frequently find one piece of research enough, there is a general tendency to hop from topic to topic ... spoiling the field [may be] less problematic for prospective researchers than might be expected.

The problems, he argues, are more likely to be for the researched, who 'may be left seething with rage and determined to skin alive the next aspiring ethnographer who seeks access'. 'We cannot', as he puts it, 'kick people in the teeth, or elsewhere, and expect them to go on smiling.'

While the threat of 'smash and grab' (Punch, 1986) research on remote communities may be primarily to future ethnographers seeking access, organizations may have more immediate and powerful means of retaliation if research is published without their consent. Even if there is no non-disclosure agreement that a researcher can be sued for breach of, the organization may still be able to damage the researcher's reputation with other organizations (foreclosing future research opportunities), with funding bodies or with the researcher's institution. Given the influence that some organizations have, as direct funders of research, through their representation on management boards of funding bodies and through their influence on government and universities, this may be no idle threat.

A third consideration, in the United Kingdom at least, is that of the threat of libel action if such publications could be construed as having the potential to damage someone's reputation. As Punch (1989) and Cavendish (1982) describe, the potential costs of a libel hearing and the damages that might be awarded mean that publishers are extremely cautious about taking on any work that might be subject to even the threat of action and may require the author to indemnify them against any risk. Cavendish (1982) had to change the name, industry and even the location of the companies that she studied and write under a pseudonym in order to get her book published. With the resources that some organizations have at their disposal, their capability to launch such actions to protect the reputation of (probably senior) organization members may make publishers particularly careful about agreeing to publish work that has not been approved by those being studied.

Reporting to other audiences

Whether or not the organization exercises any 'right' to control what is reported, the primary audience for research outputs is more likely to be the academic community than the organization that has been the research site. Indeed one of the arguments for not requiring that all research outputs should be subject to vetting by the organization is that the interests of this community are likely to be more in how the findings relate to theory and the literature than in the detail of any confidential or sensitive practices that might be disclosed and that any inadvertent disclosure is unlikely to attract attention. The potential readership of most research papers, moreover, is likely to mean that any dissemination of findings will be very limited, and an organization may draw more attention to what it perceives to be negative findings by attempts to suppress research than by letting it be published.[1] For organization members, who may not be familiar with academic literature, however, and for whom a journal article poses the same threat of disclosure as a front-page newspaper story, controlling publication, to whatever extent they are able to, may be seen as the safest option.

As with reports to the organization, one way of addressing such concerns is by anonymization, but it may be hard to persuade organizations that this can provide adequate protection of confidential findings, convinced as they are of their own distinctiveness. Interestingly, however, the commonality between organizations may be greater than they realize and it is not uncommon for members of several different organizations to be equally convinced that an anonymized research report refers to their own organization. Despite the difficulties of disguising the identity of organizations operating in sectors with a small number of well-known companies, and where there may thus be only a few possible organizations that could be 'Investment Bank X', 'Oil Company Y', or 'Car Manufacturer Z', what the researcher may need to achieve is not absolute unidentifiability, but plausible deniability. Avoiding simple errors like naming the organization in the acknowledgements, referring to unique characteristics of a particular organization, or citing documents that identify it, may therefore be sufficient.

Another way of overcoming such concerns about the academic literature may be to invite organization members to be joint authors of papers, so that they can see what is involved for themselves. Indeed for some researchers, such as proponents of participatory action research, this is the preferred mode of publication, being a tangible manifestation of joint engagement with research. It can also be seen as evidence of the reciprocity that Bell and Bryman (2007) identify as a potential ethical principle for management research. Researchers working with organizations that have their own research capacity and/or who consider themselves to be 'thought leaders', may also find that they are the recipients, rather than the originators, of proposals for joint authorship.

---

[1]This is now popularly known as the Streisand effect (after Barbara Streisand's legal efforts to suppress photographs of her Malibu beachside home led to them attracting much greater attention than they had before her intervention).

The inclusion of organization members as joint authors clearly precludes anonymization, as their affiliations will generally be listed in the paper. In some circumstances organizations, or individuals within them, may also wish to be explicitly identified in papers reporting the research, especially if the findings reflect positively on them. This argument is sometimes used to counter suggestions that anonymity should be a requirement for all research reports, and indeed some journal editors have suggested that secrecy is undesirable and that disclosure of the identity of research sites enables a richer account of organizational context to be presented and allows readers to judge the validity of accounts against their own experience (Liebenau and Smithson, 1993, 1994).

In suggesting that organization members may misunderstand academic publishing priorities, it is not intended to suggest that no researchers will ever be interested in reporting their work to a popular audience, or that newspapers or broadcasters are never interested in reporting on the outputs of academic research, but that such wider dissemination of research tends to be more the exception rather than the rule (despite the best efforts of university press offices). It may be the case, moreover, that organizations themselves have an interest in gaining publicity through the placing of stories in the media and may possess the resources (press departments, media contacts and so on) to do so particularly effectively, especially if they have what is perceived as a success story to tell. The impetus for the publication of research reports for a general public or trade audience may therefore come as much, if not more, from the organization as from the researcher. Such publications may also involve joint authorship with organization members who hope to gain credit from the stories that they tell. Since this is likely to be a concern for a relative minority of researchers, however, the focus here will be on publication for an academic audience.

Before considering the particular issues that may need to be considered in reporting research in organizations for an academic audience, one further potential audience for research reports may be identified: that of other organizations in the same industry or sector. As mentioned in Chapter 5, research in organizations may have a value in enabling benchmarking between competitors (that may translate into potential revenues for the researcher). It is not always the case that organizations are well informed about how their performance and practices compare with competitors, or whether other organizations face similar problems or have identified superior solutions. While commercial benchmarking services are available in some industries, organizations may be suspicious that these are intended more as a means of selling consultancy services than of providing sound analysis or may balk at the (often considerable) cost. Academic research may therefore be considered more independent and objective. Reporting to such an audience is likely to be tightly controlled within a closed group of organizations, each of whom is required to share data equally in exchange for equal access to others' data. Reports need not identify specific high- or low-performing organizations, though, but simply indicate to each organization how its performance compares to industry averages and highest and lowest performing cohorts.

Reporting to an academic audience

Two aspects related to fieldwork would seem likely to be particular areas of attention in reports for an academic audience: 'telling how the research was done' (Lofland, 1971) and the case description. In terms of the former, authors such as Taylor and Bogdan (1998) offer a checklist of information that should be provided to readers (see Table 7.3).

Lofland and Lofland (1995: 222) offer a similar checklist addressing: inception and social relations, private feelings, data gathering, data focusing and analysis and retrospect. Punch (1986) argues that providing such information is particularly important in studies involving field research where the reader does not have access to the original data and is heavily reliant on the integrity of the researcher in explaining how the research was carried out, the researcher's relationship with the field setting and participants, and how the data were analysed and selected for report.

In addition to describing the mechanics of the research process, the researcher also needs to find a way to present their findings. While quantitative data may lend themselves to tabular presentation and be summarized with descriptive statistics, matters are typically more complex with qualitative data. A common way in which this is done is as a narrative 'case description', telling a connected story about what was observed, or described in interviews. Getting from perhaps many hundreds of pages of fieldnotes or interview transcripts to an account that is sufficiently concise to be included in a journal article, or even a dissertation or research monograph, however, does not happen by itself.

Table 7.3 'What you should tell your readers' (after Taylor and Bogdan, 1998)

Type of information	Explanation
Methodology	Data-gathering methods and procedures
Theoretical perspective	Prior theoretical influences
Time and length of the study	
Nature and number of informants and settings	
Research design	How were sites and participants selected
Your own frame of mind	What motivated the study
Your relationship with people	
Your analysis	

Rather, there will be an often extreme process of selection. Choosing what to leave out can be difficult, though, especially if the researcher, having been so immersed in the setting, finds it hard to see the wood for the trees. Lofland and Lofland (1995: 212) talk, somewhat melodramatically, of the 'agony of omission' in relation to abandoning sections of writing that may have been laboured over many times and for long hours, but similar distress can accompany decisions not to include particular incidents or quotations. The guiding principle, as Lofland and Lofland (1995) suggest however, should be the development of a coherent and focused narrative.

As Golden-Biddle and Locke (1993: 595) argue, the construction of fieldwork accounts is not just a matter of selecting data, but involves a skilled process of rhetorical crafting to produce an account that convinces the reader of its authenticity, plausibility and criticality; appealing to readers 'to accept that the researcher was indeed present in the field and grasped how the members understood their world … that the findings make a contribution to issues of common concern [and to prompt] readers to re-examine the taken-for-granted assumptions that underly their work'. Indeed for Golden-Biddle and Locke (1993) telling how the research was done is part of this rhetorical strategy, contributing to the perceived authenticity of the presented account.

It is not just what is told to the reader that the researcher must decide, but also how it is said. Van Maanen (1988), for example, identifies three different types of tale that are employed in reporting fieldwork: realist, confessional and impressionist. Realist tales describe the case from a position of interpretive omnipotence, in which the researcher is the ultimate authority on what is reported. The researcher themself is largely absent from the account, however, except as a knowledgeable outsider able to see through the misconceptions that distort the understandings of organization members. Accounts are also rich in particular, concrete, everyday detail and lacking in drama or abstraction and close attention is paid to reporting the views of organization members in their own words.

Confessional tales, in contrast, are characterized by a personalized narrative style that presents the researcher's experience of the field and also often their biases and failures. The experience of organization members is presented, but often mediated through the researcher's own autobiography. While acknowledging the fallibility of their accounts researchers also contrive to 'argue that their materials are reasonably uncontaminated and pure despite all the bothersome problems exposed in the confession' (Van Maanen, 1988: 78). Often relegated to appendices separate from the main, realist, account, the confessional tale serves to qualify the implied omniscience while not undermining it. As Lofland and Lofland (1995: 225) observe, however, despite the apparent commitment to disclosure, 'We delude ourselves if we expect naturalistic researchers to tell all in print', rather, 'what typically goes into describing how the study was done are the "second worst things that happened".'

The last of Van Maanen's tales, the impressionist, presents the field setting from the researcher's point of view. Often written in an almost fictional style, seeking as Van Maanen (1988: 103) puts it 'to imaginatively place the audience in the fieldwork setting', interpretation is minimized and the story is presented in all its confusion and incompleteness. Fragmented knowledge, characterization and dramatic control are used to conjure up events as they were encountered by the fieldworker, rather than as subsequent interpretation would have us see them.

As Van Maanen's 'tales' illustrate, reports of fieldwork settings are not a transparent rendering of events as they occurred in the field, even if they may seem to present themselves as such. Rather, as Parker (2000: 240) writes:

> cases are partial rewritings or partial understandings of partial data ... all research must be subject to these tensions of text against experience, detachment against involvement. And of course these are not matters that can be avoided by the use of any particular set of methodological technologies.

Similarly Buchanan et al. (1988: 65) comment, in relation to reports fed back to the organisation (but it may also be taken to apply to research reports more generally), that

> researchers must accept that such accounts are imperfect (they contain gaps and mis-understandings), are frozen in time (respondents change their views); and negotiated (respondents suggest, and insist on, changes in fact, emphasis and interpretation).

That such limitations are not so apparent in some forms of organizational research, such as surveys, does not mean that they are not present.

EXERCISES

1 Outline **three** arguments for, and **three** arguments against, a researcher fixing a definite date for their departure from the field some time in advance.

2
   - Who, if anybody apart from themselves, would you consider an organizational researcher may have responsibilities to when publishing their research?
   - Describe the obligations that you consider these responsibilities to place upon the researcher.
   - How may a researcher discharge these obligations?

3
   - Describe **three** measures that may be employed to protect the confidentiality of research findings, while enabling the researcher to report on them.
   - What may limit the effectiveness of each of these measures?

Further reading

Writing

Becker, H.S. (1986) *Writing for Social Scientists: How to Start and Finish Your Thesis, Book or Article.* London: University of Chicago Press.

Booth, W.C., Colomb, G.G. and Williams, J.M. (2008) *The Craft of Research,* 3rd edn. London: University of Chicago Press.

Wolcott, H.F. (2001) *Writing Up Qualitative Research,* 2nd edn. London: SAGE.

Ethics of reporting

deLaine, M. (2000) *Fieldwork, Participation and Practice: Ethics and Dilemmas in Qualitative Research.* London: SAGE.

Hammersley, M. and Traianou, A. (2012) *Ethics in Qualitative Research: Controversies and Contexts.* London: SAGE.

Wiles, R. (2013) *What Are Qualitative Research Ethics?* London: Bloomsbury Academic.

References

Alcadipani, R. and Hodgson, D. (2009) 'By any means necessary? Ethnographic access, ethics and the critical researcher', *TAMARA: Journal of Critical Postmodern Organization Science,* 7 (3/4): 127–46.

Alvesson, M. and Deetz, S. (2000) *Doing Critical Management Research.* London: SAGE.

Becker, H.S. (1964) 'Problems in the publication of field studies', in A J. Vidich, J. Bensman, and M.R. Stein (eds), *Reflections on Community Studies.* New York: Wiley, pp. 267–84.

Becker, H.S. (1967) 'Whose side are we on?', *Social Problems,* 14 (3): 239–47.

Beech, N., Hibbert, P., MacIntosh, R. and McInnes, P. (2009) '"But I thought we were friends?" Life cycles and research relationships', in S. Ybema, D. Yanow, H. Wels and F.H. Kamsteeg (eds), *Organizational Ethnography: Studying the Complexities of Everyday Organizational Life.* London: SAGE, pp. 196–214.

Bell, E. and Bryman, A. (2007) 'The ethics of management research: an exploratory content analysis', *British Journal of Management,* 18 (1): 63.

Bell, E. and Wray Bliss, E. (2009) 'Research ethics: regulations and responsibilities', in D.A. Buchanan and A. Bryman (eds), *SAGE Handbook of Organizational Research Methods.* London: SAGE, pp. 78–92.

Berry, T., Capps, T., Cooper, D.J., Hopper, T.M. and Lowe, E.A. (1985) 'NCB accounts – a mine of mis-information?', *Accountancy,* 96 (1097): 10–12.

Bosk, C.L. (1979) *Forgive and Remember: Managing Medical Failure.* Chicago, IL: University of Chicago Press.

Braithwaite, J. (1985) 'Corporate crime research: why two interviewers are needed', *Sociology,* 19 (1): 136–8.

Brannan, M.J. and Oultram, T. (2012) 'Participant observation', in G. Symon and C. Cassell (eds), *Qualitative Organizational Research: Core Methods and Current Challenges*. London: SAGE, pp. 296–313.

Buchanan, D., Boddy, D. and McCalman, J. (1988) 'Getting in, getting on, getting out and getting back', in A. Bryman (ed.), *Doing Research in Organizations*. London: Routledge, pp. 53–67.

Bulmer, M. (1988) 'Some reflections upon research in organisations', in A. Bryman (ed.), *Doing Research in Organizations*. London: Routledge, pp. 151–61.

Burgess, R.G. (1984) *In the Field: An Introduction to Field Research*. London: Allen and Unwin.

Cavendish, R. (1982) *Women on the Line*. London: Taylor and Francis.

Cohen, S. and Taylor, L. (1977) 'Talking about prison blues', in C. Bell and H. Newby (eds), *Doing Sociological Research*. London: Allen and Unwin, pp. 67–86.

Collinson, D. (19920 *Managing the Shopfloor: Subjectivity, Masculinity, and Workplace Culture*. Berlin: Walter de Gruyter.

Crabtree, A., Rouncefield, M. and Tolmie, P. (2012) *Doing Design Ethnography*. London: Springer-Verlag.

Daniels, A.K. (1983) 'Self-deception and self-discovery in fieldwork', *Qualitative Sociology*, 6 (3): 195–214.

Denzin, N.K. (1970) *Sociological Methods: A Sourcebook*. Chicago, IL: Aldine.

Ellis, C. (1995) 'Emotional and ethical quagmires in returning to the field', *Journal of Contemporary Ethnography*, 24 (1): 68–98.

Emerson, R.M., Fretz, R.I. and Shaw, L.L. (2007) 'Participant observation and fieldnotes', in P. Atkinson, A. Coffey, S. Delamont, J. Lofland and L. Lofland (eds), *Handbook of Ethnography*. London: SAGE, pp. 352–68.

Evans-Pritchard, E.E. (1973) 'Some reminiscences and reflections on fieldwork', *Journal of the Anthropological Society of Oxford*, 4 (1): 1–12.

Feldman, M.S. (1989) *Order Without Design: Information Production and Policy Making*. Stanford, CA: Stanford University Press.

Ferdinand, J., Pearson, G., Rowe, M and Worthington, F. (2007) 'A different kind of ethics', *Ethnography*, 8 (4): 519–43.

Goffman, E. (1989) 'On fieldwork', *Journal of Contemporary Ethnography*, 18 (2): 123–32.

Glesne, C. (1989) 'Rapport and friendship in ethnographic research', *International Journal of Qualitative Studies in Education*, 2 (1): 45–54.

Golden-Biddle, K. and Locke, K. (1993) 'Appealing work: an investigation of how ethnographic texts convince', *Organization Science*, 4 (4): 595–616.

Hughes, J., King, V., Rodden, T. and Andersen, H. (1994) 'Moving out from the control room: ethnography in system design', in *Proceedings of the 1994 ACM Conference on Computer-supported Cooperative Work*. New York: Association for Computing Machinery, pp. 429–39.

Irvine, H. (2003) 'Trust me! A personal account of confidentiality issues in an organisational research project', *Accounting Forum*, 27 (2): 111–31.

Iversen, R.R. (2009) '"Getting out"' in ethnography: a seldom-told story', *Qualitative Social Work*, 8 (1): 9–26.

Janes, R.W. (1961) 'A note on phases of the community role of the participant-observer', *American Sociological Review*, 26 (3): 446–50.

Johnson, J.M. (1975) *Doing Field Research*. New York: Free Press.

Kleinman, S. and Copp, M.A. (1993) *Emotions and Fieldwork*. Newbury Park, CA: SAGE.

Leidner, R. (1993) *Fast Food, Fast Talk: Service Work and the Routinization of Everyday Life*. London: University of California Press.

Liebenau, J. and Smithson, S. (1993) 'Editorial: secrecy threatens research', *European Journal of Information Systems*, 2 (4): 239.

Liebenau, J. and Smithson, S. (1994) 'Editorial: secrecy in case studies – a response to Hirschheim and Lyytinen', *European Journal of Information Systems*, 32 (2): 84–6.

Lofland, J. (1971) *Analyzing Social Settings: A Guide to Qualitative Observation and Analysis*. London: Wadsworth.

Lofland, J. and Lofland, L. (1995) *Analyzing Social Settings: A Guide to Qualitative Observation and Analysis*, 3rd edn. London: Wadsworth.

Miles, M.B. and Huberman, A.M. (1994) *Qualitative Data Analysis: An Expanded Sourcebook*, 2nd edn. London: SAGE.

Morrison, Z.J., Gregory, D. and Thibodeau, S. (2012) '"Thanks for using me": an exploration of exit strategy in qualitative research', *International Journal of Qualitative Methods*, 11 (4): 416.

Newson, J. and Polster, C. (2001) 'Reclaiming our centre', *Science Studies*, 14 (1): 55–75.

O'Hare, P. (2009) 'Getting down to writing up: navigating from the field to the desk and the (re)presentation of fieldwork', *Anthropology Matters*, 9 (2). Available at: www.anthropologymatters.com/index.php?journal = anth_matte rs&page = article&op = view&path%5B%5D = 47&path%5B%5D = 88.

Ortiz, S.M. (2004) 'Leaving the private world of wives of professional athletes: a male sociologist's reflections', *Journal of Contemporary Ethnography*, 33 (4): 466.

Parker, M. (2000) *Organizational Culture and Identity: Unity and Division at Work*. London: SAGE.

Pettigrew, A.M. (1973) *The Politics of Organizational Decision-Making*. London: Tavistock.

Punch, M. (1986) *The Politics and Ethics of Fieldwork*. London: SAGE.

Punch, M. (1989) 'Researching police deviance: a personal encounter with the limitations and liabilities of field-work', *The British Journal of Sociology*, 40 (2): 177–204.

Randall, D., Rouncefield, M. and Harper, R. (2007) *Fieldwork for Design: Theory and Practice*. London: Springer.

Reeves, C.L. (2010) 'A difficult negotiation: fieldwork relations with gatekeepers', *Qualitative Research*, 10 (3): 315–31.

Snow, D.A. (1980) 'The disengagement process: a neglected problem in participant observation research', *Qualitative Sociology*, 3 (2): 100–22.

Stacey, J. (1988) 'Can there be a feminist ethnography?', *Women's Studies International Forum*, 11: 21–7.

Taylor, S.J. (1991) 'Leaving the field: research, relationships, and responsibilities', in W.B. Shaffir and R.A. Stebbins (eds), *Experiencing Fieldwork: An Inside View of Qualitative Research*. London: SAGE, pp. 238–47.

Taylor, S.J. and Bogdan, R. (1998) *Introduction to Qualitative Research Methods: The Search for Meanings*, 3rd edn. Chichester: John Wiley and Sons.

Tolich, M. (2004) 'Internal confidentiality: when confidentiality assurances fail relational informants', *Qualitative Sociology*, 27 (1): 101–6.

Van Maanen, J. (1988) *Tales of the Field: On Writing Ethnography*. London: University of Chicago Press.

Walford, G. (2001) *Doing Qualitative Educational Research: A Personal Guide to the Research Process*. London: Continuum International Publishing Group.

Wallis, R. (1977) 'The moral career of a research project', in C. Bell and H. Newby (eds), *Doing Sociological Research*. London: Allen and Unwin, pp. 149–67.

Wax, R.H. (1971) *Doing Fieldwork: Warnings and Advice*. London: University of Chicago Press.

Wiles, R., Crow, G., Heath, S. and Charles, V. (2008) 'The management of confidentiality and anonymity in social research', *International Journal of Social Research Methodology*, 11 (5): 417–28.

Wolf, D. (1991) 'High-risk methodology: reflections on leaving an outlaw society', in W.B. Shaffir and R.A. Stebbins (eds), *Experiencing Fieldwork: An Inside View of Qualitative Research*. London: SAGE, pp. 211–23.

8

Getting Back

Chapter objectives
• to identify reasons why a researcher may seek to return to an organization that they have previously studied
• to consider the problems that may be encountered in doing so

Having written up the research and reported it in whatever venues are considered appropriate, the research process will typically be at an end and the researcher moves on to other projects. In some situations, however, the researcher may wish to re-enter the original research site. There may be various reasons for this, as shown in Table 8.1.

To present findings

Sometimes a return to the field may not be associated with the immediate continuation of research, but with the reporting of findings from a completed study. Burawoy (2003) terms this the 'valedictory revisit'. While in some ways

Table 8.1 Reasons for returning to the field

To present findings
After a voluntary or enforced suspension of research
To validate findings
To collect new data to verify findings
To complete data collection on something that was still going on when the original fieldwork ended
To collect data on something that had not happened during the original period of fieldwork
To follow up on something that was not studied during the original fieldwork
To track a process over time
To conduct a restudy

the researcher may treat this as a straightforward visit by an organizational outsider, their history with the organization may sometimes cast a shadow over such events. Following an extended piece of fieldwork, for example, organization members may find it difficult to adjust to seeing the researcher in an 'expert' role, or to accept what are perceived as critical comments from an erstwhile 'colleague' or 'friend'. If the researcher, for their part, is sensitive to their anomalous role or holds some hope of pursuing research again in the setting they may also find the experience quite stressful. That said, such occasions can be pleasant reunions too.

After a voluntary or enforced suspension of research

The course of research does not always run smooth and events may occur that lead to the suspension of fieldwork for a period of time (although Smith [2001] suggests that this is rarely explicitly acknowledged in research reports). This may be due, say, to illness or personal difficulties of the researcher or to a crisis in the organization that necessitates the researcher's withdrawal from the field. While a voluntary interruption, if relatively brief, may not be consequential for the research, organization members may be disconcerted by the unexpected departure of the researcher and it may take time to re-establish rapport. If possible, therefore, it may help to follow a similar procedure to that for leaving the field, as discussed in Chapter 7, in terms of alerting organization members and explaining the reasons and expected duration of the suspension. Where the research is suspended due to a crisis in the organization it may be more difficult to regain entry, as the events may affect staff morale and the organizational circumstances may be sufficiently altered that resumption of the original studies may not be possible.

To validate research findings

Member validation, in which the researcher shares their findings with organization members to determine 'if the members recognize, understand and accept one's descriptions of the setting' (Douglas 1976: 131), need not involve a return to the field. In practice, however, taking findings to the research participants and engaging with them personally is likely to be more effective in eliciting a response than simply sending them a physical document or email attachment and awaiting their comments. The researcher may therefore wish to arrange follow-up meetings with key organization members to discuss various research outputs. This may not be straightforward, however. For example, Brannan and Oultram (2012: 309) discuss the very different dynamic in the relationship with participants when conducting follow-up interviews just four to six months after the completion of a participant observation study – 'people I had worked with for a year, and yet it was like they didn't know me at all'.

In the 'weak' version of member validation (Seale, 1999), the researcher may simply seek agreement to the accuracy of interview transcripts (and their use in data analysis), while the 'strong' version might involve the sharing of final research reports (either with, or without, a partial or complete veto on their eventual publication). In between might be the sharing of case descriptions, or analysis.

As Emerson (1981: 362) argues, however, unless members simply confirm their recognition, understanding and acceptance, the researcher is likely to

> obtain additional equivocal evidence; additional situationally influenced statements must then be interpreted, just as the earlier statements were, in order to establish a version of the member's perspective. Under these conditions, taking findings back to the field is not a test but an opportunity for reflexive elaboration.

Member validation, therefore, as Bloor (2001: 388) puts it, 'is not immaculately produced'. Rather, as he illustrates, even while endorsing the findings members may be defensive about the picture they present, raising concerns about the accuracy and representativeness of the researcher's account, may argue that the picture is no longer accurate (as the situation and people's understandings have changed over time), or may propose an interpretation of the findings that runs counter to that intended by the researcher. Furthermore, following Giddens' notion of the double hermeneutic (Giddens, 1993), the findings may come to shape members' understandings of their situation. Member validation exercises, as Sandelowski (2002: 108) proposes, therefore, 'are arguably less useful for validating one's (that is, the researcher's) interpretation of an experience than for providing an opportunity to collect additional data about members' responses to a new phenomenon, namely, the researcher's account'.

The underlying assumption of member validation, moreover, is that organization members will assent to an accurate account of the research setting. Yet there may be a variety of reasons why they may not do so. If, as was discussed in Chapter 7 for example, organization members tend to have an idealized view of themselves and their behaviours, they may be dismayed by a portrayal that is less than flattering, whether or not it is accurate. Alternatively, individuals' willingness to endorse findings may be influenced by organizational power relations. Thus remarks critical of practices in the organization, while genuinely expressed in the course of research (and perhaps even supported by other evidence), may be disavowed if powerful individuals deny their validity (O'Reilly and Dhanju, 2010). Similarly individuals may decide whether they endorse research findings not on their accuracy, but on whether certain powerful individuals do so too. Research findings may therefore be treated as resources in organizational politics.

To collect new data to verify findings

During analysis of fieldwork data the significance of particular features of the research setting may become apparent that were not appreciated at the time of the research, or were not recorded because, as Orr (1996) describes, they seemed obvious or unremarkable in the field context. Returning to the field to rectify such omissions may be possible where the features are relatively objective – the numbers of people in particular teams, say, the layout of a building, or the data items included in a standard report (provided, of course, that these have not changed in the time since the completion of the original research).

It is unfortunately also not uncommon during data analysis to experience regrets that a particular event was not observed, for example, a question was not followed up, or a particular person spoken to. For qualitative researchers who view data, as Bloor (2001: 388) puts it, as 'shaped by the circumstances of their production', however, it will never be possible to recreate the circumstances that gave rise to the original finding. Even if the same individuals are available and have not been primed by knowledge of the research findings, asking the same question again at a different time and under different conditions cannot be assumed to elicit the same answer. The ability of new data to verify earlier findings may therefore be limited.

This does not mean that the return to the field, per se, is the cause of this problem, as the same changes in circumstances may occur during the course of a piece of fieldwork. The potentially greater lapse of time, the need to re-establish familiarity and the possible effects of awareness of research findings, however, may all tend to diminish the continuity between the two instances of data collection. New data may therefore not so much fill in the gaps as add new variety to the picture.

To complete data collection on something that was still going on when the original fieldwork ended

Although, in an ideal world, the phenomena being studied would fit neatly into the time allotted to fieldwork, in practice there can often be delays or over-runs that mean that not everything the researcher might wish to study happens before they leave the field. While it may be possible to extend the original period of fieldwork (but with no guarantee that this will be sufficient), as was suggested in Chapter 7 it may be better to leave the field at the planned date and return later, rather than hanging around waiting for a particular event to happen or for a process to come to completion.

It can be difficult, however, to get sufficient forewarning of events to enable a timely return to the field, so the researcher may find themselves having to gather retrospective data on some or all of the event or process. Although such data may still be valuable for the research, therefore, they will not be wholly consistent with contemporaneous data that were gathered during the original fieldwork.

To collect data on something that had not happened during the original period of fieldwork

Alternatively, it may be known in advance (or discovered during the original fieldwork) that some relevant situations are not expected to occur during the planned period of the study. For example, Randall et al. (2007: 192) note: 'in the Air Traffic Control research the bulk of the research took place in the winter months. Given that controllers constantly made reference to how busy it got in the summer, it pointed to a need to return to the domain.' Such a situation, if suitably handled, however, may be able to be presented as a temporary interruption to a single continuing study rather than a separate research episode.

To follow up on something that was not studied during the original fieldwork

As there is always more in the field setting than the researcher can possibly attend to at one time, fieldwork necessarily involves choices about what to observe or to ask about in interviews. Either during fieldwork or data analysis, however, additional topics may be identified that the researcher wishes to investigate but on which the available data do not provide sufficient insight. Alternatively, the researcher may realize in later fieldwork in other settings that the original organization would provide a suitable site in which to study a new topic.

Such a possibility offers a pragmatic justification for maintaining good relations with former research sites, as it may be expected that re-entry is likely to be easier to negotiate than initial access to a new organization. To the extent, however, that the new research is independent of the earlier work it may be necessary to revisit earlier agreements, rather than to assume that they necessarily still hold.

To track a process over time

It may be recognized at the outset that the planned fieldwork will be unable to observe the entire process of, say, the growth of a firm, the commercialization of a new technology from lab to market, or the progress of a cohort of school-children. It may therefore be a component of the original design, or it may be decided at the end of the original fieldwork that the researcher should make periodic returns to the field to gather new data. Clearly such an arrangement implies a considerable commitment on both sides and may prove difficult to sustain for either party. The potential for a genuinely longitudinal study transcending the normal research life cycle, however, may be considered to merit the effort.

To conduct a restudy

In a small number of cases it may be decided to formally repeat an earlier study. This may be carried out by the original researchers, or sometimes by new researchers. Burgess (1987), for example, revisited the Bishop McGregor school that he had reported on in Burgess (1983), while Bryman (1989) revisited his earlier study of religious 'functionaries' (Anglican clergy, Methodist ministers and Roman Catholic priests). Goodwin and O'Connor (2007), in contrast, were prompted to undertake a restudy of workplace learning as a fortuitous result of the discovery of 851 archived interview schedules from the original study.

Bryman (1989) argues that a restudy should not be considered a replication of the original study because it cannot be assumed that the original findings were correct, rather its value is likely to lie in identifying changes since the original study. Burawoy (2003) identifies four possible causes of the discrepancies that may be identified in the course of such 'revisits': the relationship of observer to participant; the theory brought to the field by the ethnographer; internal processes within the field itself; and forces external to the field. Furthermore, he argues, each of these causes tends to be associated with a particular focus of the restudy: refutation of the claims of the earlier research; reconstruction of the analysis using alternative theories; description of changes and their explanation.

Undertaking a restudy can face a number of difficulties, however. As Bell (1977) and Ellis (1995) report in relation to community studies, for example, reports of the original study may have serious effects on the later findings as research participants react, sometimes with hostility, to how they have been described. There may also be strained relationships between the former research team as a result of unresolved issues from the earlier study and intervening career trajectories (Bell, 1977).

There may be problems too in the comparability of the studies. For example the survival (or rather contact) rate of original respondents may be quite low, as both Bryman (1989) and Goodwin and O'Connor (2007) report and, as Burgess (1987) argues, the organization itself may have changed so much that the extent to which it could be considered the same organization may be questioned. Potentially compounding the question of comparability may be the temptation to modify the original research design to accommodate the changes. If the value of a restudy is in the comparison across time, however, then this temptation needs to be resisted, Bryman (1989) argues, even if it might make the second study more relevant to contemporary practice.

Challenges of returning to the field

If there are various reasons why a researcher may wish to get back into an organization, the challenges they face may be quite similar. A major issue in most contemporary settings is that of organizational change. If re-entry is sought more than perhaps one or two years later, in many organizations personnel may have significantly changed. This can be particularly problematic if the original sponsor and/or gatekeeper for the research has moved or left the organization, as this may make it necessary to negotiate access again from scratch. As was emphasized in the discussion of restudies, only a small proportion of the original respondents may be available (and willing to participate in further research). In some instances even the whole activity that was originally studied may have been discontinued.

The return to the field can be the occasion in which the researcher discovers the strength of feelings aroused by what they may have perceived to be innocent and non-judgemental comments in research reports. It may not even be necessary for members to have read the reports as, perhaps exaggerated, rumours about their contents can rapidly become accepted wisdom (Davis, 1993) or press stories may misrepresent their content (Greenberg, 1993). Nor may it be just negative reactions to reports that may affect subsequent research – positive endorsement of findings may alter organization members' views and behaviours in ways that it will be impossible to reverse.

It can be hard, both practically and emotionally, therefore (though probably easier than with an initial contact), to negotiate access and re-establish relationships with organization members. While the likelihood of organizational change complicating re-entry increases with time, however, as Buchanan et al. (1988) argue, it may be 'tactful' to allow some period of time before seeking further research access. In their own studies they indicate that they left at least six months between contacts, so that organizations did not feel 'over-researched'. As Clark (2008) argues, however, complaints of research fatigue may not be primarily a product of frequency of contact, but more to do with organization members' perceptions that earlier studies did not lead to any experience of change and of the costs of participation.

1 List **four** possible reasons for the relative lack of restudies in organizational research.

Reason
1
2
3
4

2 Identify **four** types of problems that a researcher may encounter in seeking to return to an organization they have previously studied and suggest any measures that a researcher may adopt to try to overcome these problems.

Problems	Measures to overcome
1	
2	
3	
4	

Further reading

Although some organizational researchers report working with the same organization over periods of more than a decade (e.g. Huxham and Vangen, 2003; Burgelman and Grove, 2007), it would seem that issues associated with returning to the field have not received much attention in the organizational research literature, nor would there seem to be much of a tradition of restudies.

Burgelman, R.A. and Grove, A.S. (2007) 'Let chaos reign, then rein in chaos – repeatedly: managing strategic dynamics for corporate longevity', *Strategic Management Journal*, 28 (10): 965–79.

Huxham, C. and Vangen, S. (2003) 'Researching organizational practice through action research: case studies and design choices', *Organizational Research Methods*, 6 (3): 383–403.

References

Bell, C. (1977) 'Reflections on the Banbury restudy', in C. Bell and H. Newby (eds), *Doing Sociological Research*. London: Allen and Unwin, pp. 47–62.

Bloor, M. (2001) 'Notes on member validation', in R.M. Emerson (ed.) *Contemporary Field Research*, 2nd edn. Prospect Heights, IL: Waveland Press, pp. 383–95.

Brannan, M.J. and Oultram, T. (2012) 'Participant observation', in G. Symon and C. Cassell (eds), *Qualitative Organizational Research: Core Methods and Current Challenges*. London: SAGE, pp. 296–313.

Bryman, A. (1989) 'The value of re-studies in sociology: the case of clergy and ministers, 1971 to 1985', *Sociology*, 23 (1): 31–53.

Buchanan, D., Boddy, D. and McCalman, J. (1988) 'Getting in, getting on, getting out and getting back', in A. Bryman (ed.), *Doing Research in Organizations*. London: Routledge, pp. 53–67.

Burawoy, M. (2003) 'Revisits: an outline of a theory of reflexive ethnography', *American Sociological Review*, 68 (5), 645–79.

Burgess, R.G. (1983) *Experiencing Comprehensive Education: A Study of Bishop McGregor School*. London: Methuen.

Burgess, R.G. (1987) 'Studying and restudying Bishop McGregor School', in G. Walford (ed.), *Doing Sociology of Education*. London: Falmer Press, p. 67.

Clark, T. (2008) '"We're over-researched here!" Exploring accounts of research fatigue within qualitative research engagements', *Sociology*, 42 (5): 953–70.

Davis, D.L. (1993) 'Unintended consequences: the myth of '"the return" in anthropological fieldwork', in C.B. Brettell (ed.), *When They Read What We Write: The Politics of Ethnography*. Westport, CT: Bergin and Garvey, pp. 29–35.

Douglas, J.D. (1976) *Investigative Social Research*. Beverly Hills, CA: SAGE.

Ellis, C. (1995) 'Emotional and ethical quagmires in returning to the field', *Journal of Contemporary Ethnography*, 24 (1): 68–98.

Emerson, R.M. (1981) 'Observational field work', *Annual Review of Sociology*, 7 (1): 351–78.

Giddens, A. (1993) *New Rules of Sociological Method*, 2nd edn. Cambridge: Polity Press.

Goodwin, J. and O'Connor, H. (2007) 'Researching 40 years of learning for work: the experiences of one cohort of workers', *Journal of Vocational Education and Training*, 59 (3): 349–67.

Greenberg, O. (1993) 'When they read what the papers say we wrote', in C.B. Brettell (ed.), *When They Read What We Write: The Politics of Ethnography*. Westport, CT: Bergin and Garvey, pp. 107–18.

O'Reilly, K. and Dhanju, R. (2010) '"Your report is completely wrong!" (Aapkii report ek dum galat hai!): locating spaces inside NGOs for feedback and dissemination', *Human Organization*, 69 (3): 285.

Orr, J.E. (1996) *Talking About Machines: An Ethnography of a Modern Job*. London: Cornell University Press.

Randall, D., Harper, R. and Rouncefield, M. (2007) *Fieldwork for Design: Theory and Practice*. London: Springer.

Sandelowski, M. (2002) 'Reembodying qualitative inquiry', *Qualitative Health Research*, 12 (1): 104–15.

Seale, C. (1999) *The Quality of Qualitative Research*. London: SAGE.

Smith, V. (2001) 'Ethnographies of work and the work of ethnographers', in P. Atkinson, A. Coffey, S. Delamont, J. Lofland and L. Lofland (eds), *Handbook of Ethnography*. London: SAGE, pp. 220–33.

9

Emerging Issues in Research in Organizations

<hr>

Chapter objectives

- to consider how research in organizations may be affected by

  - o new modes of data collection
  - o technological change
  - o globalization
  - o new forms of organization

<hr>

Much of the discussion of research in organizations in this book so far relates to a model of fieldwork that is perhaps not so very different from the Hawthorne Studies of the 1930s (Roethlisberger and Dickson, 1939), Lipset's *Union Democracy* study (Lipset, 1964) or even that of early twentieth century social anthropologists such as E.E. Evans-Pritchard or Margaret Mead (save that the researcher is likely to be in an office block or on a factory floor rather closer to home than in a village hut in some faraway land). There is a specific location in which the phenomena the researcher wishes to study take place and by gaining access to this location the researcher can study the phenomena of interest and gather information from those involved. Admittedly, perceptions of the relationship between the researcher and their 'subjects' and the understanding of the sorts of knowledge the researcher obtains may have changed, but 'getting in' to an organization and gathering data, through interviews and/or observation, is still the essence of much fieldwork. The researcher then returns 'home' and seeks to transform these data into a persuasive account of 'what goes on' in the field setting.

That there is a long tradition of such fieldwork does not mean that it is irrelevant to contemporary researchers. Indeed, as this book has sought to illustrate, the earlier literature on the practice of fieldwork can still have much to offer in understanding the challenges that may be encountered in the practice of research in organizations. There are a number of areas, however, where relatively recent developments in data-gathering techniques and the character of organizations are posing new challenges for organizational fieldwork. As these changes are still ongoing and the measures to address them still emerging, this chapter will not pretend to offer a definitive account of their implications or of the solutions to the challenges they pose. Rather the aim will be to highlight them as potential issues for contemporary researchers and to discuss their possible implications for research practice. An annotated reading list at the end of the chapter provides some pointers to relevant literature for those wishing to pursue these issues further.

Four areas in particular will be focused on: technology and new modes of data collection; technology and organizational change; globalization; and new organizational forms. While these will be treated as separate topics, it is recognized that there are some common underlying trends, particularly the emergence of the Internet, that are manifested in each of these areas. They are discussed separately, however, to emphasize their influence in different parts of the research process.

Technology and new modes of data collection

One of the curiosities in reading earlier literature on fieldwork is the enthusiastic discussion of the potential of new-fangled devices, such as tape recorders, to transform data collection. As the logistics involved in conducting fieldwork with a typically mains-powered device the size of a large briefcase became apparent, however, enthusiasm transferred to pocket-sized cassette recorders and 'dictaphones', notwithstanding persistent comments on the cost and time required for transcription. While contemporary digital audio recorders, or even phones or portable media players, are now sufficiently cheap and ubiquitous that their use, when permitted, is unexceptional, transcription still remains a significant burden. Technological enthusiasts now look to speech recognition software to solve this problem, although it is still some way off being able to function effectively with possibly multiple, unknown voices in noisy field settings without the researcher's intervention (such as re-dictating the recording in their own voice). It may not be a bad thing that this process is not fully automated, however. While often tedious and time-consuming, manual transcription has the virtue of forcing the researcher to pay close attention to what is recorded, so re-dictation or correcting a poor transcription will require some level of engagement with the original recording that will be absent if transcription is automated or outsourced. Just as downloading a journal article doesn't mean that it has been read, so possessing a transcript of a recording does not mean that the researcher has the familiarity with its content necessary to proceed with analysis.

That it is now possible to obtain a good-quality audio recording relatively unobtrusively and to convert this to a transcript with less difficulty than previously, moreover, does not fundamentally alter the data-gathering process, except to the extent that it may make the use of formal interviews, to which the technology is best suited, more likely. If this were to lead to a decline in the use of other data-gathering methods, however, it could be considered to risk a loss of data richness and of insight on the temporally extended, naturally occurring (as opposed to researcher-provoked) informal processes that interviews are not well suited to capturing.

Other technological developments that may lead to new forms of data being gathered relate to use of video recording. As with audio recording, digitization, and reduced size and cost of equipment have made video recording easier to use and more accessible. Although there has been a long-standing tradition of ethnomethodologically and ethnographically informed work studies using video analysis (Heath et al., 2010; Szymanski and Whalen, 2011) it is only more recently that the technology has begun to attract attention in more mainstream organization research in fields such as entrepreneurship (Clarke, 2011) and health research (Iedema and Carroll, 2011).

As Hindmarsh and Pilnick (2007: 1399) argue, video recording can be particularly useful in studying tacit, ephemeral and non-verbal aspects of organizational phenomena, providing the researcher with repeated access to the 'details and contingencies of their production'. While bringing new forms of data into the scope of analysis, however, video recording is necessarily constrained by the field of view of the camera, potentially narrowing the focus of observation. At the same time, the very richness of additional data available makes the analytical task much more demanding. Assuming that it were possible to gain permission to set up a video camera in a boardroom, say, in order to study executive decision-making, there could be many hours of material to be analysed in terms of its visual, verbal and non-verbal content and even then it would only provide insight on those aspects of executive decision-making visible and/or audible within the confines of the boardroom. As a result, therefore, video-based studies tend to focus on micro-processes of interaction in a specific setting, rather than longer-term phenomena that may occur over multiple, dispersed locations.

A third way in which technology may be altering the scope of data collection is through the use of the Internet as a medium for data-gathering. This has three main aspects: the carrying out of traditional modes of data collection such as surveys (email or online), interviews (text, audio or video) or ethnography via the Internet; the collection of data from people's use of the Internet; and the use of the Internet to gather other data.

In terms of the first of these, the Internet is not necessarily leading to new forms of data being gathered, but provides a way of increasing the efficiency of data-gathering and overcoming geographical constraints. Thus online surveys have a variety of advantages over face-to-face, telephone or postal surveys (see Table 9.1).

Table 9.1   Advantages of online surveys

Low administration costs
Automatic validation of responses
Flexibility
Personalization
Speed of response
Contextual help
Capture data in immediately analysable form
More selective
More honest
Easy to style

(After www.smart-survey.co.uk/articles/10-advantages-of-online-surveys/)

These advantages will accrue to any form of social research, but may be expected to be particularly significant for research in organizations in which rates of access to the Internet may be expected to be generally high. With the increasing geographical dispersion of large organizations, discussed in more detail in the section on globalization below, moreover, staff may work regularly with remotely located colleagues and regard the Internet as a very normal context for interaction. Indeed they may expect to be contacted electronically, and may regard face-to-face or postal surveys as old-fashioned.

The key problem with Internet survey research is sample quality, because the online population may not be representative of the population being studied. Even if in principle all members of an organization have access to the Internet, for example, it may not be equally convenient for all groups of employees to do so as part of their work routine. It is also important to distinguish between invited and open Internet surveys. Invited surveys have the advantage of targeting a specific population, but face the same difficulties, discussed in relation to research access in Chapter 5, of identifying and making contact with the targets. Open surveys, perhaps publicized via public fora, face a particular problem of respondent bias, since the size of the population reached by this means, let alone its composition, may be unknown and there may be a risk of duplicate entries (where the same person is able to answer the survey several times). These disadvantages notwithstanding, convenience, cost and familiarity suggest that online surveys are likely to become the default option in much survey-based research in organizations.

The Internet also creates the possibility for interviews to be held with participants in any location with suitable network connections. If network bandwidth or speed is limited interviews can be text-based, for example using email or an instant messaging service, or audio only. Increasingly, however, video interviews are likely to be possible in most organizational locations. Although video interviews are richer than text or audio-based methods in providing some access to visual cues and to the non-vocal elements of interviewee responses, it can be harder to establish rapport and retain the interviewees' engagement compared to face-to-face interaction, and the quality of data gathered can consequently suffer (James and Busher, 2009).

Virtual ethnography (Hine, 2000) or netnography (Kozinets, 2009) applies ethnographic methods to the study of online communities. Such 'insider' studies (Sproull and Arriaga, 2007) typically involve the researcher undertaking participant observation as a member of the community. There is a huge diversity of such communities. Sproull and Arriaga (2007), for example, classify them into several types: consumer communities (of fans of particular brands, sports teams, entertainers or media properties); (a)vocation communities (of enthusiasts of particular activities); place-based communities (of residents of a particular geographical locale); condition communities (of those with experience of or interest in a particular condition, that may be based on a demographic characteristic, illness, or involvement with some organization); concern communities (of those with a common political, social or ideological interest); and collaborative work communities. Most such communities are voluntary and independent of particular organizations (even where an organization may be the focus of the community) and the majority of studies are of communities of this kind. Perhaps the major exception to this are studies of free/libre/open source software (FLOSS) development (cf. Crowston et al., 2012) that often has a significant organizational component, both in terms of the involvement of commercial business organizations and in terms of being coordinated towards common goals.

A further research possibility for Internet-based research, and particularly for the study of online communities, is the analysis of archival data. Rather than participating in the community, a researcher may be able to access and analyse records of earlier activity. While there may be issues of consent relating to access to such data they can constitute a very large and rich data set for analysis of interaction.

If online surveys, interviews and ethnography are distinguished from earlier data-gathering methods predominantly in terms of their medium of interaction, the Internet also creates the opportunity for new forms of data-gathering as a result of what Zuboff (1988) refers to as the informating capacity of information technology, that is, its textualization of previously hidden work practices, rendering them traceable. An organization member's interactions with colleagues, for example, can potentially be traced through phone, email and instant message logs without any direct observation of their work; bidding patterns on online auctions can be tracked to investigate mechanisms of price discovery, or contributions to an online community may be analysed to explore members' behaviour and attitudes.

In terms of such data it would seem useful to distinguish between those that relate to an organization's interactions with the public via the Internet, and those that are internal to the organization, generally requiring some permission to be accessed (although a few organizations, particularly in the government sector, are making some internal data publicly accessible under open data mandates). While most Internet research in organizations is likely, as it does in conventional field-work, to require access to internal data, the quantity of publicly available data that can be accessed at low cost by those with the necessary programming skills, constitutes a highly attractive resource for researchers, particularly those studying the external image of organizations, whether from the point of view of marketing, public relations or corporate social responsibility. Since the data are generally col-lected for purposes other than research, however, their quality and suitability may not always be well-matched to the particular focus of research and it may also not be straightforward to extract and transform the data into a usable format.

Many organizations hold a wealth of data, much of it a by-product of organ-ization members' informated work practices, that may be another valuable resource for research. With permission, such data may be accessible remotely, enabling researchers to significantly reduce the costs of data-gathering. Researchers may also access their own data from remote sites, for example through the provision of instrumented software. While this can greatly increase the convenience of data-gathering, it may distort findings as only those aspects of the phenomenon that are recorded in the data source will be accessible. Significant elements of work practices that do not involve information technol-ogy, such as offline communication, may therefore be rendered invisible.

Internet research is seen as giving rise to a particular set of ethical issues (McKee and Porter, 2009), especially if conducted in public fora or using data that organization members do not know are being recorded. In both cases, the fact that the researcher may be able to access data without their explicit consent is some-times countered by assertions that in posting on the Internet users should be aware that their comments may be accessed by others and that such data are therefore not private. Indeed it is argued by some that privacy is no longer a social norm. A distinction might also be made between data that are gathered directly as a result of the activity being undertaken and those that are gathered by third parties. In many circumstances the specific identity of individuals may not be relevant and the research can be done with anonymized data. Achieving this in practice, however, will reduce the convenience of data-gathering and may still not provide adequate safeguards against identification of individuals.

Technology and organizational change

The technological developments that are contributing to the emergence of new forms of research practice are also associated with changes to organizations. A number of these, as identified by Davenport (1993), may have implications for the conduct of research in organizations (see Table 9.2).

Table 9.2 Selected organizational changes associated with information technology (after Davenport, 1993)

Automational	Eliminating human labour from the process
Sequential	Changing process sequence to enable parallelism
Geographical	Coordinating processes across distances
Disintermediating	Eliminating intermediaries from the process

Thus organizations employ fewer staff for the same output, work practices are speeded up, and may be carried out over considerable geographical distances, with customers having direct access to organizational processes and performing some of the work themselves. Airline passengers book tickets and check in online, eliminating travel agents from the process and reducing the number of check-in staff required. In multinational software companies, development teams may span many geographical locations and time zones, with individuals coordinating their sometimes parallel work streams through information technology. Thus there is no longer a single location from which the whole work process may be observed and even organization members may only infrequently meet face-to-face, if at all. Only through technology, with its potentially restricted view of work, are certain practices observable and even in face-to-face interaction with organization members, important parts of their practices may be engaged with absent others.

Increasing pressures in the workplace from reduced staff numbers, compounded by economic insecurity, may make it more difficult for organization members to put aside time to help researchers. Opened to direct contact with customers, staff may be more cautious about being honest in their opinions. Aware of the surveillance potential of technology, individuals play the system to their advantage, e.g. McCabe (2007). It is not that these are necessarily completely new phenomena, but they require some adjustments in where data are sought and assumptions about what they tell us.

Globalization

Whether as a result of technology or not, it is increasingly the case that both the organizations providing goods and services in a particular location and the location of members of many large organizations are becoming more geographically dispersed. A growing proportion of the world's manufacturing takes place in China, for example. Similarly, a growing proportion of organizations operating in many developed economies are foreign-owned, while multinational companies, including those indigenous to a particular location, build virtual work teams with staff located in many different countries.

From the point of view of research in organizations this means that the potential sites in which to study particular practices may be much more widely located and the sites themselves are more diverse. Researchers in the UK studying manufacturing organizations, for example, are likely to need a significantly larger travel budget than they would have done in the past, and even if they study local sites, these are increasingly likely to be foreign-owned and to involve interactions with individuals from different countries, some of whom may be physically located at other sites, perhaps outside the UK.

The effects of diversity may be expected to influence cultural norms, both of individuals and of the organization as a whole. There may also be tensions and misunderstandings between organization members from different backgrounds. Although some organizations may seek to overcome such differences through a strong company culture, from a research perspective this does not so much eliminate differences as overlay yet another influence on local practices. For a researcher from a particular background, moreover, it may not always be easy to detect or appreciate the influence of these cultural norms.

Diversity may also have a linguistic aspect, with subcultures associated with the speakers of particular languages. Again while the organization may promote a particular lingua franca, not all members may be equally comfortable in its use and better data may be obtained by interaction in the organization member's mother tongue. Of course this has been a staple issue throughout the history of ethnographic research. What is perhaps new, however, is that in contemporary organizations there may be several languages within one location, each with its particular associations and significations that the researcher may need to be aware of.

'New organizational forms'

Early fieldwork research in organizations tended to be dominated by studies in large, formal organizations in both the public (e.g. Becker et al., 1961; Blau, 1955; Johnson, 1975) and private (e.g. Burawoy, 1979; Dalton, 1959; Gouldner, 1955) sectors. While these sorts of organizations continue to be important fieldwork sites (e.g. McCabe, 2007; Mollona, 2009), perhaps because of their economic and practical visibility, there has also been growing interest (cf. Palmer et al., 2007; Schreyögg and Sydow, 2010) in what are commonly referred to as 'new organizational forms' (even if, as Table 9.3 illustrates, many of these date back to the early 1990s).

Table 9.3 'New organizational forms'

New organizational form	Reference
Post-bureaucratic	Heckscher and Donellon (1994)
Virtual	Bleecker (1994)
Network	Nohria and Eccles (1992)
Shamrock	Handy (1995)
Horizontal	Ostroff (1999)
Fast cycle	Bower and Hout (1988)
Knowledge-based	Drucker (1992)
Boundaryless	Ashkenas et al. (2002)
Project-based	Whitley (2006)
Temporary	Lundin and Söderholm (1995)

Whether or not any of these constitute genuinely distinctive organizational forms, or are just different ways of characterizing a number of recent trends in existing organizations, the organizational changes that they reflect, such as delayering, downsizing and the promotion of 'flexible', team-based work practices, may pose new challenges for research in organizations.

As with the effects attributed to technological change above, the increased stress and uncertainty of these 'new' forms may make organizations more reluctant to provide access. The shifting structures, alliances and membership of such organizations may also cause difficulties for sustained interaction, while the shift from hierarchical to network or market coordination may make access and reporting more complex.

Another area of growing interest in research in organizations is in studies in sectors that are seen to be of growing importance (or of growing recognition of their importance), such as small- and medium-sized enterprises and third sector organizations (social enterprises, charities, voluntary organizations). From a research perspective, the typically smaller size, shorter history, instability and informality of many of these more recently studied organizations poses challenges in the identification of research sites, the negotiation and maintenance of access and their capacity to resist disruption. Not that any of these are necessarily more challenging than with conventional organizations, but processes may need to be modified. Thus passive observation may be more difficult in a smaller setting where the researcher is more likely to stand out; where access may be agreed either by just one individual, or require the consent of several independent parties, research agreements may be subject to much more rapid changes, as may the parties involved.

The increasing range of types of organization studied may also reflect an element of what Punch (1986: 47) identifies as the fieldworker's continual quest for 'new and more esoteric settings'. The lap-dancing club (Colosi, 2010), the

International Monetary Fund (Harper, 1997), or the world of professional clinical triallists (Abadie, 2010) could be considered the organizational researcher's equivalent of a biologist's undiscovered ecosystem or the mountaineer's unclimbed route, an uncharted (and previously unaccessed) domain that they can be the first to explore and perhaps to put their name to.

EXERCISES

1 • Identify what is **gained** in conducting organizational research online, rather than face to face.
  • Identify what is **lost** in conducting organizational research online, rather than face to face? What, if anything, can a researcher do to compensate for what is lost?
2 Describe **five** key challenges posed to the practice of organizational fieldwork by contemporary changes in organizational forms. How may organizational researchers respond to each challenge?

References

Abadie, R. (2010) *The Professional Guinea Pig: Big Pharma and the Risky World of Human Subjects*. London: Wiley.

Ashkenas, R.N., Ulrich, D., Jick, T. and Kerr, S. (2002) *The Boundaryless Organization: Breaking the Chains of Organizational Structure*. San Francisco, CA: Jossey-Bass.

Becker, H.S., Geer, B., Hughes, E.C. and Strauss, A.L. (1961) *Boys in White: Student Culture in Medical School*. Chicago, IL: Chicago University Press.

Blau, P.M. (1955) *The Dynamics of Bureaucracy: A Study of Interpersonal Relations in Two Government Agencies*. Chicago, IL: University of Chicago Press.

Bleecker, S.E. (1994) 'The virtual organization', *The Futurist*, (2): 9–14.

Bower, J.L. and Hout, T.M. (1988) 'Fast-cycle capability for competitive power', *Harvard Business Review*, 66 (6): 110–18.

Burawoy, M. (1979) *Manufacturing Consent: Changes in the Labor Process Under Monopoly Capitalism*. London: University of Chicago Press.

Clarke, J. (2011) 'Revitalizing entrepreneurship: how visual symbols are used in entrepreneurial performances', *Journal of Management Studies*, 48 (6): 1365–91.

Colosi, R. (2010) *Dirty Dancing? An Ethnography of Lap-dancing*. Abingdon: Willan Publishing.

Crowston, K., Wang, K., Howison, J. and Wiggins, A. (2012) 'Free/Libre open-source software development: What we know and what we do not know', *ACM Computing Surveys*, 44 (2): 7.1–7.35.

Dalton, M. (1959) *Men who Manage: Fusions of Feeling and Theory in Administration*. New York: Wiley.

Davenport, T.H. (1993) *Process Innovation: Reengineering Work through Information Technology*. London: Harvard Business School Press Books.

Drucker, P.F. (1992) 'The new society of organizations', *Harvard Business Review*, 70 (5): 95–105.

Gouldner, A.W. (1955) *Patterns of Industrial Bureaucracy*. London: Routledge and Kegan Paul.

Handy, C. (1995) *The Age of Unreason*. London: Random House UK.

Harper, R.P. (1997) *Inside the IMF: An Ethnography of Documents, Technology, and Organizational Action*. London: Academic Press.

Heath, C., Hindmarsh, J. and Luff, P. (2010) *Video in Qualitative Research: Analysing Social Interaction in Everyday Life*. London: SAGE.

Heckscher, C.C. and Donnellon, A. (1994) *The Post-bureaucratic Organization: New Perspectives on Organizational Change*. London: SAGE.

Hindmarsh, J. and Pilnick, A. (2007) 'Knowing bodies at work: embodiment and ephemeral teamwork in anaesthesia', *Organization Studies*, 28 (9): 1395–416.

Hine, C. (2000) *Virtual Ethnography*. London: SAGE.

Iedema, R. and Carroll, K. (2011) 'The "clinalyst": institutionalizing reflexive space to realize safety and flexible systematization in health care', *Journal of Organizational Change Management*, 24 (2): 175–90.

James, N. and Busher, H. (2009) *Online Interviewing*. London: SAGE.

Johnson, J.M. (1975) *Doing Field Research*. New York: Free Press.

Kozinets, R.V. (2009) *Netnography: Doing Ethnographic Research Online*. London: SAGE.

Lipset, S.M. (1964) 'The biography of a research project: union democracy', in P.E. Hammond (ed.), *Sociologists at Work*. New York: Basic Books, pp. 96–120.

Lundin, R.A. and Söderholm, A. (1995) 'A theory of the temporary organization', *Scandinavian Journal of Management*, 11 (4): 437–55.

McCabe, D. (2007) *Power at Work: How Employees Reproduce the Corporate Machine*. London: Taylor and Francis Books.

McKee, H.A. and Porter, J.E. (2009) *The Ethics of Internet Research: A Rhetorical, Case-based Process*. New York: Peter Lang.

Mollona, M. (2009) *Made in Sheffield: An Ethnography of Industrial Work and Politics*. Oxford: Berghahn Books.

Nohria, N. and Eccles, R. (1992) *Networks and Organizations: Structures, Form and Action*. Boston, MA: Harvard Business Press.

Ostroff, F. (1999) *The Horizontal Organization: What the Organization of the Future Looks Like and How it Delivers Value to Customers*. Oxford: Oxford University Press.

Palmer, I., Benveniste, J. and Dunford, R. (2007) 'New organizational forms: towards a generative dialogue', *Organization Studies*, 28 (12): 1829–47.

Punch, M. (1986) *The Politics and Ethics of Fieldwork*. London: SAGE.

Roethlisberger, F.J. and Dickson, W.J. (1939) *Management and the Worker: An Account of a Research Program Conducted by the Western Electric Company, Hawthorne Works, Chicago*. Cambridge, MA: Harvard University Press.

Schreyögg, G. and Sydow, J. (2010) 'Organizing for fluidity? Dilemmas of new organizational forms', *Organization Science*, 21 (6): 1251–62.

Sproull, L. and Arriaga, M. (2007) 'Online communities', in H. Bidgoli (ed.), *Handbook of Computer Networks*. Hoboken, NJ: Wiley, pp. 898–914.

Szymanski, M.H. and Whalen, J. (2011) *Making Work Visible: Ethnographically Grounded Case Studies of Work Practice*. Cambridge: Cambridge University Press.

Whitley, R. (2006) 'Project-based firms: new organizational form or variations on a theme?', *Industrial and Corporate Change*, 15 (1): 77–99.

Zuboff, S. (1988) *In the Age of the Smart Machine. The Future of Work and Power*. Oxford: Heinemann.

10

Conclusions

Chapter objectives

- to consider whether the issues identified in this book indicate that organizations constitute a distinctive context for research
- to propose that organizational research could benefit from greater attention to fieldwork practice

In Chapter 2, the question was raised whether organizations constitute a distinctive context for research that merits separate consideration from other social settings. As the topics discussed, and the range of literature drawn on, in this book illustrate, however, it would be hard to draw a clear distinction between organizational and other forms of social research. Even those working in organization studies might find it difficult to disagree with Bulmer (1988: 151) who, as a self-acknowledged outsider to that field, observed that 'there are relatively few issues of research method within organizations that are unique to them'.

This is hardly surprising, though, since organizations are but one specialized type of social setting. Nor are the people in them separate from the rest of society (even a closed monastic order is in some relationship, if predominantly one of exclusion, with the society in which it exists). Rather the distinctiveness of organizations as sites for research lies in the combination of characteristics that accentuate a number of major issues in the research process. In Chapter 2 these were identified as coordination, common principle(s), a relatively clear boundary and relative persistence. It was also suggested that larger, more formalized organizations may additionally exhibit significant economic power and a capability for, and interest in, research. Compared to a community, or an informal social group therefore, an organization tends to be more structured, hierarchical and formally bounded and potentially more able to control how they are researched.

Although, as discussed in Chapter 3, a wide variety of research designs may involve some measure of organizational fieldwork and these may employ a range of different data-gathering methods, the distinctive character of organizations may be particularly significant in studies adopting flexible designs that seek to gather rich qualitative data, perhaps through interviews, but especially observation. Such research is likely to depend on the researcher being able to spend an extended period inside the organization, rather than relying on data gathered from outside, for example through surveys or published statistics. In gaining access to the organizational backstage (Goffman, 1969) however, these studies may also face particular issues of research ethics, especially relating to informed consent and confidentiality. The increasing attempts to formalize ethical regulation of social research, as discussed in Chapter 4, may therefore be a significant constraint on such studies.

The characteristics of organizations also mean that gaining access may be a considerably more involved process than in other forms of social research, as discussed in Chapter 5. Because organizational boundaries are formally and legally enforceable, for example, it is rarely possible to conduct overt research in organizations without permission.[1] Given the reasonable ethical objections to deception, therefore, access will be by negotiation and the researcher may need to put considerable effort into locating 'qualified prospects', who are able to grant permission; preparing their request in a way that is likely to appeal to the organization's common principle(s); and planning and carrying out their negotiation strategy. Such efforts may sometimes be unnecessary if the researcher is lucky enough to approach an organization that is keen to participate in research, and may be in vain if the organization is unwilling to enter any discussion. On balance, however, it would seem better to risk wasting some time on preparation than to have access refused due to poorly handled negotiations.

Even once having successfully negotiated permission to undertake research in an organization, however, the difficulties of access may be far from over. Notwithstanding the relatively high degree of coordination in organizations compared to other social settings, the formalization of structure may mean that access is an ongoing process involving negotiation with successive gatekeepers at every step along the way.

The relative power of the researcher and their 'subjects' may also be rather different in research in organizations than in other forms of social research. On

---

[1]There are a few studies that have sought to get round access constraints by conducting research off-site. Ellem (2009), for example, conducted research on union derecognition in the Australian iron-ore industry, in homes, pubs, accommodation quarters, union rooms and cars as the ongoing conflict between the unions and the mining companies made it necessary to work with one side or the other. Similarly Anteby (2008) relied on interviews with retired workers, observation and archival data in his study of 'side production' (the making of homers, objects produced by a worker for their own purposes using a factory's materials and machinery and on the company's time) in an aircraft company. Such studies are very much the exception, however.

the one hand, in gaining access to organizations or in studying organizational elites, the researcher is likely to be in a subordinate position, a supplicant dependent on their subjects' favour in order to be able to conduct their work. Only for a few, elite researchers are organizations likely to be actively seeking their attention. That organization members' suspicion regarding the motives for and consequences of permitting access may be driven by misunderstandings about academic research, moreover, does not mean that their objections may be any less of a barrier.

Once access to an organization has been granted, on the other hand, the researcher may be in a relatively privileged position. That their research is approved, even if not actively supported, by senior organization members may mean that the researcher is identified with those members and involvement in the study may be influenced, both positively and negatively, by organizational politics. Individuals may participate because they are told to, or to curry favour with their superiors, or may resist or sabotage research to challenge other factions in the organization. Although not necessarily viewed favourably by all organization members, the researcher's academic associations may also give them a certain status (and perhaps open them to ridicule too). While these phenomena may be observed in other social settings, the formal structure of organizations potentially makes them more prominent.

Chapter 5 places considerable emphasis on the argument made by Walford (2001) that access negotiations can benefit from the insights offered by the literature on commercial selling. While many researchers may find such an idea disquieting it may nevertheless be salutary for them to consider that the merits of their research are not always self-evident to those they wish to study. The process may also perhaps be made more palatable by considering it more theoretically in the terminology of the sociology of translation (Callon, 1986: 196), as one in which researchers seek 'to impose themselves and their definition of the situation on others'.

Given the potential difficulties in gaining access to organizations, some authors, such as Buchanan et al. (1988: 56), suggest that it is a 'game of chance, not of skill' and recommend that researchers should adopt an opportunistic strategy, making use of personal and family contacts and improvising access requests as circumstances allow. Bulmer (1988), however, suggests that this is unsatisfactory and proposes that research in organizations could benefit from greater attention to systematic sampling, rather than, as Pugh (1988: 127) argues, treating sample as a 'euphemism for an assorted group of organizations that agreed to participate'.

While there may be particular difficulties in 'getting in' to conduct research in organizations, the challenges of such research are far from over once access has been achieved. Rather, as discussed in Chapter 6, for researchers in organizations 'getting on' once inside the organization can be demanding not just of time and effort, but of political and social sensitivit, It is not enough merely to be present in the organization, the researcher needs to build rapport with organization members to gain insight on their views and practices. This may need to be done relatively quickly, if perhaps somewhat superficially, in interview-based studies, setting the interviewees at their ease and encouraging them to talk freely and honestly. In observational studies there may be a much more extended process of fitting in and building trust and rapport to try to create the conditions where organization members' behave, as far as possible, as they would do if the researcher were not there. How easy or difficult this may be is likely to vary depending partly on the extent to which characteristics of the researcher, such as age, gender or ethnicity, fall within the norms of the particular organization, but also on the researcher's versatility in blending in.

Whether the researcher has achieved sufficient entree in a setting that their presence has minimal effect on organization members' behaviour can never be truly known. There may always be realms of organizational practice that remain beyond the reach of the researcher. This may simply be a practical matter of the layout of work settings, such that the researcher's presence requires some adjustment of practices, or of the researcher's, perhaps indirect, contribution to work activities. In some situations, however, organization members may go to considerable lengths to create an impression that their behaviour is completely natural, perhaps letting the researcher in on 'secrets' to suggest that they are seeing behind the scenes. This may be because organization members wish to keep certain practices hidden from scrutiny, either because they would be socially disapproved, or because of negative organizational consequences that may arise from their discovery. All the researcher can report, therefore, is what they see, or hear, of the setting, without assuming that this is necessarily what would have happened in their absence.

As Chapter 6 discusses, conducting fieldwork in organizations can be challenging in terms of negotiating organizational politics, ethical dilemmas and emotional demands, all of which can have an important influence not just on what is studied, but also on the validity and reliability of the findings and what can be done with them. While it may be overstating matters to assume, as authors such as Douglas (1976) and Punch (1989) discuss, that organization members are necessarily aiming to deceive the researcher, it may also be advisable to reflect on the potential motivations of organization members and the circumstances under which data were gathered.

These challenges can make fieldwork a stressful experience and place considerable demands on the researcher's social skills in developing rapport with organization members; sustaining their role in the organization in the face of difficulties such as political tensions, organizational restructuring or personal hostility from some organization members; and maintaining organization members' perceptions of them as non-threatening. Although these efforts may not always be enough to prevent premature termination of the research, they may ease the departure and avoid foreclosing future research opportunities.

Even if departure from the organization is not forced on the researcher, however, it may still not be straightforward to achieve a smooth ending to fieldwork. Negotiating a graceful departure from the setting may require careful planning to ensure that organization members are given sufficient notification, commitments are fulfilled and the social courtesies of leave-taking are properly observed. This will be particularly important if the researcher wishes to keep open the possibility of returning to the organization at a later date, to collect more data, for example, or to discuss findings or initiate new studies.

It is not just how the researcher leaves the organization that may affect the prospects for a future return, but what they do afterwards, especially in relation to publication of findings. Even if there has not been formal agreement to provide organization members with the opportunity to review research outputs, feeding back source data, such as interview transcripts, or intermediate outputs such as case descriptions, can be a valuable chance to check the accuracy of data collection and to get members' reflections on the findings.

Although, thankfully, apparently not a common problem (as yet, at least), the experience of researchers such as Punch (1986) and Irvine (2003) suggests that caution is desirable in offering organizations a veto on publication. Whether, as Bulmer (1988) proposes, researchers may be able to assert a right to publish irrespective of the views of organization members, however, would seem open to question on ethical grounds as well as the risk of spoiling the field for future research. Given organizations' increasing sensitivity about their reputation in the face of recent scandals, moreover, some negotiation over what is reported about research may be unavoidable. As the continuing high rate of publication of such research demonstrates, though, this would seem unlikely to be a significant constraint on organizational fieldwork.

If much of the discussion in this book has suggested that the classic literature on fieldwork from social anthropology and sociology is still very relevant to research in organizations, there are also some signs that the landscape of organizations and research practice may be changing in ways that create both new challenges and new opportunities for fieldwork. In particular the increasing geographical dispersion of work, both within and beyond formal organizational boundaries, means that traditional models of face-to-face observation in a specific locale need to be rethought. Similarly the Internet enables new forms of, and venues for, data collection and, with the informating capacity of information technology, makes visible new realms of organizational practice (potentially without ever venturing into an organization at all). As with earlier technological developments it may be wise to treat with some caution claims that fieldwork will be irrevocably transformed by such developments, but they would seem to offer some exciting possibilities for innovative research. Whether or not technology-facilitated, research innovation would also seem likely in new forms and types of organizations as fieldworkers seek to pioneer research in previously unstudied domains.

If future research in organizations takes place in a wider variety of locations, using a wider variety of data-gathering techniques to address a wider variety of questions, this does not necessarily mean that the practice of organizational fieldwork will be so very different from today. While by no means deliberately planned as such, the relative attention paid to different stages of the research process in the chapters of this book would seem illustrative of their relative significance in research practice. Thus the biggest challenge of organizational fieldwork, although rarely touched on in most research methods textbooks, is probably in 'getting on' in the organization. This is not to underestimate the difficulties that can be encountered in 'getting in', to which textbooks tend to give some acknowledgement, but to emphasize that it is only a necessary, but not sufficient, condition for effective research. Without the ability to get on in the organization, to gather relevant data (the difficulties of which are perhaps only really evident when trying to achieve this inside an organization), access, per se, will not achieve very much.

Although the relatively limited attention paid to 'getting out', compared to 'getting in' and 'getting on', is appropriate in terms of the research process, it would be fair to say that the issue remains almost as neglected as Snow (1980) identified it to be. While these chapters could not claim to provide a comprehensive coverage of the topic, therefore, they at least recognize that this may not always be as straightforward as the absence of discussion in the literature may be seen as implying.

The one exception to the correspondence between chapter length and significance in practice relates to research ethics. The relative brevity of Chapter 4 is not because ethical issues are not important in organizational fieldwork, but because they permeate all stages of the research process (and are thus returned to in each of the subsequent chapters). Furthermore, in a climate of increasing formalization of research ethics they may be expected to require yet greater attention. In seeking to integrate ethics into the discussion of research practice, then, the aim has been to explore ethics, not as a set of abstract principles against which the research proposal needs to be signed off before fieldwork can commence, but as a lived experience of dilemmas and trade-offs that the researcher needs to negotiate in practice. This is not to suggest that there is no place for ethical codes or that the judgement of the researcher, perhaps under pressure and in a hurry, will always be ethically correct, but rather that codes and ethical approval cannot be enough to ensure ethical practice and that educating and supporting the researcher in their handling of ethical dilemmas as they encounter them is also needed.

A similar argument may be made with respect to the relationship between the focus of this book and that of most research methods texts. It is not that it isn't important to know how to design a good study or analyse data properly, but this is not much use if the researcher doesn't know how to put the design into practice, or to actually get hold of the data to be analysed. As in the 'practice turn' in sociology and management (Reckwitz, 2002; Sandberg and Tsoukas, 2011; Schatzki et al., 2001; Whittington, 2006), it is argued that the abstract accounts of how research should be done that are provided in many research methods textbooks bear little relationship to what is actually involved in undertaking research. In seeking to redress this imbalance in the discussion of research methods, this book has sought to raise the profile of fieldwork in research in organizations and to explore the challenges and rewards that it involves.

EXERCISES

1 For each of the following characteristics of organizations, identify **three** ways in which this may affect the conduct of organizational fieldwork.

Characteristic of organizations	Effects on fieldwork
Coordination	
Common principle	
Boundary	
Relative persistence	
Economic power	
Capability for, and interest in, research	

2 For each of the following forms or aspects of research, identify:

   (a) whether they could be considered exclusive to organizational research
   (b) any problems associated with them that may be accentuated by research being conducted in an organizational setting

	Exclusive to organizational research? Y/N	Problems accentuated in organizational research
Experiments		
Surveys		
Interviews		
Observation		

(Continued)

(Continued)

Document analysis
Gaining access
Reporting of findings
Return to the field
Informed consent
Maintaining
confidentiality
Anonymity

References

Anteby, M. (2008) *Moral Gray Zones: Side Productions, Identity, and Regulation in an Aeronautic Plant.* London: Princeton University Press.

Buchanan, D., Boddy, D. and McCalman, J. (1988) 'Getting in, getting on, getting out and getting back', in A. Bryman (ed.), *Doing Research in Organizations.* London: Routledge, pp. 53–67.

Bulmer, M. (1988) 'Some reflections upon research in organisations', in A. Bryman (ed.), *Doing Research in Organisations.* London: Routledge, pp. 151–61.

Callon, M. (1986) 'Some elements of a sociology of translation: domestication of the scallops and the fishermen of St Brieuc Bay', in J. Law (ed.), *Power, Action and Belief: A New Sociology of Knowledge.* London: Routledge and Kegan Paul, pp. 196–233.

Douglas, J.D. (1976) *Investigative Social Research: Individual and Team Field Research.* Beverly Hills, CA: SAGE.

Ellem, B. (2009) 'Drinking with Dessie: research mines and life in the Pilbara', in K. Townsend and J. Burgess (eds), *Method in the Madness: Research Stories You Won't Read in Textbooks.* Oxford: Chandos Publishing, pp. 39–50.

Goffman, E. (1969) *The Presentation of Self in Everday Life.* London: Penguin.

Irvine, H. (2003) 'Trust me! A personal account of confidentiality issues in an organisational research project', *Accounting Forum*, 27 (1): 111–31.

Pugh, D.S. (1988) 'The Aston research programme', in A. Bryman (ed.), *Doing Research in Organisations.* London: Routledge, pp. 123–35.

Punch, M. (1986) *The Politics and Ethics of Fieldwork.* London: SAGE.

Punch, M. (1989) 'Researching police deviance: a personal encounter with the limitations and liabilities of field-work', *British Journal of Sociology*, 40 (2): 177–204.

Reckwitz, A. (2002) 'Toward a theory of social practices', *European Journal of Social Theory*, 5 (2): 243.

Sandberg, J. and Tsoukas, H. (2011) 'Grasping the logic of practice: theorizing through practical rationality', *Academy of Management Review*, 36 (2): 338–60.

Schatzki, T.R., Knorr-Cetina, K. and Von Savigny, E. (2001) *The Practice Turn in Contemporary Theory.* London: Psychology Press.

Snow, D.A. (1980) 'The disengagement process: a neglected problem in participant observation research', *Qualitative Sociology*, 3 (2): 100–22.

Walford, G. (2001) *Doing Qualitative Educational Research: A Personal Guide to the Research Process.* London: Continuum International Publishing Group.

Whittington, R. (2006) 'Completing the practice turn in strategy research', *Organization Studies*, 27 (5): 613.

Index

academic journals
  as venue for reporting research in
    organizations 7, 54, 164, 176–180
acceptance 119, 122, 123
access
  bottom-up 101
  ethics of 130
  ladder 87
  letter 90–94,104
  to organization, gaining 13, 26, 35,
    74–116, 121, 141
  problems of 5, 87, 142
  top-down 101,118
accountability
  relationships of 64
accuracy 166, 168. 171, 187, 211
action research 15,20,23,95,168,176
  see also participative inquiry
age
  as influence on fieldwork 83,119,127
agony of omission 179
altruism 135
anger 167
anonymity 8, 66, 99, 172, 177
anthropology 15, 76, 211
anxiety 67, 122, 141
appropriateness
  as evaluation criterion for research site 82
asking questions 41–44
Atkinson, Paul x,117
audience 7, 8, 12, 35, 54, 101, 147, 165–168,
  175–180
audio-recording 50–53, 132, 171, 197
authority 25, 90, 101, 115, 137, 140,
  143–145

bargain 7, 99, 157, 159, 162–165
Becker, Howard S. 104, 140, 167, 174
becoming part of the furniture 130
Bell, Colin 190
Belmont principles 65
benchmarking 96, 177
beneficence 65, 66, 143, 169
benefits 13, 20, 66, 95–99, 105, 136, 169
betrayal 162, 173

bias 21, 45, 48, 120, 139–141, 166, 171,
  174, 179
biographical reconstruction 122–123
biomedical model 68–69,75
Blau, Peter, M. 101, 129, 133, 134, 139
boredom
  as incentive for participation 136
  researcher's experience of 141, 142, 161
boundary 1, 12, 207
Bryman, Alan 2, 39, 40, 106, 190, 191
Buchanan, Boddy and McCalman 3, 5, 85,
  90, 91, 95, 97, 106, 140, 157, 165, 172,
  180, 191, 209
Bulmer, Martin 107, 146, 172–174, 207,
  209, 211
bureaucratic organizations 13, 165
Burgess, Robert 103, 119, 138, 170, 190, 191

case study 22, 38, 81, 82
chameleon quality 140
check questions 45
co-location 49
coding 41, 54, 164
cold calling 85, 88, 89
common principles 1, 12, 13, 140, 207, 208
comparability 27, 68, 96, 190, 191
comparative design 38
competence 35, 75, 90, 97
completeness rule
  lack of 159
Computer-Assisted Qualitative Data Analysis
  (CAQDAS) 54
confessional appendices x,2
confidante
  researcher as 137
confidentiality 7, 8, 26, 62, 66, 94, 95, 96,
  99–101, 121, 122, 130, 141, 143–145,
  160, 165, 170, 172, 173, 208
confidentiality commercial 24, 167
confidentiality internal vs external 170
conflict methodology 146
  see also investigative social research
consequentialism 62, 63, 64
consultancy 6, 15, 18, 20, 23–24, 95, 96, 125,
  168, 173, 177